GENDER AND MINISTRY IN EARLY CHRISTIANITY AND THE CHURCH TODAY

Adolphus Chinedu Amadi-Azuogu

D1270407

WITHDRAWN

University Press of America,® Inc.
Lanham · Boulder · New York · Toronto · Plymouth, UK

This book is dedicated to the following:

Edith Chima Amadi-Azuogu (my wife and sweetheart)
Ebere Peter Amadi-Azuogu (my first son)
Ikechi Adolphus Amadi-Azuogu (my second son)
Cordelia Amadi-Azuogu (my beloved mother)
Jacinta Nwoko (my sister-in-law)

Table of Contents

Foreword

It is with great enthusiasm that I am writing the foreword to this great book dedicated to women, whom I may describe as *the oppressed creatures of every epoch of human history.* In this regard, sacred history has made no difference. As women we are facing oppression on all sides, even in some of the Christian churches where masculine sacraments are created to continue to trample down on the womenfolk. Everything is done in the name of God and on his behalf. I am overjoyed that the writer has dedicated this book entirely to the course and welfare of women all over of the world.

Really, he has said what many women have longed to say but could not say it. Since they are wary of their patriarchal environment they either lacked the courage to say it or the theological and exegetical expertise needed to convey the message. Of course, solidly armed with the tools of biblical scholarship, this author is best qualified to undertake a work of this kind *on women's behalf.* He has become our plenipotentiary and special ambassador before a world that oppresses its female members, whether it is in the state or in the church, it makes no difference. Indeed, he has become our embassy to this world and to the Holy church of God, where women are constantly profiled *because they are women.*

I have no doubts in my mind that through this work the writer has become the voice of "the oppressed women" of our time. Indeed, he is an honorable fellow worker in our freedom movements. His research, as the reader will see, is *thorough, extensive, solid* and *convincing.* He has hit the hammer correctly at the nail. He has called a spade, a spade. He has an unrivaled originality in his mode of presentation.

If women in past centuries were exploited and subordinated by the men controlling their societies, this still remains a feature of our society today, be it *the church* or *the state*. The call made in this book is a call for men and women to work together as *joint heirs of grace* (1Pet 3,7). It is by no means a call for the male class to continue to hierarchically subordinate the female members of the Christian church, using unexplained and obscure biblical texts as their basis. It is not right to pretend as if women have simply no divine vocation to be leaders in the Christian community, or to be ordained priests and deacons, or to occupy high places in the hierarchy of the church. *The gift of anointing is not, could not, and cannot be a male prerogative.* So let us not reduce God to a mere "gynecologist".

Indeed, this author has sounded the trumpet for the equality of man and woman. This egalitarian principle is needed more in our present day church in which the men controlling our destiny keep issuing documents to continue to decree us into silence in God's name, or to exclude us from the center of power in the church. Everything is done under the false pretext that *it is not the mind of a Jesus* who chose to manifest his resurrected self first to us, the women, as all the gospel accounts testify. Unless this patriarchal attitude is contained religion will be presented to the womenfolk as an oppressive mystical experience, an opium which sedates us. It could even be sees as an instrument put in place to help men to keep us in check so that power will be forever theirs. Accordingly, in this foreword, my clarion call is, *Women of all continents arise!*

Indeed, this is a book worth-reading by all and sundry. This author has taken an honest and courageous step in this work, on behalf of women. What many men lack the courage and honesty to do, he has done for us. To you we shall be ever grateful. As the reader will see, this is a bold attempt to call a *spade, a spade*. To my fellow women, you have become the "St. Paul" of our century and millennium. What the ancient goddess *Isis* was to the Egyptian women movement and Paul to the oppressed women of his Jewish society, you have now become to the women of our age.

Really, it is my belief that every woman who reads this work will no doubt be happy with it. Therefore, I do not hesitate to recommend it to everyone, especially the women for whose sake it was written. I have no doubt in my mind that this scholarly work will strengthen the resolve of the contemporary woman to continue to fight for equal treatment with her male counterparts and for her rightful place in the society, *including the Holy Church of God.* In my own assessment and evaluation, this work is indeed a wonderful scholarly contribution towards the "emancipation of women" from a male dominated *world* and *church*. As the reader will soon discover this is a masterpiece. *It is in this light that I call upon all, who are not afraid of the truth, to read, own and treasure this work.*

Jo Ann Bynum
Dean/Doctor of Ministry
Southern California School of Ministry
Los Angeles, California, USA
May 13, 2004

Preface

The word *liberation* is now becoming a household terminology in many women circles due to the activities of the *Women Liberation Movement* throughout the world. Obviously, this is an indication that all is not well in terms of the male-female relationship. In other words, there are soft spots in the world's dealing with women including the Christian church. Normally, a free person does not really think about liberating the self. This means that liberation is for those whose freedom and human rights have been trampled upon, as women are today in many parts of the world. This means that it is for the deprived and dispossessed. Hence, the present day clamor among women is to fix what went wrong in the relationship between women and the world around them. On a more precise note, this work is about fixing this same problem in the *church of God* where women are treated as second class Christians or secondary creatures, on account of their gender, in allocating ministry roles in the church. This has created the problem of *gender and inequality* in Christianity, especially in relation to the *ministry of the church*. At the secular level, the principle of equal protection applies. But at the religious level, it is all about the principle of unequal protection defended in God's name. In view of this, the relationship between gender and ministry is now one of the flash points in theology in discussing gender issues today.

In the time of the OT Exodus there was a similar situation. Then it was all about the deliverance of the *biblical Israelites* from the Egypt of the ancient Pharaohs. The *inequality,* which existed in the Exodus story, could not be condoned by God. The reason for this divine displeasure is because *discrimination* and *unequal opportunity* existed, just as it still exists in the Christian church today in relation to the womenfolk. These excruciating conditions in the Exodus story were not considered to be the plan of the Holy God. Neither racial nor gender profiling is taken to be the benchmark for the ideal order. They do not fit into the overall divine plan, which preordained freedom and equality for the created human beings. In effect, the resulting act of oppression, humiliation, human degradation and loss of human rights in the narratives of Exodus could not be tolerated by God. This is considered an obvious aberration in need of rectification.

In view of this worrying situation in Exodus a point was reached when God could no longer watch the unfolding human tragedy from the fence, nor even keep further silence. To be merely a divine spectator served no further useful purpose. Something decisive needed to happen to bring a swift and hilarious end to this distortion of the plan of God. Consequently, Moses was sent to rectify this anomaly and set free those in chains. He had the mission to break their shackles of oppression, just as we are called today to break the fetters that bind and inhibit women in the *household of faith*, especially in relation to gender and ministry. In the Exodus narratives, as far as God is concerned, the yoke of oppression needed to be removed and human rights restored to those who did not have them. Freedom should be restored to those who have lost it. This is what the women liberation movement is all about – to restore a lost freedom to women. In a sense, it plays the role of a new "Moses" for the 21st century women.

In the light of the Exodus experience there is no gainsaying that a similar yoke of oppression exists in relation to *women and the ministry of the Christian church today*. This needs to be removed in our own day as well. To prevent women from participating *fully* in the ministry of the church is to downgrade them to the status of the oppressed in the Egypt of the Pharaohs where the Israelites were treated as second class people. As Christians, in our own way, we re-enact this ugly saga by refusing to unconditionally admit women to the top echelon of the church's hierarchy. As a result, we make them "slaves" in the *household of faith* by re-imposing the OT temple boundaries which prevented them from having unfettered access to the "holy of holies", the supposed place of divine presence. In our own day, we have restored the veil of the temple that Jesus tore (Matt 27,51; Mk 15,38 and Luke 23,45) to grant every Christian, including women, unconditional access to the divine throne. Unfortunately, today, we veil women off from the divine presence *in order to protect male privileges*. In this regard, some of the Christian churches have recruited men as the only ritual officials, who *alone* could offer ritual intercession on behalf of women. Hence, the equality of man and woman continues to be foreign to the Christian churches involved, thereby intensifying the womanist struggle.

As the facts of biblical history and tradition show the OT that should have upheld a radical equality between man and woman *in all things* failed in this respect. Even though it told us that God created man and woman in his own image and likeness (Gen 1,26.27), yet the later pages seem to say that God created the man more in his own image and likeness than the woman. This makes the woman to be a secondary creature to the man. Accordingly, we are left with a situation similar to George Orwell's *Animal Farm* where he stated the principle of *all animals are equal, but some are more equal than others*. The final outcome is that the woman has been made to become a *secondary creature*. She is presented almost always in a deficit situation. Stories are told to maintain this. Hence, this woman is always at the mercy of men. This ugly condition necessitates some urgent action in this 21st century. The woman has to take her own destiny into her own hands since most of the men are very reluctant and quite unwilling to help her out of the present impasse. It is interesting that there are many women liberation movements today throughout the world to address this question of female marginalization in our world and in the church of Christ. This is very positive.

In view of this marginalization, there is today a new situation of oppression, degradation and loss of human rights needing another Moses. Creation is again undergoing a distortion, this time not by Pharaoh and his henchmen but by the men who have "usurped" divine powers and hijacked his work and the ministry of the church. Accordingly, the woman is discriminated against, sidelined in ritual leadership in many of the Christian churches. Unfortunately, her ministry position in the church is said to be inconsistent with the holy plan of God. Here the thesis of Genesis 3,16 (*and he shall rule over you*) is meticulously remembered and radically enforced. This becomes the only scripture that a patriarchal society quickly remembers when dealing with women and the ministry of the church. Of course, this leads to an aberration in creation. The reason for this is that the authority that God gave to man and woman in Genesis 1,28 ("And God blessed them, and God said unto them, Be fruitful, and multiply, and replenish the earth, and subdue it: and have dominion over the fish of the sea, and over the fowl of the air, and over every living thing that moveth upon the earth" KJV) is now forgotten or *faintly* remembered. The fact that the Petrine community recognized man and woman as joint heirs of grace (1Pet 3,7) is now *de-emphasized* and *watered* down. This anomaly needs to be rectified in 21st century Christianity. The time to do it is now.

It is in view of this that I am writing this book on *Gender and Ministry* in the church today. If the racial intolerance against the biblical Israelites was bad, the present day discriminatory practices against women are equally bad. In addition, these acts are morally reprehensible no matter where they are practiced and enforced. To carry them out, even in the name of the Holy God and his Christ, does not in any way justify them. The fact that religion is used to sedate the woman, making it look like the opium of Karl Marx for her, does not provide any justification for this odious and blameworthy act. God does not become the author of sexual discriminations and gender profiling simply because we are operating these in his name, using him as our "religious trademark". The time has come to recognize and uphold the equality of man and woman as Paul and some segments of early Christianity did. One area to begin this immediate implementation is in the area of *the ministry of women in the Christian church today*.

The urgency of this implementation arises from the known fact that throughout sacred and secular history women have suffered more than those liberated from Egypt. As the facts show, for centuries, men have held them captive, taken them hostage both at the religious and secular level. Even, till today, men monopolize the political arena. And in the religious sphere they monopolize ritual leadership. As a result, almost everything is defined with patriarchal terminology and on patriarchal terms. This explains why some of my religious contemporaries resent the idea of a woman bishop, priestess, deaconess, pastor or senior pastor in some of the Christian churches. It is for this same reason that one of the male professors from a renowned theological seminary in Southern California approached to write the foreword to this work declined to do so because he felt that male chauvinism was uncompromisingly challenged in this work. If he is part of the system challenged in this book it was understandable that he would not want to be part of the critique, though he recognized me as a *prophetic writer*, which is what I am.

In view of this patriarchal situation, a male-oriented idea of God pervades and permeates theology and the ministry of the Christian church. As a result, man has produced a theology in which God is never a "She", but always a "He". Accordingly, it is not surprising that the idea of a "She-God" is repugnant to a people with a patriarchal mindset in which everything about God has to be expressed in almost exclusive male categories. In this way, God too has become a victim of our patriarchalisation of revelation and religion. In our zeal to make God a "He" our anthropomorphic conception of him has helped to water theology down to the level of anthropologizing it since God has been made to become a "he" like the rest of men. In this way, gender has been made to become a factor in theology. In effect, this brings God into the raging gender struggle between the "he" and the "she". Here, God is made to take sides with the "he" to the disadvantage of the "she". Sadly enough we forget that the Christian God transcends sex and gender. We cannot specify his gender since this would mean quantifying him. Gender is part of this quantification process. One can see that the gender we attribute to God is only a patriarchal *modus loquendi* - mode of speech. Otherwise, to be so certain about his sex is to reduce him to the level of anthropology. Yet God is the "Neither, Nor", without implying that he or she is a hermaphrodite.

In this regard, the German theologian - Rudolf Bultmann - was right in saying that God is *der unsagbare Gott* – the "unsayable" God. In view of this, Exo 3,14 is right in insisting that this God is simply the "I AM WHO I AM" (אֶהְיֶה אֲשֶׁר אֶהְיֶה). This shows how incomprehensible he is to the finite mind. This is only logical since the finite cannot adequately comprehend the infinite, the fact of revelation notwithstanding. It requires an infinite mind to adequately comprehend an infinite being. Therefore, to assign a specific gender to him is nothing but an attempt, as Bultmann himself pointed out, *to talk about the otherworldly in terms of this worldly*. Luckily, God transcends sex and gender. Hence, he is above the present gender-squabbles among us. Any effort to make him part of this is already a failure. Whether we attribute "He" to God or "She" to him, they are all attempts to say something about him. If men can say that God is a "he", women can also say that God is a "she". Here we simply have the case of the *tale of two cities*.

Indeed, the woman has to be equal with man since both of them are equally *joint heirs of grace* (1Peter 3,7). Consequently, there has to be true emancipation for the woman. She has to be released from her "detention", from the "house arrest" where men have kept her a "prisoner" for centuries. She has to break loose her chains. A new act of deliverance is needed for her to guarantee her freedom. This is why this book is written *so that men and women can be equal partners in the ministry of the Christian church*.

However, this act of emancipating the woman is not intended to lead her to *absolute* independence. By no means! This work is all about the *inter-dependence* of the sexes. It is about *mutual coexistence* of the genders, based on unbiased principles of *equality, equity, fairness* and *human dignity.* It is about *equal opportunity for all,* irrespective of gender, color, race or national origin. Therefore, a relationship of reciprocal respect has to exist and equal protection has to be the hallmark of this new relationship. Indeed, the *equality of the sexes has to be the defining principle of this new situation.* Without this the one-sided relationship between gender and ministry will continue. It is in view of this that Paul and the early church are considered relevant to this work.

Accordingly, this work will try to show how Paul championed the cause of women by granting them equal status with men in the ministry of the church and how later Christianity adopted and adapted the Pauline ecclesiological principles. With this in mind, all lovers of justice, champions of human rights and civil liberties throughout the world will find this book very useful and quite appealing. Of course, women activists will equally appreciate the thoughts in this scholarly work since they help to move the arguments in favor of the equality of the sexes in the church forward. So read on.

Chinedu Adolphus Amadi-Azuogu
Director of Doctor of Ministry Program
Southern California School of Ministry
Los Angeles, California, USA
May 13, 2004

Acknowledgments

This is the time for a roll call of those who have contributed in different ways towards the production of this work. My first word of thanks goes to my most dearly beloved wife, *Edith Chima Amadi-Azuogu* (nee Edith Chima Aririguzo), who has inspired this work on the role of women in the church today, having herself worked for the Christian church in a lesser capacity. She has all it takes for a man to risk and possess her. Hence, she is my "Treasure Island". It is not surprising therefore that she is the "jewel of my life" and a great source of inspiration for this work. Her wisdom and love have permeated and punctuated this work.

Also I recognize two other indirect family movers of this work, our young sons *Ebere* and *Ikechi*. They have remained our great source of inspiration. Looking at them I was always motivated into leaving a legacy for them in the form of this book so that they too shall grow up to say, "Long live the women!" I am happy that I have succeeded.

My next word of thanks goes to my mother, *Cordelia Amadi-Azuogu*. I thank her for all that she has been to me and to all my brothers and sisters. During the Biafra-Nigeria war (the bloody Nigerian civil war for Igbo self-determination) of 1967-70, when my father enrolled in the Biafran army in defense of the defunct Federal Republic of Biafra, she became a father and mother to us. During the period she carried the burden of family alone. Now that our father is regrettably dead, she continues to fill the created father-vacuum. Besides, in my greatest hours of need, preceding the writing of this book, she stood firmly with me and for me, when the weather was unnecessarily stormy because people could not understand why a celibate should legally marry. When confronted with the choice of choosing between an "amorphous public" and a beloved son, she did the virtuous thing and risked choosing the correct thing, in the form of a son. I cannot thank her enough. In the same vein, I remain grateful to my mother-in-law *Philomena Nwoko Aririguzo*, who has equally been highly supportive of us in our supreme decision in life, despite her ailment. And to all my sisters I also express my profound gratitude. They have supported my course and identified with it. My gratitude goes also to my late father, *Cajetan Amadi Azuogu*, whose life was cut short on the 6th of July, 1998 at the age of sixty-five. He is fondly remembered in this work. May he rest in Peace!

My next word of thanks goes to *John* and *Jacinta Nwoko*, a Nigerian couple of Igbo descent now residing in California, USA. At the beginning of my sojourn here in the US they provided me with initial temporary shelter where I stayed and developed the main thoughts of this book. They are remembered in this work.

I am also grateful to *Emeka Okoro* the director of UMU-IGBO USA, a non-profit cultural organization with headquarters in Ontario, California. This organization helps African-American children of Nigerian descent and other African Americans to know their cultural roots. Emeka has been a very close Nigerian friend. He helped to provide me with indirect financial support during the time of writing this book. I cannot thank him enough.

I wish also to thank Pastors *Blessing* and *Pauline Ubani*, a Nigerian couple now resident in California, USA, who have been very good to me and my wife. Their support and encouragement contributed in the production of this work.

I am very grateful to the men and women of the *University Press of America* who accepted to publish this manuscript on *Gender and Ministry*. They have afforded me the opportunity to display my scholarship. If they rejected it, I would not have had the chance to make this contribution to biblical scholarship.

To my former colleagues in the ministry at the *Claretian Missionary Congregation* in Nigeria *I continue to be very grateful.* We were great friends and collaborators in the work of the gospel. *This Christian spirit is unchangeable*; though our states in life have now changed. I wish to use this medium to assure them of my continued friendship with all of them. It was such a wonderful time with every "Tom, Dick and Harry" among them. Those smiles on my face have in no way evaporated. *Though theological principles and human exigencies now separate us the same Spirit of Christ continues to unite us.* Whether we die or live, we are for him.

If we believe that it is the same Lord, *I should now be seen as your special embassy to the world.* My missionary life continues in the Lord. As you can see, in this book, the task of preaching the good news of salvation continues with me *unabated* and *unhindered.* Wherever I am, I continue to be *an anointed of the Lord.* Nothing can change this reality. So let us continue to pray for one another in the one Lord Jesus. We parted peacefully, may peace continue to follow us, especially those of us who wish and desire it. *From wherever I am, I continue to hold out the olive branch and right hand of fellowship to all of you.*

Finally, as we read in the *Acts of the Apostles,* the Athenians decided to dedicate a temple to the "unknown God" (ἀγνώστῳ θεῷ) less they have forgotten any of the ancient Greek gods without knowing it (Acts 17,23). Here, I am doing a similar thing. Accordingly, I wish also to dedicate an "altar of thanksgiving" to all those who should have been specifically acknowledged in this work but have either escaped my memory or were simply omitted to avoid publishing a "book of names". This omission is not due to malice. However, like the Athenians, I am also dedicating a "temple" to them to assure them that I have not forgotten them, though their names were not specifically mentioned here. For fear of publishing a long register I have limited the names to the ones mentioned here. All the same, I remain grateful to everyone who has collaborated with me in any way, either in the past or in the present. Let us move together to produce the next work. This leads us now to make a general introduction to this work.

General Introduction

The relationship between gender and ministry has long been established in the Christian church. On the one hand, all the levels of ministry are taken to be compatible with the male gender. On the other hand, the relationship between *ministry and female gender* is contentious and controversial.

In a minority of the Christian churches some progress has been made in recent years to recognize equal ministry status for the two genders. This, notwithstanding, the majority trend shows that many of the Christian churches still believe that women are not supposed to be ministers in the church, worse still to be senior pastors or serve in ordained capacity. In view of this, the female gender is taken to be incongruous to certain ministry positions in the majority of the churches. For instance, the idea of a deaconess, priestess or female bishop is thought to be a contradiction in terms, a theological illogicality, an ecclesiological abnormality. For some of the Christian churches this is even considered a *taboo*.

Hence, in these churches, these women are denied senior ministry and administrative positions without any qualms of conscience. The result is that they cannot be ordained priests or deacons, or be consecrated as bishops, or appointed senior pastors in some of those churches accepting their ministry as pastors.[1] In view of this, ecclesiastical appointments are strictly made along gender lines to *the disadvantage of women*. Here, *gender* and *ministry* are made to be two eternal parallel lines that can never meet. As a result, female gender becomes incompatible with ordination and leadership positions in the Christian churches.

On the one hand, God is presented as a deity who patronizes male leadership and endorses the role of men in the church as leaders in the highest places. Hence, the topmost hierarchy of the church is seen as something reserved for men by God. On the other hand, this same God is depicted as one who abhors female leadership in the church and rejects the participation of women in the top echelon of the church's hierarchy. *As a result, gender discrimination in ministry becomes the hallmark of the Christian churches involved.* This is made to be an indispensable element of ecclesiology. Hence, Christian ministry is characterized by *gender profiling.* In this way, *gender separation* and *gender distinction* become important elements of the ministry of the Christian church today.

Even though Christianity is home to the great democracies of the world, yet this idea of profiling women in the church falsely portrays Christianity as *the religion of unequal opportunity,* where gender profiling is extolled and cherished as a religious virtue to be defended at all cost. Here, the principle of inequality in George Orwell's *Animal Farm* becomes apparent: *all animals are equal, but some are more equal than others.* In our own context, this becomes the case of *all Christians are equal, but some are more equal than others.* The "some" in our own situation becomes the *male class* now established as superior to the female class. Tension is thus created in which there is now the *male versus the female.* This is what has provoked a feminist reaction now called *the women liberation movement.* There is now a precipitation of gender struggle, which fortunately has not yet deteriorated into gender warfare. Nonetheless, the problem is there and needs *real* solution.

In the light of the male argument favoring male monopoly of power in the church, this Platonic saying, "ruling and not serving is proper to man",[2] becomes relevant here. Hence, Plato calls the *diakonos* (servant) a "contemptible flatterer."[3] It is in this light that the Sophist philosophers asked, "how can a man be happy when he has to serve someone?"[4] The only service considered to have a higher value was the one rendered to the state.[5] This philosophical thinking helps to explain why men hold onto leadership in the churches to the exclusion of women. They continue to take women to be like the Platonic *contemptible flatterers.* Consequently, they are considered to be unfit for leadership in the church.

As we shall see in this work, the reason for this is not because God has willed this "upside down situation". On the contrary, it is because men want to assert their "will-to-rule" in a Christian church that has become over-patriarchalised in the course of church history. Since ministry today is mainly about *power, privilege, prestige and wealth,* one sees why there is a constant link between ministry and gender. A powerful male clergy arrogates these to the male members and prevents women from joining its rank and file.

Unfortunately, this clergy tightly controls the theological instruments needed to change the status quo. Hence, every effort is made to use theology as an instrument of female subjugation in the church. Certainly, this is a theological camouflage. No wonder, then, Jesus is zealously invoked to maintain the power structures instituted on patriarchal foundations. As a result, every obscure text relating to men is blown out of proportion and magnified to maintain the status quo favoring men. But every biblical text, which supports the position of women, is either explained away, downplayed or watered down to the point of no importance. Here, we see the "theology of convenience" at work. In the end, Christian theology becomes, *ipso facto,* patriarchal theology.

Indeed, the relationship between gender and the ministry of the Christian church is seen very clearly in this example from the law book of Roman Catholicism, called the *canon law.* Here, canon 1024 of this code unambiguously says: "Only a baptized man can validly receive sacred ordination".[6] In view of this legal provision, a male sacrament is *de iure* (by law) established. Hence, *de iure* (by law), only men can be ritual leaders in Roman Catholicism, though this should not have been the case based on a holistic interpretation of the NT evidence. Regrettably, through the legal provision of canon 1024, Roman Catholicism has made God to be a deity who can only confer sacred ordination on the male members of the church. In this way, women have been legislated out of church office because of *gender discrimination.*

As one can see, in this denomination and the others resisting the ministry of women in the church at all levels, "maleness" is considered to be consistent with sacred ministry, while "femaleness" is taken to be irreconcilable with it. On account of this, there is an indisputable tension between *gender* and *ministry.* These realities are presented as two parallel lines that can never meet. Here, the "sacred" is shown to be at odds with what is feminine. Hence, God can only confer sacred ordination or other ministry positions only on the male members of these churches.

As a result, the priesthood and other senior ministry positions become *exclusively* male. In addition, the sacrament of ordination becomes the "sacrament of men". This is a form of *religious apartheid.* The only difference here is, instead of designating a "white only area", we have a *"men only area"*. Nonetheless, the principle involved is the same: segregation, discrimination, exclusion and separation. Here, the reader sees clearly the inherent lack of fairness towards the female members of this church. Whereas, there is an *exclusive* male ministry, there is no such thing as an exclusive female ministry. Nothing is reserved for women, *except childbearing*. This puts the Christian God in an awkward situation in which he is *falsely* portrayed as the "Grand Patron" of inequality and the "God of Partiality"; who plays this favoritism always in favor of men. This is a regrettable situation and constitutes *blasphemy* against the Holy Trinity.

The irony of this whole situation is that secular authorities should not discriminate against women, but the church of God can do this in his name and on his behalf. What a contradiction! Here, we see that the male gender is taken to be the *super gender* of the Christian religion. The male Christians *de facto* (by fact) become more equal than women – a reenactment of George Orwell's *Animal Farm* already cited above. Hence, men are made to be a *divinely favored gender*. Consequently, *only* men can be high-ranking church leaders in many of the Christian churches. In this situation, all Christians are equal *only* in principle *and not in reality*.

However, some questions still remain to be answered. Does God really go to the extreme of examining the gender of the members of the Christian church before determining their roles in the ministry of the church or before granting them ministry favors? Is he to be construed as a *Sacred Gynecologist* interested in establishing sex and gender before allotting ministry positions to Christians? Certainly, it will be naive to say or even contemplate this.

Indeed, God does not worry about sex and gender, as we do in the church today. To make him to be preoccupied with this is to reduce him to the level of irrationality. The fact still remains that he is the Transcendent God. This means that he goes beyond our limited mode of reasoning. As a result, *he does not favor any of the genders*. And he is certainly not one of the gynecologists around, not even a sacred one.

Therefore, let us not, under whatever pretext, try to make him look like a "Holy Gynecologist", *which he is not*. Let us not recruit him to be in the vanguard of gender profiling or discrimination against women. Certainly, he stands above this unjust situation and does not even countenance it, as this work will show. It is in vain to mask God this way because this is not what he is. This grotesque God is not our God. The God of Christianity stands above the worldly situation of *sex* and *gender*. To bring him down to this level is to demean him.

It is in view of this that anti-womanist statements are viewed with regret in this work. One example of these is from Tertullian, one of the early Church Fathers. Once, he said, "A woman may not speak, nor baptise, or 'offer' [the Eucharist], nor claim the right to any masculine function, still less to the priestly office."[7] Here, this relationship between *gender and ministry* is brought into a sharper focus. Clearly, one sees that ministry is taken to be a masculine function, *an all-male affair*. According to Tertullian, as well as the Catholic code of canon law cited above, being female is inconsistent with sacred duties, since ministry pertains to the sacred. As can be seen from the text of Tertullian, such sacred things as baptism, presiding over the Eucharist and the priestly office are tied to the male gender. This work will try to establish whether this is correct or not.

The churches resenting women in senior ministry positions give one the impression that *being a woman is incompatible with being a minister of God.* Hence, obscure biblical texts are used to maintain this. One of such is 1Tim 2,11-15.[8] Whereas Roman Catholicism, for instance, uses this text as one of the basis to exclude women from ordained ministry in the church, it turns a blind eye to 1Tim 3,1-7[9] *that emphatically resents and possibly rejects a celibate minister.*[10] This gives one the impression that the main thing is not about maintaining the integrity of sacred scripture but to "pick and choose" in order to protect the power base of the male oligarchy ruling the church.

In the light of the problems just highlighted above, this work helps to bring the early church face to face with the Christian church today. In this regard, different contemporary attitudes towards the ministry of women in the church will be examined. The problems involved will be examined from the standpoint of Paul and early Christianity. The fundamental questions to be addressed will be: What is the relationship between *gender and ministry* in early Christianity? How is this related to the church today? It is our intention in this work to see whether early Christianity was run on gender basis. Or was it a patriarchal Christianity? What role did egalitarianism play in such a church? These and some others will be the guiding questions.

As the study progresses, we shall see that ministry in the church of Paul, for instance, was not gender based. The charismatic nature of such a church recognized the importance of the Holy Spirit, which created openness towards the ministry of the female members. Since this Holy Spirit is the giver of gifts, he had no favored gender and no reserved gifts. The confession of Jesus as Lord was all that was needed.

In other words, what determined qualification for ministry in the community was not biological.

As we shall see in this work, the argument that Jesus chose only men is an anthropomorphic language that the church of Paul resisted. The transcendent nature of the Holy Spirit placed him above gynecological examinations in determining ministry roles in the community. It is not good to engage the Holy Spirit in gender disputes or try to make him the author of gender struggle or warfare. This can only demean him. Hence, Christians should refrain from doing this. We have to resist this in this 21st century.

At this juncture, I wish to say a few things about the exegetical method to be used in this work. As is usually the case, no one method is sufficient. This means that there will be a combination of exegetical techniques. Accordingly, this work will make use of the textual, literary and historical critical methods. In addition, there will be grammatical analysis and morphological evaluations of both Hebrew and Greek.

The historical critical method will try to put some of the texts and problems to be analyzed in their proper historical contexts. The literary method takes literary evidence backed by external evidence. The textual critical method tries, whenever the need arises, to establish original texts for analysis. The morphological approach will examine the forms of the Greek and Hebrew words used. Grammatical analysis will make syntactical evaluations whenever it is necessary to do so.

Indeed, this work will be both analytic and deductive. It will also be contextual and existential – relating the fruit of research to the contemporary situation in the church today. Some of the texts will best be interpreted within their contextual situations or *Sitz im Leben*[11] in order to know *per se* what the text means irrespective of what later Christian tradition thinks or makes of it. At this juncture, we shall now begin with the first chapter of the book dealing with the relationship between Paul and his fellow workers.

Chinedu Adolphus Amadi-Azuogu
Director of Doctoral Program
Southern California School of Ministry,
Los Angeles, California, USA
May 13, 2004 (Edith, my wife's birthday)

Notes

[1] This is part of what has led a good number of these women, who feel that they have also a calling, to establish independent churches of their own, answerable to no one, where they could function as senior pastors, like their male counterparts. In other words, this reluctance on the part of men to recognize the role of women in the churches is helping to create an inflation of Christian churches and denominations.

[2] Beyer, "διακονέω", TDNT II, 82.

[3] Beyer, "διακονέω", TDNT II, 82.

[4] Beyer, "διακονέω", TDNT II, 82.

[5] Beyer, "διακονέω", TDNT II, 82.

[6] *The New Code of canon law: in English translation*, Prepared by: The Canon Law Society Of Great Britain and Ireland, London 1983, 183.

[7] Tertullian, "De Virginibus Velandis 9", in: H. Bettenson, *The Early Christian Fathers*, 151.

[8] This text reads: "Let a woman learn in silence with all submissiveness. [12] I permit no woman to teach or to have authority over men; she is to keep silent. [13] For Adam was formed first, then Eve; [14] and Adam was not deceived, but the woman was deceived and became a transgressor. [15] Yet woman will be saved through bearing children, if she continues in faith and love and holiness, with modesty" (1Tim 2,11-15).

[9] Against the celibate teaching of Roman Catholicism, this text expressly insists on the marriage of the pastors and leaders of the church in these words: "Now a bishop must be above reproach, *the husband of one wife*, temperate, sensible, dignified, hospitable, an apt teacher, 3 no drunkard, not violent but gentle, not quarrelsome, and no lover of money. 4 *He must manage his own household well, keeping his children submissive* and respectful in every way; 5 *for if a man does not know how to manage his own household, how can he care for God's church?*" (1Tim 3,2-5).

[10] One reason for this resentment is seen in the following text, which was fighting the Gnosticism of the day that forbade marriage. The text in question reads: "Now the Spirit expressly says that in later times some will depart from the faith by giving heed to deceitful spirits and doctrines of demons, 2 through the pretensions of liars whose consciences are seared, 3 *who forbid marriage* and enjoin abstinence from foods which God created to be received with thanksgiving by those who believe and know the truth. 4 For everything created by God is good, and nothing is to be rejected if it is received with thanksgiving" (1Tim 4,1-3).

[11] This is a German word. Literally, it is translated as, "situation in life".

Chapter 1

Paul and his Fellow Workers

Our study of the relationship between gender and ministry in early Christianity begins with an examination of the relationship between Paul and those he called his *fellow workers*. This is considered necessary because it will help us to establish the connection between gender and ministry in the Christianity represented by Paul. What was his attitude towards the ministry of women in the church? In the light of this question, this present discussion will help to highlight how Paul cherished and esteemed the women members of his church alongside with men. It will show us that there was no connecting nexus between *gender* and *ministry* as such. In other words, gender was not a condition for distributing ministry roles in the community of Paul. The association, which we make today between the male gender and sacred ministry, disappears here. Hence, this chapter will show what type of ministry roles Paul assigned to women.

Apart from this, it will also help to demonstrate to the 21st century Christians that the equality of man and woman, in both the early church and Pauline Christianity, was not just something theoretical. By all accounts, it was a characteristic feature of this Christianity, as seen in the examples of Paul. Here, one continues to see the true Pauline attitude towards the men and women in his church.

1) Statistical and Lexical Analysis [1]

The first thing we wish to do here is to examine the available statistical evidence to see how the Greek word *synergós* (συνεργός),[2] which Paul used to designate those whom he called his "fellow workers", is distributed in the New Testament canonical literature.

συνεργός (synergós)		Rom	1Cor	2Cor	Phil	Phm	1Th	Col*	3Jo*
συνεργός (synergós)		Rom 16,3 16,9 16,21	1Cor 3,9	2Cor 1,24 8,23	Phil 2,25 4,3	Phm 1 24	1Th 3,2	Col* 4,11	3Jo* 8
συνεργέω (synergéô)	Mk** 16,20	Rom 8,28	1Cor 16,16	2Cor 6,1					Ja* 2,22

As the reader can see, both the noun *synergós* (συνεργός) and its verb *synergêo* (συνεργέω) belong almost exclusively to the undisputed Pauline literature. This evidence shows that the subordination-letters,[3] apart from Colossians, do not show interest in it. In view of this, it can be said that, though this word exists outside Paul, nevertheless, he is the *only* New Testament writer who used it to describe the ministry of some of the members of his church community, *including women*. As we shall soon see, this word *synergós* expresses a special relationship between Paul and some members of his charismatic church community.

Lexically, *synergós* means fellow worker, coworker, or helper. Its corresponding verb *synergeô* (συνεργέω) means to help or to work with.[4] In other words, the *synergói* of Paul were his special *helpers* in the task of preaching the good news of the kingdom. Both men and women participated in this special task. Hence, they were special collaborators of the apostle in carrying out this sacred task. In other words, they labored together with Paul. Hence, they were Paul's fellow laborers in the vineyard of the Lord.

To be one's fellow worker is to be a partner, or an associate. This creates a situation of comradeship. Hence, those involved become colleagues. An atmosphere of friendship begins to exist. In view of this, the *fellow workers* of Paul were also his special friends and trusted companions. A close bond existed among them. Paul could even express this in the way he presented them in his writings. In the heated struggle involved in proclaiming the gospel in the 1st century AD, these were the *allies* of Paul in spreading the good news of salvation. In a sense, then, they can truly be called the *special confreres* of the apostle.

In line with this, Bertram says that Paul "honoured his companions by using this and similar terms, thereby consolidating their authority in the churches".[5] In which case, these people were highly placed church officials of the day, wielding authority in the name and on behalf of the apostle. It is in view of this that the use of the term *synergós* becomes an important benchmark for measuring the attitude of Paul towards the ministry of women in the church. As the *synergoi* of Paul, women equally wielded authority in the Pauline churches. Let us now examine the texts where Paul addressed men and women as his *fellow workers*. Below are the relevant ones.

Greet Prisca and Aquila, my fellow workers [*tous synergous mou*] in Christ Jesus (Rom 16,3).

Greet Urbanus, our fellow worker [*ton synergon hêmôn*] in Christ. (Rom 16,9).

Timothy my fellow [*ho synergós mou*] worker greets you Rom 16,21.

I have thought it necessary to send you Epaphroditus my brother and fellow worker [*synergon*] and fellow soldier, and your messenger and minister to my need. Phil 2,25 (see also Phil 4,2-3).

To Philemon our beloved fellow worker [*synergô hêmôn*] Philemon 1,2.

Epahras, my fellow prisoner in Christ Jesus, sends greetings to you, and so do Mark, Aristrachus, Demans, and Luke, my fellow workers [*synergoi mou*].

In this list, one sees a constant and frequent use of the word *synergós* (fellow worker). This suggests to us that those involved were prominent Christians who cooperated with Paul, in an outstanding way, in the spread of the gospel. With this special ministry status, these people stood above many Christians in the community of Paul. No doubt they occupied a special place in Pauline Christianity. So we are dealing with a very special group. In view of this, it is fair to say that they were among the core ministers of the apostle. With this in mind, let us now analyze the evidence in the table above, beginning with the Roman church.

2) Women as "Fellow Workers" in the Church of Rome

The text of Rom 16,1-16 looks like a type of *roll call* of recognized personalities in the Church of Rome. Paul seems to know the activities of each of those mentioned, even though he is neither the founder of this church, nor has he visited it at the time of writing. Nonetheless, his influence in this church was equally felt. Besides, he shows that he has intimate knowledge of the church community in Rome. As can be seen from the text of Rom 16,1-2, he could even write this church in advance to announce the impending arrival of a certain deaconess, called Phoebe. Indeed, the fact that he was greeting so many people by their names suggests that he was quite at home with this church.

The people greeted seem to be some eminent members of the *Roman church* with reputation of unquestionable and undiluted partnership with the apostle. Hence, we see him giving "honor to whom honor is due". He recognizes that these people have played some remarkable roles in the preaching of the good news. They have been very outstanding in their activities. It is in view of this that the use of *synergós* in the list of greetings in Rom 16,3-16 is very interesting for this study. The reason is that it helps to demonstrate that Paul did not discriminate between woman and man in granting this special status. He was not gender-obsessed, as is the case with some church authorities today. Hence, gender profiling is out of the question here. The following are those recognized as the *fellow workers* of Paul in Rom 16,3-16.

a) Prisca
b) Aquila
c) Urbanus
d) Timothy

As one can see, among these four fellow workers in the church of Rome, one of them is a woman called *Prisca.* Indeed, it is quite an interesting thing that *Prisca,* though a woman, was also recognized as a church dignitary, alongside with other men. Here, we have strong indication that there was no discrimination between the sexes in distributing roles in Pauline Christianity. This is intensified by the fact that Paul made no distinction between the greeting to Prisca and the one to Aquila. In fact, we see that he even mentioned the name of Prisca first before that of Aquila and the other men in the list. If Paul advocated for male chauvinism, he would not have done it this way. This invites us to examine this couple more closely.

3) Prisca and Aquila

The texts of Rom 16,5 and 1Cor 16,19 help to shed more light on the status of Prisca[6] and Aquila.[7] They were among the first urban Christians in the metropolitan city of ancient Rome. This couple was also among those expelled from Rome by the emperor Claudius in AD 49.[8] As a result of this expulsion Prisca and Aquila moved to Corinth where Paul met them.[9] Later, they moved to Ephesus where they established a *house church.*[10] In this regard, 1Cor 16,19 says, "the churches of Asia send you greetings. Aquila and Prisca together with the church at their house send you many greetings in the Lord." It is not to be imagined that Aquila excluded his wife (Prisca) from running the affairs of this *church* in their house. It makes sense to say that they jointly presided over it.

This relationship between Aquila and Prisca is also seen in the case of another couple-Apphia and Archippus-in the letter to Philemom. The couple had also a *house church.* The relevant text to this effect says, "and to Apphia our sister, and to Archippus our fellow soldier, and to the *church in your house*" (Philemon 2). One sees that women were playing meaningful roles in Pauline Christianity. Since they were playing host to the house churches they could be called "pastors" of such churches, to use our present day terminology. In a sense, they were also church planters. They labored so that the faith might be kept alive.

If one argues that the men (Aquila and Archippus) mentioned in the texts above were the ones presiding over the house church in their homes, another text punctures such an argument. This time it is about a woman in Col. 4,15 who also played host to the house church in Colossia. The relevant text says, "Greet the brethren who are in Laodicea and also Nympha and the church that is in her house." This shows that women were leaders of house churches. They did not play second class Christians. In which case, the women mentioned, Prisca, Apphia and Nympha were leaders in the New Testament house churches. The ordination of women deacons in early Christianity is to be seen in this context. *And the debate about the priestly ordination of women should also note this ministry position in the early church.*

On another note, we have also evidence of women participation in the leadership of the house churches in Acts. This time it has to do with the mother of John Mark (Acts 12.25), who was a fellow missionary of Paul. Her mother Mary housed also a prayer group of the apostolic Christians. The relevant text says:

> And when he [Peter] had considered the thing, he came to the house of Mary the mother of John, whose surname was Mark; where many were gathered together praying. And as Peter knocked at the door of the gate, a damsel came to hearken, named Rhoda. And when she knew Peter's voice, she opened not the gate for gladness, but ran in, and told how Peter stood before the gate (KJV: Acts 12,12-14).

The context of this text is the miraculous release of Peter from prison (Acts 12,7-11). Upon his release, he went straight to the home of Mary, the mother of John Mark. The fact that Peter went straight to the house of this woman is an indication that it is a place well known to him for the early Christian liturgical gathering. He was clearly aware that this was an accepted meeting place for the apostolic Christians. In other words, this place where these Christians were gathered was simply a *church*. Otherwise, how else does one define one in the context of Acts?

So one sees that Peter was not a stranger to this place. This is further supported by the fact that another woman in the praying community, named Rhoda, quickly recognized his voice. Of course, the fact that she ran to tell the others of the sudden appearance of Peter means that they too were aware of his imprisonment. Hence, the woman ran to bring the good news to the others in the church community, possibly still praying for the release of Peter.

We can also deduce from the text that Mary herself seemed to be a person of nobility and perhaps wealthy. It is possible that her social standing enabled her son, John Mark, to find his feet quickly within the missionary community. Hence, Paul and Barnabas did not hesitate to include him in their missionary expeditions.

Here, we have evidence of the house church in Acts. Of course, this was already a reality in Acts 2,46, where the early Christians went to the temple and broke bread in their houses. In this regard, Luke says: "And they, continuing daily with one accord in the temple, and breaking bread from house to house, did eat their meat with gladness and singleness of heart" (KJV: Acts 2,46). The "breaking of bread" here is the Eucharistic celebration. As Luke tells us, it took place from "house to house". This shows that the early celebration of the Eucharist was a house affair. The early Jewish Christians had no need of cathedrals, or pro-cathedrals or mega churches. The house church satisfied their needs.[11]

In view of this, what was taking place in the house of Mary is to be seen in this light. There is every reason to believe that Mary was presiding over this church in her house. And of course, Peter did not even go to his fellow apostles but to this church in this woman's house. This is also interesting for the ministry of women in the church today. The apostolic church was not even anti-women's ministry. As we have seen in the text above, the leadership role of women was even recognized and endorsed. Hence, Peter went straight to the house of this woman where the church community was gathered. This makes it all the more perplexing that we should be resenting the role of women in the ministry of the church today. As we can see, the apostolic church integrated gender and ministry. It tried to harmonize the two of them.

In the case of Prisca and Aquila the fact that Paul mentioned the church in their house twice in two separate letters means that it was recognized by him. There is no doubt that he equally knew that Prisca was playing a leadership role in this church. This helps to explain further why Paul singles out this couple in his list of greetings (Rom 16,3) and thanks them in a very special way (Rom 16,4). In a sense, then, Prisca was also an official of this house church. She was actively involved in its ministry. This is in consonance with Rom 16.1-2, which recognizes the presence of a deaconess in the Cenchrean church and Rom 16.7, which recognized the presence of women apostles in Pauline Christianity.

It is striking that Paul places the name Prisca first. In this regard, Lampe says, "references to Prisca before Aquila more likely indicate that she was even more active in church life than her craftsman husband."[12] Further, he says, "the couple has often been depicted as wealthy, with Prisca of ever higher social status than Aquila since her name in most cases is placed before his"[13] This points to Phoebe, the deaconess, in Rom 16,1-2.

Apart from being mentioned in connection with a house church Prisca and Aquila were fairly known in the New Testament times. Excluding the instances already mentioned, they are also known in Acts 18,2[14] and 2Tim 4,19.[15] This means that they had a recognized personality in the apostolic church and beyond. There is no gainsaying that they were high profile Christians and outstanding church leaders. This helps to make them distinguished members of the *synergói* of Paul.

4) Other Women in Rom 16

At this point, I wish also to say a few words about some of the other eminent women mentioned in the litany of greetings contained in Rom 16, though not specifically named as *fellow workers*. As the evidence shows, not only did Paul recognize certain women as his *fellow workers*, he also recognized other highly placed women in the church. He did not discriminate against them. The relevant texts are Rom 16,6 and 16,12. Let us look at them.

Rom 16,6: ἀσπασασθε Μαρίαν, ἥτις πολλὰ ἐκοπίασεν εἰς ὑμας	Greet *Maria* who has labored hard for you.
Rom 16,12: ἀσπάσασθε Τρύφαιναν καὶ Τρύφωσαν τὰς κοπιώσας ἐν κυρίῳ. Ἀσπάσασθε Περσίδα τὴν ἀγαπητήν, ἥτις πολλὰ ἐκοπίασεν ἐν κυρίῳ.	Greet *Tryphaena* and *Tryphosa* who labor in the Lord. Greet *Persida* the beloved who has labored hard in the Lord.

Excluding Phoebe (Rom 16,1-2) and Julia (Rom 16,7) who were deaconess and apostle, here we have four other women in addition to Prisca. All these have labored hard *en kyriô* (ἐν κυρίῳ) in the Lord. In the case of the *Persida* of the text, Paul describes her in a very warm and affectionate way. She is called "Persida the beloved" (Περσίδα τὴν ἀγαπητήν). Here, cordiality is expressed and affection is poured out lavishly. This is not a characteristic feature of someone who precluded women from active ministry in the church or disliked them. Based on this information, here in Rom 16, Byrne rightly said: "If later generations saw fit to curtail and even forbid the engagement of women in the apostolic mission, then the evidence of these texts suggests that that can hardly be regarded as something to be laid at the feet of Paul."[16] As the reader will see, this work will demonstrate this in the clearest possible way. Truncated hermeneutics has led to the use of Paul and the early church against women. In view of this, we intend to set scripture walking once more on its feet and no longer on its head.

Indeed, Paul recognizes these women fully as genuine *fellow workers* in the οἰκεῖος της πίστεως (*oikeíos tês písteôs*) *household of faith* (cf. Gal 6,10). As far as he is concerned, they have also labored hard *en kyriô* (in the Lord). This is not to be forgotten in analyzing the attitude of Paul and the early church towards women. It has also to be kept in mind in discussing the place of women in the ministry of the church in the 21st century. In all instances, Paul describes the contribution of these women to the church as "laboring". All the women involved have labored. In other words, they are his fellow laborers in the vineyard of the Lord. What, then, does this mean in the ministry of Paul? This leads us now to examine the verb used in describing the labor of these women, as the fellow workers of the apostle.

5) The Greek Verb Κοπιάω

This is the verb used to describe the type of function the women involved performed. We are attracted to it because it was also used to describe the same group of people in the Thessalonian church. Its analysis will help us to know the identity of the women mentioned.

Lexically, this Greek verb *kopiáô* (κοπιάω) means to tire, to make great exertions, to wear oneself out whether through mental or physical effort.[17] Also it means to labor. This lexical information shows that the women mentioned in Rom 16,6.12 were not just casual laborers in the vineyard of the Lord. The type of job they performed involved a severe and strenuous effort. It involved exhaustion. The reader sees that these women performed a difficult task, which made great exertions on them. They were really worn out in the course of their missionary activity.

In this regard, Paul even refers to his own missionary activity as *work* (1Cor 15,10). Here, he boasted, saying, περισσότερον αὐτων πάντων εκοπιασα – I *labored* more than all of them. Judging from this text, it is not difficult to see that the missionary activity of Paul is described with this verb κοπιάω (*kopiáô*), just as he uses it now to describe the work of these women. Of course, this is not just any type of work or labor. It is the "work of the Lord" and a "laboring for the Lord". Hence, it should not be in vain (1Cor 15,58). In using this term to describe his own missionary work, Paul compares it with manual labor, to point out how laborious it is. This special usage in Paul applies also to other missionaries (2Cor 10,15-16). One, then, sees that *kopiaô*, as a term, is used to apply to *church ministry* in Paul.

Although this work or ministry is a burden, yet Paul takes it up for the sake of Christ (1Thes 2,9). This work is described as "labor in the Lord" (Rom 16,12) and work for the community (Rom 16,6). The reward is from God. This is what motivates the laborer, whether a man or a woman. Notwithstanding, the laborers of the Lord deserve esteem. Hence, Paul advises the Thessalonian community in these words:

Greek Text:	Translation: But we appeal to you,
ἐρωτωμεν δὲ ὑμας, ἀδελφοί, εἰδέναι τοὺς *κοπιωντας* ἐν ὑμιν καὶ προϊσταμένους ὑμων ἐν κυρίῳ καὶ νουθετουντας ὑμας	brothers and sisters, to respect those who labor among you and are in authority over you in the Lord and advise you,

| καὶ ἡγεῖσθαι αὐτοὺς ὑπερεκ-
περισσοῦ ἐν ἀγάπῃ διὰ τὸ ἔργον
αὐτῶν. Εἰρηνεύετε ἐν ἑαυτοῖς | 13 and to regard them beyond measure in
love because of their work. Be at peace
among yourselves (1Thes 5,12-13). |

A breakdown of this text shows that those for whom respect is solicited in the Thessalonian community have the following credentials:

a) They labor among the Thessalonians (τοὺς κοπιωντας ἐν ὑμιν), just as the women in Rom 16,6.12 labored among the Romans. Their ministry in the church is described as "work".

b) They are leaders in the community (πρόϊσταμένους ὑμων), and have authority over it. This authority is described as ἐν κυρίῳ (in the Lord). This gives it an ecclesiastical dimension. These Christians were not just ordinary members of the church community. They had *authority* in the community. This applies also to the women mentioned as *laborers* in the text of Romans cited above.

c) These "ecclesiastical officials" had the duty to advise and counsel the community (νουθετουντας ὑμας). So they were considered to be the wise men and women of the church. They had Christian wisdom, which places them in the best position to advise the community. This shows that Paul considered them to have impeccable and unquestionable orthodoxy. In the case of the women mentioned in Rom 16,6.12, this becomes outstanding in relation to one of them described by Paul as "Persida the beloved" (*Persída tên agapêtên*). This woman is said to have labored very hard in the Lord.

All the three elements listed above show that these "special laborers" have solid credentials as Christian community leaders. In other words, those who labor, as in the text of Romans above, are laboring as "church officials" of the day. Hence, Paul appeals to the community to treat them in the following ways.

a) They should be treated with respect.

b) The nature of their work demands that they should be highly esteemed. Hence, the community should have high regards for them beyond measure (ἡγεῖσθαι αὐτοὺς ὑπερεκπερισσοῦ).

c) All these are to be done ἐν ἀγάπῃ (in love).

One sees that these people stand above the community.

In view of this analysis, Hauch suggests that the τοὺς κοπιωντας ἐν ὑμιν (those who labor among you) with the πρόϊσταμένοι (those in authority) of 1Thes 5,12 is a reference to the office bearers of the community.[18] This position is entirely endorsed in this work. The text clearly shows that the reference here is to church office, even if it is not yet as developed as it is today. In the context of the day, it certainly passes. This means that the women who labored and even labored very hard in Rom 16 were accepted church officials, who labored side by side with their male counterparts. They were not discriminated against. Hence, they had the same privileges with men. One sees, in the period closer to the Jesus-event, that women performed ecclesiastical tasks, which are denied them in later Christianity. This is the problem facing Christianity in the 21st century. It belongs to us to solve it without any more foot-dragging or dilly-dallying.

From the standpoint of Pauline Christianity the exclusion of women from any aspect of the apostolic mission is not Christian. As the facts of New Testament history and practice show these women did not debase the ministry of Paul and the early church. Instead, they enriched it. Pauline Christianity was the "Christianity of equal opportunity". Hence, it belonged equally to every member, with full and unhindered participation for all. Discrimination of the sexes was neither remembered nor practiced. Gender profiling was not in force. Hence, it could neither determine nor influence the official church policy of the time towards the ministry of women. The principle of *justice and fairness* was allowed to run its course. This is something that Pauline interpreters and historians of New Testament history in the 21st century are not to forget. It is important to do this especially when one wants to apportion blames for the later New Testament subordination of women, which still remains the feature of many of the Christian churches, even in this third millennium. At this point, we shall focus attention on the church at Phillipi to see more information on the women fellow workers of Paul.

6) Women as Fellow Workers in the Philippian Church[19]

The practice of designating women as *fellow workers* was not only limited to the Roman church. Other Pauline churches, like the Christian Church at Philippi, equally experienced this. Hence, in the Philippian church, other persons mentioned as the *synergói* (fellow workers) of Paul include Epaphroditus, Philemon and Luke. To be mentioned in a very special way, as the *synergói* of Paul, are two prominent women in this church. These are *Euodia* and *Syntyche* named in Phil 4,2-3. Since this text contains important clarifications, let us review it briefly.

Greek:[20] 4:2 Εὐοδίαν παρακαλω καὶ Συντύχην παρακαλω τὸ αὐτο' φρονειν ἐν κυρίῳ4:3 ναὶ ἐρωτω καὶ σέ γνήσιε σύζυγε, συλλαμβάνου αὐταις, ἅιτινες ἐν τω εὐαγγελίῳ συνήθλησάν μοι μετὰ καὶ Κλήμεντος καὶ των λοιπων συνεργων μου, ὧν τὰ ὀνόματα ἐν βίβλῳ ζωῆς.	Translation: I appeal to Euodia and I appeal to Syntyche to live in harmony in the Lord. Yes I ask you also, true yoke-fellow, help them, for they struggled along with me in spreading the good news together with Clement and the rest of my fellow workers, whose names are in the book of life (Phil 4,2-3).

Paul makes this solemn appeal to these two women in a very special way, not just as members of the Philippian church, but as eminent leaders of the church community. This means that these were local church leaders with a recognized position of prominence in the community. In which case, these women (Euodia and Syntyche) had an authoritative position in Pauline Christianity.

It seems that they were having some unspecified problems. This is maintained because of the use of this imperative form *syllambánou* (συλλαμβάνου). It comes from the deponent verb *syllambánomai* (συλλαμβάνομαι), which means to come to the aid of, help or assist.[21] However, our principal consideration here is not their disagreement but their role in preaching the good news of salvation which has a bearing on the ministry of women in the New Testament churches.

In this regard, the information given by the grammatical construction ἅιτινες ἐν τῷ εὐαγγελίῳ συνήθλησάν μοι μετα (they struggled along with me in spreading the good news) becomes crucial in understanding their role as *synergói* (fellow workers) of Paul. The main word here is the verb *synêthlêsán* (συνήθλησάν) used in the text above. It will help us to know more about these *fellow workers*. What, then, does it mean?

7) Women as "Fellow Athletes" of Paul

We are led to this discussion by the use of the verb *synêthlêsán* in the grammatical construction of Phil 4,3. This verb is from *synathléô* (συναθλέω) which is a compound word made up of *syn* + *athléô*. It is also found in Phil 1,27.[22] In both instances, the verb is used in connection with the preaching of the good news. This is one obvious indication that these fellow workers of Paul, including women, *were preachers of the gospel*, though presented as competitors in athletic events.

As we have seen above, one component part of *synathléô* is the verb *athléô* (ἀθλέω). It means to contest in an athletic event. Two nouns are derived from it. The first one is *athléma* (ἀθλήμα), which means a contest, or a struggle. And the second is *athlêtês* (ἀθλήτης), which means a combatant or champion.[23] The derived adjective is *athlêtikos* (ἀθλητικός).[24] In all these forms, one sees that a continuous struggle is involved. In order to be in top form, the athlete must train and prepare well. This applies also to the mission of the Christian. It is in vain for a Christian to claim salvation when one has not even trained to be a good "athlete".

In the New Testament the verbal form *athléô* is found only in Paul. Here, it means *to be an athlete*.[25] So this imagery of an athlete is akin to Paul, though it also influenced later Christianity.[26] Further, it means to undergo a struggle, to contend in battle.[27] This battle imagery is strongly kept in the forefront. It shows how difficult life was for the first century

Christian missionaries, described as "athletes". In this regard, Ignatius of Antioch writes to Polycarp as follows:

> You must not be panic-stricken by those who have an air of credibility but who teach heresy. Stand your ground like an anvil under the hammer. A great athlete must suffer blows to conquer. And especially for God's sake must we put up with [2] everything, so that he will put up with us. Show more enthusiasm than you do. Mark the times. Be on the alert for him who is above time, the Timeless, the Unseen, the One who became visible for our sakes, who was beyond touch and passion, yet who for our sakes became subject to suffering, and endured everything for us.[28]

The difficulty involved is shown with the imagery of the anvil under the hammer. This shows that the Christian "athlete" functioned under very adverse conditions, as the use of the Greek verb *kopiáo* (to labor) above shows. It was all about suffering. The life of Paul shows this very clearly. However, the struggle involved is not in vain. There is a motivation fueling and sustaining it. Hence, *athléô* also means to contend for a prize.[29] In which case, there is a reward. The battle involved is not aimless, because there is a reason for the contest.

This means that the contestants should make every preparation to win in order to get the prestigious prize in the end, as in an Olympic event. This was precisely the motivating principle for Paul and his fellow workers. Hence, the Paul of second Timothy says:

> For I am now ready to be offered, and the time of my departure is at hand. [7] I have fought a good fight, I have finished my course, I have kept the faith: [8] Henceforth there is laid up for me a crown of righteousness, which the Lord, the righteous judge, shall give me at that day: and not to me only, but unto all them also that love his appearing (KJV: 2Tim 4,6-8).

Here, one sees a link between the *good struggle* and *reward*. The Pauline athlete hopes for the crown of righteousness. This is what makes him or her to count everything as nothing. In view of this, it is not enough to take part in the contest. One should endeavor to fight well and to keep the faith and win. The emphasis is on winning the contest. It is in view of this that Paul addresses his "athletes" in these words:

> Do you not know that the runners in the stadium all run in the race, but only one wins the prize? Run so as to win. [25] Every athlete exercises discipline in every way. They do it to win a perishable crown, but we an imperishable one. [26] Thus I do not run aimlessly; I do not fight as if I were shadowboxing. [27] No, I drive my body and train it, for fear that, after having preached to others, I myself should be disqualified (1Cor 9, 24-27).

In this text, one sees a relationship between reward and the work of the evangelist. If he or she pays the price, he or she should also win the prize. As Paul says, the prize of the evangelist is an imperishable crown. Hence, it is very important not to run aimlessly but to aim at winning. Since it is said that *no sweat, no sweet* and *no cross, no crown*, it therefore makes sense that some strain on the body is inevitable. This shows what "laboring in the Lord" meant for the fellow workers of Paul.

Finally, *athléô* also means to engage in a competition or conflict.[30] Of course, Paul was faced with a situation of competition in his preaching career, which created a conflict situation. This became fiercer in 2Corinthians where he took on his opponents head-on. He spent time in this letter trying to show that he is even a better competitor. *One, then, can say that a synergós is one who has fought on the side of Paul in this difficult competition.* He or she is one who has competed alongside with Paul as an "athletic squad". As Stauffer pointed out, "the fight in which the leader of the community is engaged demands not only extreme exertion and readiness for sacrifice, but also discipline and ordered conduct".[31] This was the situation in the case of Paul and his "fellow competitors", *among whom were women.* As we have seen above, two of them (Euodia and Syntyche) are mentioned in a special way in the Philippian church.

At this juncture, I wish to point out that the noun *athlêtês* (ἀθλήτης), which is anglicized as athlete, is derived from the verb (*athléô*). This word (*athlêtês*) was used fairly widely in early Christianity to describe the laborious endeavors of the preachers of the good news who were likened to athletes. Hence, in his letter to Polycarp Ignatius of Antioch wrote about these "athletes"as follows: "Bear the diseases of everyone, like an athlete in perfect form. The greater the toil, the greater the gain".[32] Further, he says, "as God's athlete, be sober. The prize, as you very well know, is immortality and eternal life".[33] The reader sees that this imagery of an athlete was very strong both in apostolic and post-apostolic Christianity. This shows also the extent of the influence of Paul on early Christianity.

As Stauffer further said, this "athlete" is the leader of the community "who is tested by battle and equal to every demand or conflict.[34] This means that the *synergói* of Paul, including the two women in the Philippian church, were his "fellow athletes". All of them belonged to one "athletic squad", under one leader, Paul. In the language of Ignatius of Antioch above, all of them were the "athletes of God".

In choosing these *synergói* Paul continued his policy of "non-discrimination". No one was gender profiled. As fellow athletes competing alongside with men, women equally qualified to be priests and deacons in this community. If they participated in every level of leadership in the community, there is no reason to believe that they would have been disqualified as priests in the community. Nothing could be more elevated than being either the *synergós* (fellow worker) or *synathlêtês* (fellow athlete) of Paul. If these women enjoyed these highest privileges available in the community, they would have equally enjoyed the privileges of being a priest or a deacon or a senior pastor.

The last lexical step to be taken concerns the verb *synathléô* (συ-ναθλέω) which corroborates the information we have so far. In this regard, it also means to contend or struggle along with someone.[35] One sees that these *synergói*, including women, struggled along with Paul. They fought together with him. What, then, does this *struggle* mean in the practical life of Paul and his fellow workers?

8) The Pains of an Evangelist as an "Athlete"[36]

The missionary experiences of Paul show that *preaching the gospel* was indeed a painful and bitter struggle for him. Indeed, it involved being an "athlete". As the facts of New Testament history show, not everybody was happy with him because of his revolutionary theological perspectives.

Several instances in the theology of Paul illustrate this point. For instance, he revolutionized the concept of circumcision, when in Rom 2 he tried to wipe out the line between Jews and Gentiles by introducing the element of "circumcision in the heart". Secondly, his doctrine of justification was also a critique of orthodox Jewish concept of justification. Whereas Paul makes Jesus the center of his doctrine of justification, the Jewish orthodoxy before him makes the torah the center of righteousness. Thirdly, whereas Jewish belief extolled the covenant of God with Abraham in Gen 17, Paul extolled the promises of God to Abraham (cf. Gen 15) in Gal 3,15-17. Finally, whereas orthodox Jewish belief makes Isaac to be the child of the promise, on the other hand, Paul makes Jesus to be the real child of the promise. Hence, for Paul, the fulfillment of the promise to Abraham is not in Isaac but in Jesus (see Gal 3,16)..

In addition to these theological perspectives, Paul championed the spread of Gentile or Hellenistic Christianity. As another "version" of Christianity, with its non-Jewish characteristics, many Jewish Christians could not come to terms with it (cf. 2Pet 3,15b-16).[37] This was considered by many as a departure from what was considered to be orthodox. Hence, it came constantly under attack from those who were not happy with this development understood to be a deviation from the "true faith" of Israel. For these people it was seen as a movement away from "orthodoxy". Therefore, it was considered to be an unwelcome digression.

Under this unfavorable situation the apostle had to fight to defend this "new" Christianity. Often times, he and his Christianity were placed on trial. His apostolic authority was equally questioned (cf. 1Cor 9,1-5; Gal 1,1). This was simply an attempt to degrade him and his Christianity. The ultimate aim was to discredit both preacher and gospel.

On account of this unpleasant situation, in pursuit of his *Gentile mission*, Paul suffered greatly even in the hands of his fellow Jewish Christians who sharply disagreed with him. In view of this, sometimes, they resorted to violence against him in order to subdue him or coerce him into submitting to their own perceived "orthodoxy". Accordingly, he was humiliated for the sake of the gospel. His pathetic experiences are summarized well in the following text:

[24] Of the Jews five times received I forty stripes save one. [25] Thrice was I beaten with rods, once was I stoned, thrice I suffered shipwreck, a night and a day I have been in the deep; [26] In journeyings often, in perils of waters, in perils of robbers, in perils by mine own countrymen, in perils by the heathen, in perils in the city, in perils in the wilderness, in perils in the sea, in perils among false brethren; [27] In weariness and painfulness, in watchings often, in hunger and thirst, in fastings often, in cold and nakedness. [28] Beside those things that are without, that which cometh upon me daily, the care of all the churches (KJV: 2Cor 11,24-28).

This text clearly shows how greatly he suffered in the hands of both Gentiles and Jews alike. As the text points out, it was by no means an easy road for this great apostle of Gentile Christianity. Preaching the good news was an arduous task for him. It was wearisome and burdensome. In other words, exhaustion characterized his ministry as an apostle. The dangers and perils that surrounded him made his work quite a laborious and toilsome one. He had to operate under a very strenuous and tough circumstance. In a sense, then, he had a arduous task. As a result, he was always ridiculed and dishonored. Hence, he says:

[8] We are troubled on every side, yet not distressed; we are perplexed, but not in despair; [9] Persecuted, but not forsaken; cast down, but not destroyed; [10] Always bearing about in the body the dying of the Lord Jesus, that the life also of Jesus might be made manifest in our body. [11] For we which live are always delivered unto death for Jesus' sake, that the life also of Jesus might be made manifest in our mortal flesh. (KJV: 2Cor 4,8-11).

As we can see, the apostle was badly tormented. Things were by no means easy for him. As a result, life was made to be miserable and unbearable for him. Hence, he was placed in an uncomfortable position. His opponents mounted roadblocks upon roadblocks for him. They caused serious problems for him. Every attempt was made to frustrate him and wreck his missionary foundation. Steps were taken to destroy the gospel that he preached. Indeed, efforts were made to ruin it, to reduce it to mere rubble. His fellow Jewish Christians ill-treated him for the simple reason that he was ministering to the Gentile Christians without insisting on circumcision. Certainly, missionary life was too difficult for him, as he further says:

> [3] Giving no offence in any thing, that the ministry be not blamed: [4] But in all things approving ourselves as the ministers of God, in much patience, in afflictions, in necessities, in distresses, [5] In stripes, in imprisonments, in tumults, in labours, in watchings, in fastings; [6] By pureness, by knowledge, by longsuffering, by kindness, by the Holy Ghost, by love unfeigned, [7] By the word of truth, by the power of God, by the armour of righteousness on the right hand and on the left, [8] By honour and dishonour, by evil report and good report: as deceivers, and yet true; [9] As unknown, and yet well known; as dying, and, behold, we live; as chastened, and not killed; [10] As sorrowful, yet always rejoicing; as poor, yet making many rich; as having nothing, and yet possessing all things (KJV: 2Cor 6,3-10).

As can be seen, Paul was called names to the extent of portraying him as an impostor before his missionary clients. This means that he was presented as a charlatan, as a fake and fraudulent evangelist of the gospel. In the language of the Christians of today, he was considered by his fellow Jewish Christians to be a "heretic", a non-orthodox preacher. He was seen as one propagating unsound and unhealthy doctrine. His orthodoxy was constantly questioned by his fellow Jewish Christians who felt that he was not propagating the accepted belief. In view of this, his teaching was considered to be heterodox. Hence, efforts were made to jettison it. In other words, Paul was taken to be preaching contrary to the Jerusalem accepted position. It is in this context that he was constantly dishonored and shamed just to disrupt the course of the Christianity that he was propagating. One sees that preaching the gospel was a painful and bitter struggle for him. Notwithstanding, he endured till the end and his Christianity survived the possibility of extinction. He ran the good race and won the noble prize. Today, he is the great apostle of our faith, but it was not an easy road for him.

In the light of this unenviable plight of the apostle one now sees what it actually means to struggle with him in the gospel. In other words, the women and the others called his *fellow workers* not only helped in spreading the gospel under these harsh and adverse conditions but also suffered with him in his humiliations. Since "a friend in need is a friend indeed," they emerged as his true friends and companions. They helped him to carry the cross of Jesus Christ. No wonder he singles them out because of their great evangelical act. This is to say that these women were female evangelists (women-preachers) of the word.

If they shared the cost of preaching the gospel, why should they now be excluded from the ministry of the church? *If they were not gender profiled when sharing this cost, is it not an act of gross injustice to gender profile them now so as to prevent them from acting in ordained capacity and senior ministry positions?* Since they helped to pay the missionary price together with Paul, why should they not get the prize of ordination and all levels of leadership position in the church now? Is it a justifiable act that the one who pays the ultimate price should be purposely prevented from getting the prize? Is it church justice that the one who wins the crown should be prevented from wearing the crown? This is what the present day church practice shows, when it denies women certain leadership positions in the church.

Fortunately, Pauline examples negate this ugly situation. It is wrong to exclude women from the ministry of the church under whatever pretext. It does not matter who is championing this discrimination against them. After all *a big name does not make a wrong right.* Nor does office, no matter how high and how exalted, justify a wrong action or decision. This anomaly against women has to be rectified in this 21st century.

In the light of the difficult circumstances enumerated above one sees that it was by no means easy for the women followers of Paul to have associated themselves with him. Since his life was constantly placed on the firing line by his opponents, these women were equally on this same firing line. They were also the "fellow soldiers" of the apostle in the "warfront" of salvation. They too were soft and easy targets, like Paul their master. On account of this, it needed a lot of courage to be associated with Paul in his ministry to the Gentiles. This shows that laboring for the gospel was equally a fatiguing and fastidious thing for them. Life was hard for them. Their ministry was not simply about "honey and sugar" or "bread and butter".

This special characteristic of 1st century Pauline ministry leads us to make this reflection about contemporary ministry. From what has been said so far about women and the ministry of Paul we can see what contradistinguishes these women with the present day ministers of the church who see ministry as a means of comfort and subsistence. This was not the case with the fellow workers of Paul, including women, who are today excluded from the ministry of the church. As the fellow soldiers of Paul, they sacrificed in order to witness to Christ, when many of today's pastors and ministers[38] witness to the dollar and to material things.[39] In our own time, ministry is seen as a "bed of roses", a "crown of jewel". This explains why today there are so many independent and privately owned churches, many of them with no more than fifty active members. The desire is not to minister to the people of God but to extort money and materials things from them in God's name. This gives easy money, especially in a place like the *United States of America* where the tax law grants the non-exempt status to these so-called churches[40] as non-profit organizations. In order to maximize "profit", the paying of tithes becomes the principal gospel preached. People are psychologically intimidated to pay their tithes. Hence, there is an economic boom from which these women are not wanted.

The unfortunate thing about this is that the Middle Ages' sale of indulgence by the church of the time is condemned as evil by many of these pastors, while their *sale of salvation* through the payment of tithes is condoned. *This is equally wrong.* Christians are reminded in this book that *the payment or non-payment of tithes has absolutely nothing to do with the salvation of the individual or persons involved.* In the theology of justification by Paul, salvation is a *gratis* from God. It cannot be bought by whatever means. No amount of tithe-payment can merit the individual the salvation from God, made possible in Christ. Tithe is only a form of religious tax. It does not go beyond this. Christians should note this important clarification. Otherwise, hungry and money-minded pastors will continue to exploit their theological ignorance to continue to fleece and cheat them in the name of God.

However, this clarification made here should not be misconstrued as an argument against the payment of tithes in those churches fancying it. Obviously, the Christian church needs money. However, it should not get this money through ways and means that give the false and mistaken impression that salvation is for sale or on sale through monetary contributions. It is blasphemous to link the payment of tithes and offerings with salvation. Pastors should appeal to the goodwill and generosity of their members instead of telling falsely telling them that they are robbing God if they do not tithe. This is totally wrong. *It is nothing but "money earning" made easy.*

This short digression, notwithstanding, ministry for the women followers of Paul was a painstaking assignment. They had to participate in the worries and troubles of Paul, the master, in preaching the good news of salvation. Their situation could not have been different from his hazardous predicament. The opponents of Paul could have equally associated them with him. As people on the forefront of a perilous situation, their lot could not have been any different from that of Paul himself. Together with Paul they sat on a keg of gunpowder. They carried the loose canon around just to preach the gospel. It is in view of this that it becomes more comprehensible that Paul says that these women fellow workers in the Philippian church *have labored hard in the gospel.*

The mention of *tôn loipôn synergôn mou* (the rest of my fellow workers) in Phil 4,3 indicates, perhaps, that Paul has only mentioned the names of the most outstanding members among these *fellow workers.* In which case, these women were among the eminent members of the Philippian church. This could even explain why Paul was urging them to agree with one another.

8) Final Remarks

Finally, one now sees that both *men and women* were actively involved in the pastoral ministry of the church at all levels in Pauline Christianity. In a very special way, they participated in the ministry of preaching and spreading the gospel. Men and women, as the *synergói* of Paul, were his fellow "athletes". Together, they were the "soldiers" of Christ. They played as a team, with Paul as their "team manager". They fought as an army and suffered together. In the end, they paid the costly price together and hoped for the noble prize together. Their sacrifices for the sake of the gospel ought not be in vain.

In this Christianity, the *authority* to preach the good news was in no way an exclusive reserve or prerogative of men. Paul had no inhibition to address the women-members of his church communities as his *fellow workers.* To do this neither diminished his importance nor reduced his stature as an apostle. It neither degraded, nor devalued, nor demeaned him or his apostolic ministry.

Above all, in his usage of this term, we do not see the subordination of women seen in the New Testament house codes and later Christianity. Instead of subordination, he offered "ordination" to the womenfolk. So this was not a *profiling Christianity.* In addition, it was not gender-based. It was a *"Christianity of equal opportunity".* Here, the principle of "non-discrimination" was upheld. In this Christianity, instead of ritual segregation, there was true congregation of *equal participants.* Here, the principle of *equal protection* applied to all the members.

Therefore, Paul has laid down solid principles to guide the course of women liberation in the 21st century. This becomes a movement to return to the original ideals of early Christianity. It is a movement to recognize the fact that man and woman are *fellow workers* in preaching the good news of the kingdom. It becomes a sincere Christian effort to recognize the equality of the sexes in the 21st century. It is fair, just and legitimate to demand an equality of this kind. In so doing, women are not begging for a favor. They are not even asking for a privilege. On the contrary, they are demanding for a Pauline *guaranteed* but *denied* rights.

Later Christians caused these rights to become elusive. Unfortunately, this "pipeline-error" has continued till this day. Its correction is of paramount importance in this 21st century. This is the urgent task facing the 21st century Christians. Hence, the women liberation movement becomes also a struggle for what is right, just and noble. This is not just a feminist demand or a womanist agitation. Hence, the movement is not simply a feminist or womanist movement. It is based on sound ethical and moral principles. In view of this, fair-minded persons are called upon to help to champion the course of this "sacred crusade" in search of the truth. It is a noble task to join in this liberation struggle.

This leads us now to discuss another topic of importance concerning another aspect of the ministry of women in early Christianity. This time it is about the place of women apostles in early Pauline Christianity. As controversial as this topic may seem, it is our intention to find out whether Paul recognized women as apostles in his churches. The next chapter investigates this. There we shall see how Paul deviated from the patriarchy of the time. In other words, he crossed the patriarchal line in order to integrate women into all aspects of his apostolic ministry. With this in mind let us turn the searchlight now on the question of women and the ministry of apostles in early Christianity.

Chapter 2
Women Apostles in early Pauline Christianity

Early Pauline Christianity recognized being an apostle as a gift of the Spirit, contrary to the views of Palestinian Christian traditions. As one sees in the charismatic list in 1Cor 12,28 *apostles* are mentioned first. This is also mirrored in the deutero-Pauline list in Eph 4,11. The deduction from this is that the charismatic community recognized being an apostle as one of the gifts of the Spirit to the community, something which Jewish Christianity did not do.[41] In the Pauline church, the talk was not about the subordination of women but about their "ordination". It was about each person playing the role given to him or her *by the Spirit* for the benefit of the ecclesial community.

In the light of this, the present chapter puts ecclesiastical functions in Pauline Christianity in their correct context and perspective. A church that is based on charismatic gifts will certainly understand ecclesiastical office differently from a hierarchy-minded one. This means that we should not be nervous to learn that women were apostles in the church of Paul. It fits squarely into the picture of a charismatic church, which is different from the institutionalized churches of the 21st century that are highly "hierarchicalized".

The reason for this difference is that a charismatic church is more flexible and responsive to circumstances and needs than an institutionalized church where the structures are firmly buried in traditions that are insulated from change. Besides, there is a rigid bureaucratic apparatus in place, not seen in the charismatic church. Elsewhere, in my study of the charismatic church, I have shown that this type of church is neither discriminatory nor segregationist in assigning ecclesiastical roles to its members. Fairness is its motto. Here, there is no gender-obsession. In other words, this is not a church that is based on sexual discrimination. A gender-conditioned ministry or apostolate is not its *modus operandi.* This Pauline belief that *you are all one in Christ* (Gal 3,28) is its guiding principle.

With this in mind, it is not simply mere fantasy to talk about women apostles in early Pauline Christianity. This was a fact of life in this Christianity. Hence, the Pauline church was neither taken captive by the concept of the *twelve,* nor held hostage by norms of biology. Certainly, it did not simply limit the number of apostles it knew to the synoptic number *twelve.* This explains why this church recognized *being an apostle* as one of the charismatic gifts of the community. As we can see in the charismatic list in 1Cor 12,28, Paul himself endorsed this position. The fact that this was recognized, as a gift of the Spirit, has an obvious implication for our study of "gender and ministry" in early Christianity. *It opened up the possibility of being an apostle to every member of the community, including women.* So this was not a reserved ministry.

Indeed, since nothing is based on gender-distinction a charismatic church would readily admit women to the topmost echelon of its hierarchy. The discriminatory assignment of ritual roles, for whatever reason, will also be avoided, since it is the same Spirit who is responsible for our calling as men and women. *So this church will be ever ready to admit women as deacons, even as priests.* In other words, women ordination (either at the diaconal or priestly level) would not be problematic for such a church. The appointment of women as pastors and senior pastors will also not be a problem. This is what makes it normal for early Pauline Christianity to raise women as apostles and deacons in the church.

However, this idea would be quite problematic for a church where institutionalized structures have displaced and taken over the functions of the Holy Spirit of the charismatic church. Falsely, this makes the "Spirit of truth" to look like the "spirit of partiality". Hence, in such a church, ritual leadership can only be conferred on men, the supposedly favored gender of the Holy Spirit. Also senior ministry positions are reserved for these men thereby affirming the radical relationship between gender and ministry. Here, only men can offer ritual intercessions for women and provide leadership in the church. They alone can offer sacrifices on their behalf. In a church like this, Paul is freely and consistently invoked to talk about a celibate institution (for the Catholic clergy holding onto this). On the contrary, he is poorly invoked, when church orders are discussed because he will not favor the bigotry of our time.

In such a church, the excision of women from the center of church power is justified as coming from Jesus, though the practice of Paul directly contradicts this. Since he (Paul) would challenge and accuse us, as he did in Antioch (cf. Gal 2,11-14), he is meticulously and carefully avoided, being used only when he clearly supports a held position or when male convenience is not compromised. When this is not the case, he is mentioned with great reluctance and lack of enthusiasm. This is what makes the present topic somewhat difficult.

All the same, in this chapter, Paul is brought face-to-face with the Christian church today. Without doubt his Christianity challenges the 21st century Christians to stop walking on their heads. Those Christian churches with male-domination are hereby confronted to imitate the noble example of Paul and his liberating Christianity. Unfortunately, the hard-liners and the ultra-traditionalists among us continue to be insulated from every wind of change. They have buried themselves so deep in traditions that the voice of the Holy Spirit is no longer heard where they are. Ironically, they continue to believe that they hear his voice from where they are hidden.

If you have a church ruled almost exclusively by "seniors", this becomes also an understandable pitiable predicament. Their motto is, *as it has been from the beginning, so it shall now be and so it shall ever be.* This becomes a church without the dynamics of change. Hence, the leaders continue to insist on doing it only the archaic way, the old way, but in our name, on our behalf and in the name of God. In this way, they make the Holy Spirit resistant to change, even though we are also seriously praying *that he may renew the face of the earth.* How, then, can he do this, when we are so static and uncooperative?

The usual veiled reason given to justify this theological obstinacy is that "tradition supports it". But the real reason is that the privileges of such men are better guaranteed and protected by maintaining the status quo as it is. The fear of competition with women, who are in the majority in all our churches, is enough discouragement from doing something to change the "male-made" rules of the game. We see a situation where men dread the possibility of being eclipsed in a Christian church where they are daily becoming the minority like endangered species. *In a sense, one sees the instinct of self-preservation at work here.*

Of course, this mirrors the predicament of those Christian churches resenting and resisting the ministry of women in the church as Christian leaders. As one can see, it typifies an Old Testament patriarchal mentality and the Christianity of the New Testament household codes. This is simply chauvinistic. It is a disproportionate use of religious authority against the female members of the Christian church. In this way, women have been *legislated* out of sacred ordination by a male oligarchy in the church.

It is against this background that we wish now to discuss the question of church "offices" in Pauline Christianity, as it relates to the "office" of apostles. What was the practice in this apostolic church? Is there any evidence to the contrary or in favor? In other words, were there women apostles in early Pauline Christianity? We shall now focus attention on this for a moment. In view of the nature of this discussion, this chapter has been divided into two sections. The first deals with general matters. The second concentrates on the technical analysis of Rom 16,7. Let us now begin with the first part of the discussion.

A) Preliminary Investigation

This section is concerned with general information leading to the main discussion on women apostles in the second part. In this preliminary part it is important to know what an apostle means in early Christianity. Otherwise, one may approach the main discussion with only the narrow concept of the "twelve apostles" of the Palestinian Christian tradition which seems to dominate our Christian understanding of the apostle today. In view of this, it is our intention to begin with terminological clarification.

1) The Term ἀπόστολος Explained[42]

The English word *apostle* is an Anglicization of the Greek word *apóstolos* (ἀπόστολος). Similarly, the Latin *apostolus* is also a Latinization of the same word.[43] In its original Greek sense, *apóstolos* was a naval term. It was used for seafaring and military expeditions. Based on this original meaning, we see that there were many apostles before the advent of Christianity. *This means that the concept of a "twelve only apostles" is superfluous.* In other words, the term *apóstolos* is older than the Christian religion. It predates Christianity. It is not an idea that exclusively came from Jesus. The Hellenistic world was at home with it long before Jesus and his disciples since it had military and naval connotations. The reader sees that this was a non-religious terminology taken over by the early Christians to describe a group of the followers of Jesus.

Next, the verb from *apóstolos* is *apostéllô* (ἀποστέλλω). It means the dispatch of a naval fleet on a military expedition.[44] Again, this confirms what has just been said above. It re-emphasizes the fact that the *apóstolos* in its original context is related more to military activities than to religious ones. Here, the word is used in an impersonal way since it is relating to actions performed by persons and not to the persons themselves. In other words, it was not used as a title for individuals *per se*, as later New Testament sources did.

In view of this secular meaning, one can see that the early Christians introduced novelty to this term. However, it has also to be pointed out that the later Greek period also used it in the sense of a *messenger*. This seems to be what helped to encourage its usage in the New Testament. In other words, the *apóstolos* is a *special messenger*, a *religious plenipotentiary*. Like every other messenger, the *apóstolos* is a carrier or bearer of the New Testament message. In a sense, he or she is a "religious courier". This means that the number of these messengers couldn't have been only twelve, as we see in some Christian traditions.

a) The Old Testament

Since the Palestinian Jews had no direct access to the sea, they were not used to maritime expeditions. In view of this, the term *apóstolos* was not of much use to them. Hence, it is poorly attested, even in Philo,[45] who was himself an Alexandrian Jew. As for Josephus, he understands *apóstolos* as the *sending of an emissary*. This refers to a Jewish embassy to Rome, which at the time involved seafaring.[46] One begins to see that this term *apóstolos* is heavily Hellenistic, signaling a contribution from Hellenism and Hellenistic Christianity.

b) The Greek Septuagint (LXX)

This term *apóstolos* is a *hapax legommenon*[47] in the Greek bible, called the Septuagint (LXX). It is found only in 1Kg 14,6. This is relevant to this study. The text reads:[48]

LXX: ἐγω εἰμι ἀπόστολος προς σε σκληρός *Egô eimi apóstolos pros se sklêrós*	**Translation** I am **sent** to you with a harsh message
Hebrew: וְאָנֹכִי שָׁלוּחַ אֵלַיִךְ קָשָׁה *'ānokî šālûach 'ēlayik qāšāh*	I am **sent** to you with a severe message

We shall begin the analysis involved with a text critical observation. In this regard, the first thing to be noted is that the unit, 1kg 14,1-20 containing 14,6 in the table above, is missing in the *Codex Vaticanus*.[49] The text of the *Codex Alexandrinus*[50] is used here.[51] Next, the context of this saying is the sickness of Abijah, the son of king Jeroboam 1 (1kg 14,1). In view of this health problem, the nervous Jeroboam instructed the wife to disguise herself to avoid recognition and go to the prophet Ahijah in Shiloh (1kg 14,2). Though the prophet Ahijah was unable to see because of his age (1kg 14.4b), the Lord revealed to him in advance that Jeroboam's wife was on her way coming to see him in connection with the sickness of the son (1kg 14,5a). Then the Lord told Ahijah what to say to her (1kg 14,5b).

As soon as the prophet Ahijah heard the sound of the feet of Jeroboam's wife as she was coming into the entrance, he said: "Come in, you wife of Jeroboam. Why is it that you are making yourself unrecognizable while I am being *sent* to you with a severe message" (1Kg 14,6)? Here, we see that while Jeroboam was sending his disguised wife to the prophet, the Lord was also sending Ahijah to deliver a very harsh message to Jeroboam through the wife. As the rest of the story shows the message was indeed very bitter for the prophet told the woman that Abijah, the son, must surely die (1kg 14,7-20).

Two things are relevant from the text of 1kg 14,6. The first is the use of the word *šālûach* (שָׁלוּחַ) in the Masoretic text (MT) or the Hebrew bible. The second is the use of *apóstolos*, in the LXX, to translate this *šālûach*. Let us now concentrate on this terminology.

2) Rabbinism and the שָׁלוּחַ

This word *šālûach* (שָׁלוּחַ) <also *šālîach* (שָׁלִיחַ)> comes from the Hebrew verb *šālach* (שָׁלַח), which means to send. It is the verb used for sending messengers.[52] The nominal form is *šālûach* (שָׁלוּחַ). As can be seen from both the lexical meaning and the context of 1Kgs 14,6 above, it has the sense of *one who is sent with a message from a higher person or being*. In the text of 1Kgs 14.6 above, this *šālûach*, translated in the LXX as *apóstolos* (apostle), is the prophet Ahijah. This has the later Hellenistic meaning of the *apóstolos* as a messenger, which we have already seen above. As the one sent with a message this prophet is seen in the Greek Septuagint as an *apóstolos*. With this in mind, one can say that the LXX recognized the Hebrew *šālûach* as an *apóstolos*. This shows that the LXX understands the *apóstolos* as one commissioned to deliver a divine message.

In a sense, then, the *šālûach* is one, who is sent with a mandate from the sender, who is higher than the one sent. The message he is supposed to deliver is not his own. He is more of a mouthpiece, an oracle, an instrument of delivery. This fact of sending expresses authorization and mandate from the sender. However, the fact that the Old Testament has its own distinctive legal term is an indication that the *šālûach* has a Semitic origin. In other words, even though the LXX translated it as *apóstolos*, as seen above, *it is not exactly the same thing with it.* In view of this, Rengstorf says:

> In its legal basis the whole circle of ideas bond up with the שָׁלִיחַ goes back to the Semitic law of the messenger as presupposed in the OT. Here the messenger fully represents in his person the one who sends him, usually the king; and this is the original meaning of the sending of a plenipotentiary.[53]

Here, the Old Testament participates in the world around it. In the rabbinical period, the time after AD 70, these commissioned Jewish messengers, then called the *šelûachîm* (שְׁלוּחִים) were usually *ordained rabbis*. They were set apart for their task by the "laying on of hands" in the name of the community which sent them.[54] Whereas we can talk about the Jewish *šelûachîm*, we cannot really talk about Jewish *apóstoloi* (apostles), especially in the time of Jesus.[55]

One can, then, say that though similarities exist between the *šelûachîm* and the *apóstolos*, they are not identical. Further, whereas the *šelûachîm* has a Semitic origin, the *apóstolos* is Hellenistic. Lastly, as we have seen above, whereas the *šālûach* (שָׁלוּחַ) has a legal basis, the *apóstolos* developed from naval expedition. However, these differences are not intended to inoculate the New Testament *apóstolos* against influences from the Hebrew *šālûach*.

3) The New Testament *apóstolos* and the *šālûach*

Here, the *apóstolos* is used to refer to the bearers of the New Testament message. As we have already noted above, this idea corresponds to the meaning of *apóstolos* in late Hellenistic period. In view of this, the number of these "New Testament couriers" couldn't be definitively determined. The concept of the New Testament *apóstolos* goes beyond the idea of the *twelve*. Notwithstanding what I have already said, in the synoptic gospels, it was first borne by the circle of the twelve. The *apóstolos* is a "commissioned representative of a congregation".[56] He is a messenger or a delegate who is sent forth with orders. This same idea of sending in the name of the community, found in the case of the *šᵉlûachîm* above, seems to have influenced the concept of apostle in the late apostolic period. In this regard, John 13,16 shows evidence that the Old Testament and the New Testament, to some degree, agreed on this point. The text of John 13,16 reads:

| Ἀμὴν ἀμὴν λέγω ὑμῖν οὐκ ἔστιν δοῦλος μείζων τοῦ κυρίου αὐτοῦ οὐδὲ ἀπόστολος μείζων τοῦ πέμψαντος αὐτόν. | The slave is not greater than his master, nor is the *apostle* greater than the one who sent him or her. |

The use of *apóstolos* here is in the legal sense of the *šᵉlûachîm*. Here, John tells us that Jesus understands *apóstolos* as *one who is lawfully sent to stand for another*. This is corroborated from evidence from Acts. Let us now review it.

Since the first missionaries of Christianity were Jews, it is reasonable to argue that the institution of the *šᵉlûachîm* had some influence on their understanding of the *apóstolos* in both apostolic and post-apostolic periods of Christianity. In this regard, we recall the text of Acts 13,2-3. It says:

> While they were worshipping the Lord and fasting, the Holy Spirit said, 'Set apart for me Barnabas and Saul for the work to which I have called them.' Then after fasting and praying they laid their hands on them and sent them off.

As can be deduced from this text, in a typical rabbinical style, there was the "laying on of hands" which signaled the commissioning of these two people in the name of the community. Hence, the two are now legally sent on a mission in the name of the community. Here, these people become "ambassadors plenipotentiary" for their church community. They carry a "message" from this community. They will now speak in its name and preach on its behalf. This seems to link up well with the *šālûach*. Hence, from Acts 14,14 Paul and Barnabas began to be referred to as *apostles*. This is significant. Before their commissioning and sending by the community no one gave them this title. But after it, they became recognized as apostles. This suggests an influence of the Jewish *šālûach* on the New Testament understanding of the *apóstolos*. Also it points out that the apostolic church and beyond did not simply tie the fact of being apostle with Jesus alone. *The practice of naming and sending apostles continued long after him.* In view of this, our mission now is to establish whether women participated in this process or not. In other words, were their commissioned female apostles in early Christianity? Were women also sent on a mission in the name of their respective church communities? If the answer turns out to be yes, the next question would be, then, why can't women be deaconesses, priests, senior pastors and even bishops since we take it that these are the successor of the apostles?

Of course, a reader who is used to the widely known tradition of the "twelve male apostles" of the Palestinian Christians will probably be unease with the possibility of a woman apostle in the early church. In view of this, I wish to point out that to talk about an apostle is not necessarily to imply a member of the Palestinian twelve, as we have just seen above in the case of Barnabas and Paul. Hellenistic Christianity had its own apostles as well. In fact, *the number of biblical apostles is more than twelve.* This is what prompted Rengstorf to say, "although the twelve are ἀπόστολοι [apostles] for Luke, they are not the only ἀπόστολοι [apostles]".[57] *In this regard, it is noteworthy that the "community of the beloved disciple" did not recognize the twelve as apostles, though it knew of the existence of apostles* (cf. John 13,16). John knew them only as "the twelve" (ὁι δώδεκα).

4) Statistical Information

In fact, the available statistical evidence shows that Hellenistic Christianity showed a lot of interest in this term *apóstolos*, which, as we have seen, is derived from Hellenistic culture. In this regard, it is found about 29 times in Paul. This reflects the level of Hellenistic Christian interest in the term. In the gospels, John does not know of any twelve apostles, *though he knew of the "twelve".* In the synoptic gospels, both Mark and Matthew were *reluctant* to use it. Each of them used this term only *once*. In Luke, however, it occurred about 6 times in his gospel and 28 in Acts. As one can see, only Luke appeared enthusiastic about it. This was also influenced by his interest in Gentile or Hellenistic Christianity. In view of this, his overall interest goes beyond the arithmetic of the twelve.

In the instances where *apóstolos* occurred in the synoptic gospels, whereas Matthew and Luke know of the "twelve apostles" <ὁι δώδεκα ἀπόστολοι> (Matt 10,2; Luke 6.13), or the twelve disciples <ὁι δώδεκα μαθηταὶ> of Matt 10.1, *Mark knows only of "the apostles"* <ὁι ἀπόστολοι> (Mk 6,30, Luke 9,10). *This shows that, Mark the earliest gospel account, though knew about the apostles of Jesus, did not care to tell us how many they were.* This is significant. It indicates that the idea of pegging the number of apostles to twelve did not begin from the earliest moments of the tradition. It developed later on. On account of this, number was not an issue for Mark. His silence on this means that the number of the synoptic apostles could have equally been more than the twelve recognized casually by Matthew and emphatically by Luke. In which case, the concept of the *twelve apostles* is largely a Lucan idea, which represents an early development in the Lucan tradition about Jesus and the early church. However, once Christianity reached the Hellenistic world in Acts, Luke abandoned this number and embraced other apostles as well.

5) Ἀπόστολος (apostle) outside the Gospel Traditions

As I have indicated above there is an overwhelming evidence showing that this term *apóstolos* was not restricted to the Palestinian Christian tradition alone. It is applied differently to different people, depending on whether one is in a Palestinian or Hellenistic community. All the same, there is no doubt that it refers also to the *twelve* of the Palestinian Christian tradition. As we know, in this community, the number of apostles is limited and known to be *only* twelve (Luke 6:13, 9:10), though at some point they were only **eleven** apostles (Luke 24,9.33).

However, in Hellenistic Christianity, it is seen differently. In the light of this, I wish now to go over the list of texts outside the gospel traditions that show that the notion of *apóstolos* in the New Testament is not reserved *only* for the twelve. There were other people, not belonging to this group, who were nevertheless recognized as apostles.[58]

a) The Acts of the Apostles

The evidence from this book opens our investigation here. Although the early part of this Lucan church is largely controlled by those belonging to the twelve, yet Acts testifies that not only this group was recognized as apostles in the apostolic church. The first indication to this was given by Acts 14,14-15. It says:

> But when the apostles [οἱ απόστολοι] Barnabas and Paul heard of it, they tore their garments and rushed out among the multitude, crying, [15] "Men, why are you doing this? We also are men, of like nature with you, and bring you good news, that you should turn from these vain things to a living God who made the heaven and the earth and the sea and all that is in them (Acts 14,14-15).

Here, we can see that even Acts, partly the church of the "twelve apostles", clearly recognizes some others as apostles even though they did not belong to the Palestinian twelve. Interesting is the fact that the community of Acts even knew the names of the apostles in questions. They are Paul and Barnabas. So they were not anonymous persons. We are not dealing with mere symbols here.

Apart from this the choosing of Matthias (Acts 1,21-26) is also the election of *another* apostle, *not chosen by Jesus himself*. We can see that, gradually, early Christianity has started to increase the number of apostles. It is now moving away from the concept of the twelve. As we can see, even in the Palestinian Christian community, the *twelve* never always remained the *twelve*. The community witnessed addition (the election of Matthias) and subtraction (the death of Judas). Human beings had to make up what is missing, but in the name of God.

b) Hellenistic Christianity

The first thing to be noted here is that Hellenistic Christianity recognized being an apostle as a charismatic gift (1Cor 12,28), and not as an institution. In fact, this tops the charismatic list. It occupies a central place in the community. As a charismatic gift, it was not re-served for any defined group or persons, nor was it gender-based. In other words, it was not a gender affair. Here, it is seen as a charismatic gift like any other one. In which case, the number of apostles in Helle-nistic Christianity was not defined. In view of this, it is only when one talks about the "apostolic college", or the "apostolic institution" that women are excluded, since these notions give the idea of something fixed, determined and concluded. However, early Christianity did not see it this way. Hence, the Pauline charismatic community recognized it as a gift of the Holy Spirit.

In line with what has just been said, there is no gainsaying that Pauline Christianity recognized the presence of many apostles. Of course, if this is accepted as a charismatic gift, it is only to be expected, since no one could limit the choice of the Holy Spirit. Nobody could determine for him how many people to choose and which gender to choose. This was freely available to all the members of the church, irrespective of gender, race, or color. The first evidence to this effect comes from the text of 2Cor 8,23 where Paul himself tells us that there were many apostles in his community. The text in question reads:

Greek Text	Translation
8,23: εἴτε ὑπὲρ Τίτου, κοινωνὸς ἐμὸς καὶ εἰ ὑμας συνεργός· εἴτε ἀδελφοὶ ἡμων, ἀπόστολοι ἐκκλησίων δόξα Χριστου.	If it is Timothy, [he is] my partner and a fellow worker for you; if [it is] our brothers, [they are] the *apostles* of the churches, [who are] the glory of Christ.

In this text, we see the use of *apóstoloi* (apostles) in the plural.[59] It seems that the various Hellenistic churches had their own apostles. Hence, Paul talks of ἀπόστολοι ἐκκλησίων (apostles of the churches). This corroborates the fact that the New Testament apostle was not only a messenger sent by Christ himself but also by the Churches representing him. Indeed, the fact of being an apostle was a real feature of Pauline and post Pauline Christianity. This explains why Paul had to include it in his list of charismatic gifts. In which case, the number of Christians to possess this gift is indeterminate. In addition, it is not gender-conditioned.

Of course, we have not forgotten our point of departure, which is Rom 16,7. The two mentioned there, *Andronicus* and *Julia,* were also apostles. Further, this term is also applied to Timothy and Silas (1Thess 2,6). In Phil 2,25 Epaphroditus is referred to as "your apostle" (ὑμων δὲ ἀπόστολον)· Now the reader sees that the definition of the number of apostles as "twelve" is *too narrow* and begs the question. The problem goes beyond the arithmetic of the twelve.

c) Paul as ἀπόστολος (apostle)

Apart from these general instances, with a rigorous, undiluted and unmitigated insistence, Paul himself consistently maintains that he is also an apostle. Even, he claims to have worked more than every other. Hence, in 2Cor 11.21-23, he boasted as follows:

> But whatever any one dares to boast of - I am speaking as a fool - I also dare to boast of that. [22] Are they Hebrews? So am I. Are they Israelites? So am I. Are they descendants of Abraham? So am I. [23] Are they servants of Christ? I am a better one - I am talking like a madman - with far greater labors, far more imprisonment, with countless beatings, and often near death.

Not only this, although he was not a member of the Palestinian twelve, yet he was in no mood to consider himself inferior to any of the traditional "twelve apostles". He could neither renounce his claim to apostleship nor was he prepared to compromise it. In which case, he did not accept the recognized twelve apostles to be superior to the other apostles. In view of this, Paul says:

For I am not at all inferior to these superlative apostles [ὑπερλίαν ἀποστόλων], even though I am nothing. The signs of a true apostle were performed among you in all patience, with signs and wonders and mighty works (2Cor 12.11b-12).

One sees here a defensive strategy characterizing someone, who seems to be under attack. Hence, we see Paul counter-attacking, trying to uphold the validity and authenticity of his own apostleship. Consequently, he tries to dismiss any suggestion that he is inferior to those whom he calls the "super-apostles" both in 2Cor 11,5 and 12,11. The reader sees that Paul regarded himself to be an apostle, notwithstanding the synoptic traditions.

d) The *Didache*

This is one of the earliest documents of post-apostolic Christianity. It has sixteen short chapters. The document purports to be the teaching of the twelve apostles, hence, it begins, "The Lord's Teaching to the Heathen by the Twelve". The word *didachē* (διδαχή) itself is a Greek word meaning teaching or instruction. The one carrying out this teaching is the *didáskalos* (διδάσκαλος)-teacher. Even though the document claims that the twelve apostles wrote it, yet internal evidence betrays this assertion. For instance, the document characteristically was using a singular subject form of the verbs used. Instead of "our child" to reflect the fact that twelve people were writing, it simply says "my child" (cf. Didache, 3,1-6). *Consequently, the question of authorship is immediately raised.* Certainly, we have a spurious author here. So this is a pseudonymous early Christian document.

The most relevant point here is that this second century literature recognized some other apostles outside the gospel traditions. It knew of those whom it called *apostles* and *prophets*. In view of this, it gave the following instructions :

Regarding apostles and prophets act according to the instruction of the gospel. Let every apostle who comes to you be received as the Lord. But he shall stay only one day; and a second day, in case of special need. If he stays for three days he is a false prophet. When the apostle goes away let him receive only bread, to suffice until he finds his next lodging: if he asks for money he is a false prophet.[60]

The *didache* appears to be interchanging apostles and prophets. As one sees, these apostles were more like roving missionaries. This agrees with the lexical meaning above where we said that *apóstolos* means a messenger sent on an errand with a mission. In the time of the *Didache* these apostles were special messengers of the gospel. Today, we would call them missionaries. However, their number was not simply restricted to *twelve*. As Craig Keener pointed out, "Paul nowhere limits the apostolic company to the Twelve plus himself".[61] The New Testament did not do this either. Therefore, it is wrong for us to do it.

Indeed, the time has come to correct the mistaken notion that the number of apostles is "twelve". This error has disadvantaged women throughout the course of Christian history, since people use it to argue that there were *only* twelve apostles and they were only men. A thinking of this nature shuts the door on women. Unfortunately, people use a myopic understanding of the apostolic ministry to exclude women from the ministry of the church.

For the patriarchal church, whenever apostles are mentioned, what is remembered, is only the "twelve apostles" of the gospel of Luke. No one remembers that Mark was unaware of this and that Hellenistic Christianity had many apostles, beyond the number twelve. It is only when we correct ourselves that we can truly allow the Holy Spirit to operate in his church, as he should. But as long as we are in our avoidable "error", it is difficult for the "Spirit of Truth" to direct us. The tendency will always be to resist him, thinking that we are being misled. Of course, if we believe "error" to be the truth, this becomes the logical consequence of our false belief.

In fact, what has just been said is reminiscent of the "allegory of the cave", where the one in the cave resists coming out from the darkness of the place because such a one resents light. Our centuries of traditions may have put us in a similar predicament, where we now resent the truth. This work invites all of us to be open to the "Spirit of Truth", knowing quite well that he is not as "immutable" as we take him to be. He has some flexibility. If we call on him to renew the fact of the earth, this confirms what has just been said that he is not "immutable". If we are open, he can change certain situations in the church for better. Therefore, let us resolve not to resist him any more, *even with the best of intentions*.

This invites us to open up to the possibility that, outside the gospels, other New Testament sources and some early Christian literature knew of some other people called apostles; *among whom were women*. Having said this, so far, we have only shown that men were apostles. The next task facing us now is to establish that there were also women apostles. With this in mind, let us now begin the complicated investigation, which involves the text of Rom 16,7. The reader is reminded beforehand that the analysis to be made is going to be somewhat technical since the problem involved is itself a technical one.

B) Exegetical Details

The time has now come to concentrate on the main text of Romans to be analyzed. The previous section has enabled us to establish that it is not just mere gimmick to talk about a woman apostle because *there were other apostles outside the Palestinian twelve.* In view of this, let us now go forward to advance the technical arguments in favor of women apostles in early Pauline Christianity. There will be a two-track approach in this section. The first thrust of the argument will be morphological, while the second will be textual criticism. First of all, let us begin by reading the text in question.

1) Rom 16,7:Text and Translation

The investigation to be made here is not a simple one. However, our main interest now is to try to establish the truth of what happened in the Roman church, based on the evidence from Paul himself. Since the text to be analyzed has variant readings relevant to this discussion, a *technical* analysis is quite unavoidable. Also since Rom 16,15 has a bearing on Rom 16.7, the two of them will be placed together for a comparative evaluation.

Greek Text: (Rom 16,7): ἀσπάσασθε Ἀνδρόνικον καὶ Ιουλι'αν[62] [or Ιου-νιαν] τοὺς συγγενεις μου καὶ συ-ναιχμαλώτους μου, ὅιτινες εἰσιν ἐπίσημοι ἐν τοις αποστολόις, ὅι καὶ πρό ἐμου γέγοναν ἐν Χριστω.	Translation: Greet Andronicus and Julia [or Junia?] my kin and my fellow prisoners, these are notable among the *apostles*, they have been before me in Christ.
Rom 16,15: ἀσπάσασθε Φιλόλογον καὶ Ιουλίαν [or Ιουνιαν?], Νηρέα καὶ τὴν αδελφὴν αὐτου, καὶ Ολυμπαν καὶ τοὺς σὺν αὐτοις πάντας ἁγίους.	Rom 16,15: Greet Philologus and Julia [or Junias?], Nereus and her sister, and Olumpas and all the saints [who are] with them.

2) Textual Critical Notes

I am aware of the fact that the whole of Rom 16 presents the exegete with some textual critical problems based on the doxology in 16,25-27. Also the elaborate and familiar nature of the greetings in the whole of this chapter, made to a church that Paul did not know, makes it suspect. These textual problems will not be handled here since they do not have a bearing on our discussion nor affect the outcome of our exegetical investigation. In addition, their outcome do not affect the Pauline authenticity of the text. What is important is that it is recognized as coming from Paul himself. This is the guiding principle in this work.[63]The reader is reminded to bear this in mind.

3) Preliminary Objections

I wish to begin the analysis involved by first playing the "devil's advocate." In this regard, the first thing to be noted here is that the use of *apóstolos* (ἀπόστολος) in Paul, in relation to a woman, is a *hapax legomenon*.[64] In which case, the existing evidence in support of a female apostle in Pauline Christianity may not appear to be overwhelming. If we have incontrovertible evidence in support of women called the συνεργόι (*synergói*) fellow workers of Paul, we seem to lack that here. We do not have abundance of literary evidence in support of what we seek to establish. We are faced here with a poverty of sources which slows down the case for women apostles in antiquity. Clearly, this shows that we are somehow constrained in our quest to determine the place of women apostles in early Pauline Christianity and beyond.

In view of this special handicap, one could validly argue that the *apóstolos* in Rom 16,7 is a lone case and possibly an exception to the rule. Hence, it did not represent the trend in Pauline Christianity or elsewhere. One could even go further to doubt whether this practice was widespread in the time of Paul.

This is a tolerable objection since we cannot deny the fact that this discussion is going to be made from a deficit position due to the lack of abundant evidence, unlike in the case of men apostles. All the same, this poverty can easily be addressed. If we do not have abundant New Testament sources for this study, it is due to the patriarchalisation of the New Testament, where the male writers tried to downplay everything feminine.

All the same, by drawing attention to this *other side of the coin*, I have in no way signaled a watering down of this investigation, or even of lowering the standard. It is true that the burden of proof is so high. At the same time, it is not insurmountable. I do not even intend to imply that the objection raised in this work is sustained. First of all, *the fact that something occurred once does not mean that it never took place*. It does not constitute a valid argument against the reality of such a thing. The question in this work is about *whether women were ever apostles in early Christianity and not whether the practice was a widespread one*. This is the crux of the matter.

Besides, one does not have to push this "*hapax-legomenon* argument" too far since we may be caught up in our own trap. We may end up laying up snares for ourselves. This is maintained because Roman

Catholicism has built entire ecclesiology and "hierarchology" on the text of Matt 16,18-19,[65] even though no other New Testament tradition bears this same witness. This is also a *hapax legomenon* case. Similarly, many people have also relied heavily on the eunuchs of Matt 19,12 to defend the catholic celibate institution, even though this is directly contradicted by the text of later New Testament Christianity in 1Tim 3,2-5. If we did not simply ignore these texts as a case of *hapax legomenon*, an isolated incidence, this means that we have no just reason to dismiss either the text of Rom 16,7 (dealing with the question of women apostles) or Rom 16,1-2 (dealing with deaconesses). The problem is that whenever the ministry of women is involved in a biblical text, people try to explain it away or to water down the text involved. The same vigor, with which similar texts treating male issues are tackled, dissipates once women are involved. This is the situation surrounding Rom 16,7.

Indeed, let us not try to show that we are a church of "pick and choose". Let us not present ourselves as a church that can go to any length to support male domination, while using the same vigor to suppress the rights of women in the church. Let us not show that we can do everything humanly possible to explain away anything that helps to liberate women from the shackles of the subordination that we have put in place for them, though in the name of God. It is time to live up to the truth presented by an objective reading of Holy Scripture. This is the task facing us in this 21st century. Having said this, I shall now go ahead to examine the only available evidence which points to the existence of women apostles in early Pauline Christianity.

4) The Textual Problem

As one can see from the table of Rom 16,7 above the text has two slightly differing names: *Iounian* (Ιουνιαν) for the English translation Junia and *Ioulian* (Ιουλίαν) for the female name Julia. One striking thing about these two names – *Junia* and *Julia* – is that they sound alike. Whether in English or Greek, the only thing differentiating them is the letter "N" and "L". As the textual evidence shows most of the manuscripts favor the former (*Iounian*), while a tiny minority favors the latter (*Ioulian*). This same problem is repeated in 16.15, but in a reversed order. Hence, here, the majority favors *Ioulian* (Julia), with the minority favoring *Iounian* (Junia).

Now we have a hard nut to crack. Which of these two names is the apostle mentioned in Rom 16,7? And what is the biological gender of the apostle in question? Is the one *Junia*, which could be a woman or a man?) Or is she *Julia*, which is conspicuously a woman? Did Paul ever know of any woman apostle either called Junia or Julia? In other words, was a woman **ever** recognized as an apostle in Pauline Christianity? In the different manuscript readings presented to us, which one is the correct name: *Iounian* (Junia) or *Ioulían* (Julia)? How, then, do we decide? A two-fold argument will be advanced here. The first will be morphological, while the second will be based on the textual technicality, called textual criticism. Let us begin with the first.

5) Argument from Morphology

As we probably know, morphology deals with the forms of words used. In New Testament exegesis, this is an essential part of the hermeneutic process since morphology is the bedrock of New Testament Greek. For instance, if the exegete or interpreter of the Bible does not know whether the form of the word used is masculine, feminine or a neuter gender, the one can neither translate nor interpret well. The verbal or nominal form of the word used has to be well understood, especially in the Greek language when the position of the accent on a word can change the meaning completely. One example here will suffice.

The definite article and the relative pronoun in Greek have the same letters. The only thing that distinguishes some of the gender forms from the others is the position of the accent. In order to understand well the importance of morphology in exegesis, let us look at the various grammatical genders of the definite article and the relative pronoun in the table below.

	Masculine	Feminine	Neuter
The definite article	ὁ (ho)	ἡ (hê)	τό (tó)
Relative pronoun	ὅς (hós)	ἥ (hê)	ὅ (hó)

Looking at this table it is not quite easy for a novice to Greek grammar to notice the subtlety involved. The small trick is in the morphology of the feminine genders of the definite article and the relative pronoun, on the one hand, and the masculine and neuter genders, on the other. Accordingly, we have ἡ (hê) for the article and ἥ (hê) for the pronoun. Next, we have ὁ (ho) for the masculine definite article and ὅ (hó) for the neuter relative pronoun. Unless one is at home with Greek morphology, one can easily mistake the relative pronoun for the definite article and vice versa.

In view of this clarification, the main discussion now begins with this question: Is the name *Iounian* (Ἰουνιαν) masculine or feminine?

This question is enigmatic for translators and exegetes alike. Hence, from the point of view of translation, it is an *unsettled* question. This is due to the fact that the name has a somewhat *ambiguous* morphology, which creates the possibility of translating it in one direction or the other. Whereas the Andronicus that goes with it is an indisputable masculine name, *Iounian* does not enjoy this unchallenged clarity. *Of course, the main reason is that a woman is involved. If the morphology favored a masculine form, no one would worry whether it is pronounced one way or the other.* But for a church based on Old Testament patriarchy, the possibility of a woman apostle raises the stakes higher. This is part of the confusion surrounding this study.

The first thing to be pointed out here is that this name *Iounian* is in the Greek *accusative case*. Its nominative case has *two morphological* possibilities.

a) It could be *Junias* < Ἰουνιας> (a masculine name?)

b) Or it could be *Junia* < Ἰουνια> (a feminine name).

Here, one sees, against a masculine-oriented argument that the morphological form of *Iounian* does not even show an obvious masculine name. In other words, the apostle mentioned in the text is not *self-evidently* a man. In view of this, translators are divided, without a consensus on the matter. Hence, two camps emerge, with one translating it as Junias,[66] and the other translating it as Junia.[67]

However, in either of the morphological cases above, the accusative is the same *Iounian* (Ἰουνιαν). In relation to this, Fitzmyer, while maintaining that Junias is a masculine name, nevertheless says, "*Iounian* could also be the acc. of 'Junia,' a woman's name."[68] One sees that he is equally as confused as the manuscripts and translators.

Contrary to Fitzmyer's leaning, available evidence does not support a masculine morphology. In view of this, Craig Keener said, "'Andronicus' is a Greek name borne by some Diaspora Jews, and 'Junia' is a Latin name that was also sometimes used by Jews".[69] This favors *Iounia* (Ἰουνια), #b above, as the correct nominative case of the name in question. In this case, the apostle in question is a woman and the text in question should read: *Andronicus and Junia.*

As James Dunn further pointed out, those who translate the name as masculine (Junian) take it to be a contraction of Junianus.[70] He argues that this "masculine form has been found nowhere else",[71] a position which Craig Keener has reinforced in the following words:

> An even less plausible way to get around Junia being an apostle is to claim that Junian (the direct object form of the common female Junia, not of the male Junius) is really a contraction for the male

name Junianus. But this contraction never appears in Greek literature
(including in Rome's inscriptions). Indeed, because of the way Latin
names are transcribed into Greek, Junia grammatically can be nothing other than a woman's name here, though many earlier scholars
failed to notice this.[72]

Many others take also a similar view.[73] From Keener's statement
we see that the proponents of a masculine name are simply using "the
more obscure to explain the obscure". Instead of explaining the difficulty involved, these people try to find some convenient means to explain it away because a woman is involved. In this way, they make
what is simple to be complicated. This is why they are not succeeding.
Their approach is similar to a situation where one has seen a spade, but
refuses to call it a spade, instead trying to prove that it is tree. In our
own context, the simplest thing to do is *to call a spade a spade,* but the
male oligarchy is not willing to do this. For these people, it does not
even matter, as we have seen from Keener's text above, that the masculine form being advocated by some is not even attested. In which
case, it is mere conjecture, a *figmentum mentis* (figment of the mind),
non cum fundamentum in re (without foundation in reality).

In view of this, Kenner interestingly said, "those who favor the
view that Junia was not a female apostle do so because of their prior
assumption that women could not be apostles, not because of any evidence in the text."[74] I am totally in agreement with this. Hence, I have
set out to do a detailed exegesis of the text involved so that doubts can
be eliminated in *honest and sincere minds* once and for all.

In line with what Keener has just said, Dunn maintains that Junia
is attested over 250 times,[75] showing that the name in Rom 16,7 is
obviously feminine. Finally, Dunn concludes, "the assumption that it
must be male is a striking indictment of male presumption regarding
the character and structure of earliest Christianity".[76] Dunn also pointed
out that Lagrange, Barrett, Cranfield, and Wilckens favor Junia as the
apostle in question.[77] Bernadette Brooten took this position as well.[78]
Also David Aune supports it.[79] In other words, the name is *feminine*
and not masculine.

One of the most interesting aspect of this discussion is that John
Chrysostom, one of the Fathers of the church, took the apostle in question to be a woman. This is quite striking because his writings, more
often than not, have misogynist tendencies. However, he makes an
apparent "U-turn" in his commentary on Rom 16.7, when he wrote as
follows: "O how great is the devotion of this woman that she should be
counted worthy of the appellation of apostle!"[80] Accordingly, in this

same commentary on Romans, he translated the name in question as *Junia*[81] and not Junius or Junianus

Apart from Chrysostom, other ancient commentators also took this apostle to be a woman.[82] This is interesting for the women liberation movement today. If a conservative like Chrysostom and others could make this assertion what reasons do we have today to disagree with them? Accordingly, Raymond Brown maintains that a study of the name Junia makes John Chrysostom's view plausible.[83] This is also the position taken in this work. It is not only possible, *but also true.*

According to Fitzmyer some ancient commentators took this *Iounian* to be the name of "Andronicus' wife."[84] This is also the position taken by Dunn. Hence, he says, "the most natural way to read the two names in the phrase is as husband and wife".[85] Conclusively, Craig Keener writes:

> If Junia is a woman apostle traveling with Andronicus, a male apostle, certain scandal would result if they were not brother and sister or husband and wife. Since most apostles, unlike Paul, were Married (1Cor 9.5), the early church was probably right when it understood them as a husband-wife apostolic team. There were husband-and-wife teams in some other professions, for instance, physicians, so there is no reason to think that a couple could not have functioned as apostles together.[86]

Keener is right here. The early celibate mind of Christianity, continued today in Catholicism, poisoned our minds towards certain ministry roles for a married pair. In this regard, marriage was made to be incompatible with the clerical office, which the apostles are *presumed* to have occupied. Hence, to talk about a married couple as apostles raises theological eyebrows. This is the mirror with which Andronicus and Julia have been seen for ages. On this, people ignore the evidence and extol sexual bias.

The unfortunate thing is that we forget that there is no evidence of celibacy for church officials in the New Testament churches. In this regard, Peter was married (Matt 8,14;[87] 1Cor 9,5). Paul was also married, as well as the other apostles (1Cor 9,3-5); Even in the time of the pastorals, bishops married (1Tim 3,2-5).[88] In fact, the pastorals frowned at any idea of abstention from marriage, showing that they disapproved of the celibate practice (1Tim 4,3).

These are facts of the New Testament church. In which case, it was compatible at the time for married couples to be active in the ministry. Marriage was not inconsistent with the ministry of the Christian church, though the celibate practice of some of the Christian churches turns this upside down. In any case, it is entirely plausible that Andronicus and Junia (or Julia) were an apostolic couple, just as Aquila and Prisca were missionary companions of Paul with a church in their house, as already seen in chapter one of this work. Of course, if the apostle Peter was undoubtedly married, we have no further reason to argue against them.

Based on the available evidence it is my own position that Junias or Junius is a mistranslation of *Ioulia* or *Iounia*, both of which are morphologically feminine, suggesting feminine names. Bernadette Brooten agrees with this conclusion by maintaining that this was not questioned by any commentator of Rom 16,7 prior to the 13th century BC.[89] Of the hypothetical name "Junias", Bernadette Brooten writes:

> What can a modern philologist say about Junias? Just this: it is un-attested. To date, not a single reference in ancient literature has been cited by any of the proponents of the Junias hypothesis. My own search for an attestation has also proved fruitless. This means that we do not have a single shred of evidence that the name Junias ever existed.[90]

Indeed, it seems to me that the scribes of those manuscripts retaining this name <*Iounian*> attempted to make it masculine in order to change the gender of the apostle in question. But they did not quite succeed in doing so. After all, the only thing which changed from the *Julia* of Rom 16,15 is only the letter "L" which was changed to "N". This similarity between <Junia> and <Julia> creates the suspicion that the scribes were trying to emend the text containing an obvious feminine name. This is conceivable. The simple reason for this is that emendation is also part of scribal errors.

In view of this, even if we were to take it that the name of the apostle mentioned in Rom 16,7 is *Iounian*, we will still take it as a feminine name and translate it as *Junia*. In this case, it would mean that the apostle mentioned in Rom 16,7 is a woman called *Junia*. This means that even if we retain the *Iounian* of the majority of the Greek manuscripts, the name would still be feminine. Hence, *Junia* becomes the name of a woman apostle in Pauline Christianity. At this point let us change frequency. It is now time to make the case for Julia as the name of this woman apostle.

6) Textual Critical Investigation

The first thing to be noted is that we are dealing with variant readings. In view of this, the approach to be used in resolving this complex problem is mainly the *textual critical method*. This exegetical technique seeks to establish the most likely authentic text whenever there is a variety of manuscripts with conflicting or differing readings. In our own context, the question is, which manuscript is most likely the one closest to the original tradition it seeks to represent? If we are able to establish this, it will enable us to determine whether the name of the apostle in the text is *Julia* or *Junia*. This will enable us to avoid the confusion surrounding the name *Iounian*. In view of this, let me present the manuscript evidence for the two names.[91]

a) The Manuscript Evidence

Each of these manuscripts will now be presented to the reader. Their dates will accompany them, since chronology may prove to be a vital tool necessary to make the final determination on this subject matter.

ἰουνιαν – **(Junia)**	Date (AD)	ἰουλίαν– **(Julia)**	Date (AD)
ℵ = eapr	IV	p^{46}	Ca 200
A = eapr	V	Copbo (Coptic)	III & IV
B = eap	IV	Ambrosiaster	IV
C = eapr	V	Eth (Ethiopic)	VI
D (06)=P[92]	VI		
G (012)=P[93]	IX		
P (025)=apr	IX		
Y=eap	VIII/IX		
33= eap	IX		
88=apr	XII		
181=ap	XI		
326=ap	XII		
330 =eap	XII		

i) The Textual Evidence for *Junia*

As the facts in this table show, there is an undeniable massive support for the name *Iounian* (Junia). The manuscript evidence for this is doubtless *solid* and *overwhelming*. To strengthen this position further, the four major and important manuscripts in textual criticism, called the uncials,[94] are clearly in support of it. If one takes this group of manuscripts to be the most original, it means that the apostle involved in Rom 16,7 is named *Junia*. However, this is not yet conclusive since there is another variant reading.

ii) The Textual Evidence for *Julia*

Looking at the table above, the manuscript evidence for Julia is apparently very *weak* and *scanty*. In fact, only one serious document p^{46} supports *Julia* as the apostle in Rom 16,7. However, textual critical decisions are not simply based on the principle of "majority carries the vote". In as much as the majority is important, yet it is not always conclusive in textual matters. In other words, the fact that there is overwhelming majority evidence in favor of *Iounian* (Junia) has not ended the argument. We will still allow the earliest possible witness to prevail. So let us further examine the manuscripts involved from the point of view of chronology.

b) Chronological Table[95]

Ca 200	IV AD	V AD	IX AD	XI AD	XII AD
P^{46}	א	A	Y	181	88
	B	C	33		326
	D (06)		G (012)		330
			P (025)		

In this table, all the main manuscripts supporting either *Junia* or *Julia* have been chronologically arranged. We have six possible dates ranging from AD 200 (in the first column) to the 12th century (in the last column). As the reader can see, the earliest among them is p^{46} in the first column, which dates around AD 200. According to its testimony the person mentioned in Rom 16.7, as an apostle, is *Julia*. In other words, from the standpoint of this manuscript, *the apostle in question is decidedly a woman*. This becomes a witness to the fact that the community of Paul knew about a *woman apostle*.

Further, when the manuscript p^{46} is compared with all the other ones supporting *Junia*, we see that they are later witnesses. Looking at the table, one sees that about *two centuries* elapsed before the emergence of the next closest group of manuscripts which are found in the second column above (IV A.D).

Consequently, based on chronological consideration, the conclusion to be deduced from this is that p^{46} containing *Julia,* as a woman apostle, is the earliest possible Pauline witness. In which case, its evidence should be considered to be prior to the later ones found in the other manuscripts which are in the majority. It seems that these later ones corrupted the text of Rom 16,7.

Indeed, the change found in the other manuscripts for the confusing name *Iounian* fits into a patriarchal pattern. Anxious to maintain a patriarchal logic the scribes of these manuscripts simply *emended* the text of p^{46} to reflect the patriarchal atmosphere of the time. A scribe brought up in a Palestinian Christian tradition, where only men were supposed to be apostles, will find it much easier to correct any text which says otherwise. This explains the conflicting variant readings in Rom 16,7 and 16,15.

On the other hand, the scribe of p^{46} had no reason to *fabricate*, at this early stage of the tradition, that a woman was an apostle, if she was not and if there was no evidence to this effect. This would have appeared highly offensive to his Jewish Christian contemporaries. Hence, it would have discouraged him from any falsification of such a highly sensitive matter. It is true that some maintain that p^{46} and others in support of it were misled in Rom 16,7 by the occurrence of *Julia* in Rom 16,15. If this were so, the fact that this Julia is connected with a woman should have sent off the alarm bell to the scribe. If he copied down Julia in p^{46} as a woman apostle it suggests that this scribe knew of a tradition of this kind. Alternatively, he was copying down something that he saw. *After all, in a culture in which men dominated all facets of life it was easier for a scribe to delete the name of a woman as an apostle than to manufacture it, especially in a sacred text.*

If this scribe did not have the name *Julia* in Rom 16,7 nothing would have encouraged him to *insert* this feminine name as an apostle. *In fact, he had more reasons to change it to an incontestable masculine name than to forge a conspicuous feminine one.* So the reading in p^{46}, for this study, is the *lectio difficilior* (the difficult reading). According to the principle of textual criticism, in a confusion of this nature, the more difficult text is to be preferred. From my own standpoint, this is the case in Rom 16,7. Therefore, the argument favors p^{46} *and the apostle in question is Julia, incontestably a woman.* The hullabaloo about the correct translation of *Iounian* lies in this fact that p^{46} is completely forgotten. On account of this, we split hair as if there is no other extant witness.

7) Conclusion

It is my own opinion that the later manuscripts bearing *Junia*, perhaps, influenced by the patriarchal mentality of the early church Fathers, like Ignatius of Antioch, changed this name from *Julia* to *Junia*. The reason for doing this was to avoid giving the impression that a woman was also an apostle in early Christianity. In other words, there was an *unsuccessful* attempt to make this feminine name look masculine through morphological alteration. However, this shrewd theological move did not quite succeed. In this period, church orders have started to emerge and men have started seizing church power in every respect. Patristic literature reflects this. In this regard, the writings of Ignatius of Antioch bear eloquent testimony to this. In effect, the accepted reading is the one of p[46] containing the name Julia, as a female apostle.

However, even if one refuses to accept this "Julia-conclusion"; it is not to be forgotten that Junia is also accepted in this work to be a feminine name. Either way, the person mentioned in Rom 16.7, as an apostle, is a woman. Consequently, the community of Paul knew of a woman called either Junia or Julia, who was also an apostle in Hellenistic Christianity.[96] Since the *apóstolos* originally was a naval term connected with seafaring, nothing precluded a woman from performing this task in Hellenistic culture. This was not an all-male affair. Following this model, women also became *apóstoloi* in Hellenistic Christianity. This tallies with the charismatic nature of Pauline Christianity.

Indeed, since Paul regarded being an apostle as a charismatic gift (1Cor 12.28), this means that he was under no illusion to think that it was the exclusive right or prerogative of men. Otherwise, this would have meant that the Spirit has charismatic gifts reserved for men alone, something that would not have been consistent with the charismatic nature of Pauline Christianity.

I think that it is not good to conscript this Spirit to fight in favor of our extreme patriarchal-mindedness in the church today. Let us not make him the author of the discrimination that we have put in place to service our male desire and passion to rule. The time has come to stop hiding under his canopy in order to hold on to power. The 21st century offers us the best opportunity to do this. Let us no longer make this Spirit to appear over-sympathetic to everything masculine. Let us not make him to be seen as a Spirit who has aversion for women.

The time has come to stop enlisting the Spirit of God to defend male bigotry. It is time to remember that this Spirit blows wherever he wills. Yet we forget this and create an imaginary pipeline for this Spirit through which he must necessarily operate. In this way, man has taken the Spirit of God captive, placing him under "house arrest". This encourages the women liberation movement of our day to challenge the present alienating status quo. The Spirit of God shows no partiality and is not a respecter of persons. The present day women liberation movement wants men to note this. At this juncture, we shall go over to the next chapter, which hinges on the role of prophetesses in the early church. Here, we shall see how gender got married to prophecy. There was no tension between the two.

Chapter 3
Gender and Prophecy

The prophetic ministry was an important aspect of the missionary activities of the early church. As the facts of the New Testament show, it was accepted as a gift of the Spirit in the Pauline charismatic communities (1Cor 12,28; Rom 12,6 and Eph 4,11). Both the apostolic church and post-Pauline Christianity were aware of it.

As the pieces of evidence show, the activities of Christian prophets and prophetesses in the early church are well documented. This is in contrast to the priesthood, where the New Testament and early church history knew of no Christian priests. As a result, this work will underline the radical relationship between *gender and prophecy*. Instead of resentment, there is contentment. The prophetic ministry is not taken captive by gender squabbles. It joins the hands of both genders as collaborators of the kingdom. In a sense, then, the prophetic ministry can be called the "ministry of non-discrimination".

As far as we know, the prophetic ministry was a "free for all" genders. It has no gender preference. This is understandable since the Pauline charismatic church recognized it as a free gift of the Holy Spirit. In other words, it was not a male-reserved ministry. Both men and women exercised this ministry. It was such an important ministry that Paul highly treasured it (1Cor 14,1). Before we continue, let us do a brief lexical analysis of the various words for prophet.

1) Lexical Analysis

The available lexical evidence shows that the Greek word for prophet is *prophêtês* (προφήτης). Its verbal form is *prophêteúô* (προφητεύω), which means to be a prophet,[97] to have the gift of prophecy,[98] or to be one who proclaims[99] The Hebrew word for this prophet in the Old Testament is *nābî'* (נָבִיא). This means one who proclaims the message of a deity, foretells, or proclaims the future in advance.[100] However, in the New Testament especially in Paul, it means to teach, admonish or comfort[101] In view of this, Friedrich says:

> The prophet is very different in Paul. He certainly receives revelations but he is not characterised by visions and auditions which transport him out of the world. His chief mark is the Word which God has given him to proclaim. The prophet in the Pauline congregations is not the seer but the recipient and preacher of the Word.[102]

This means that the prophetic function in the New Testament is not essentially about foreseeing the future, though this is also attested, as in the case of the passion predictions of Jesus (Matt 16,21; 20,18) and the prophet Agabus in the apostolic church (Acts 11,28; 21,10-11). All the same, this idea of future prediction was not the norm. Indeed, the main feature of the prophetic charism is not about predicting the future. This explains why the early New Testament and post New Testament prophets played both didactic and missionary roles. They functioned as *didáskalos* (διδάσκαλος)-teachers and *euaggelistês* (εὐαγγελιστής)-evangelists. They were like mobile preachers.

Next, the prophetic charism has oracular functions. In this sense, it can be said to be the gift of interpreting the will of the gods[103] and the proclamation of the divine will.[104] Somehow, this corresponds to the function of the Greek *prophêtês* (προφήτης) where the word means one who proclaims.[105] In line with this, Rengstorf says that "the Greek προφήται are proclaimers of a truth, and in so far as they belong to a sanctuary they are thus mouthpieces for the deity which they serve".[106] In ancient Israel, the prophet was originally called *rō'eh* (רֹאֶה)-a seer (1Sam 9,9). Of course, this represents the primitive stage of the prophetic institution in Israel.

In the New Testament, the prophet is essentially one who proclaims the word of God.[107] In view of this, Friedrich says that "the one who prophesies utters the divine call of judgment and repentance which is burdensome and tormenting to many. . . but which convicts others of sin and leads them to the worship of God".[108] It is in this sense that

John the Baptist is recognized as the prophet of God most high (Lk 1.76), even though he was not a seer. In view of this, it becomes understandable that the *prophêtês* in the early church was like a peripatetic preacher. He or she played missionary roles. Not only had the one a role to play in liturgical assemblies, some of these New Testament prophets functioned also as *community leaders*, as we see in the case of Silas and Barnabas, who were leaders in the church of Jerusalem (Acts 15,22.32). Given the high profile nature of some of the women in the apostolic church (Acts 9,36; 12,12-14; 18,18.26), it makes sense to say that the recognized women prophets equally played this leadership role.

2) Prophetesses in the Old Testament

The use of this word, *prophetess*, is very interesting for the study of the role of women in the ministry of the church today. The simple reason for this is that it shows that the prophetic ministry was not a men-only ministry. It was not exclusively masculine like the ministry of the Old Testament priesthood where women were not allowed to officiate as priests nor even enter the "Holy of Holies."

As far as the evidence shows, the prophetic ministry has no cultic connotation. Besides, it did not require a cultic place for its exercise. By implication, also, the prophet or prophetess was not a person of the sanctuary In view of this, the prophetic model accommodates the ministry of men and women very well. It's elastic nature makes it to transcend gender discrimination. Hence, prophets and prophetesses existed in both the Old Testament and New Testament.

This was also the case in the Hellenistic culture of the time. Accordingly, Krämer said that the *prophêtês* denotes "appointed men and women and their work, which is to declare something whose content is not derived from themselves but from the god who reveals his will at the particular site".[109] As can be seen from this text, women also enjoyed this privilege. Indeed, in Greek culture, being a prophet was not the exclusive reserve of men. It was not a male prerogative. Both Paul and the New Testament agree with this practice. Hence, women were also prophetesses in some of the New Testament communities.

In view of the non-sexist character of the prophetic ministry, morphologically, the Old Testament has the word *nābî* (נָבִיא) for the male prophet and *nəbî'āh* (נְבִיאָה) for the woman prophet. This means that there were recognized prophets, as well as prophetesses in ancient Israel. The reader sees that the prophetic ministry was not gender-based. In this regard, Exo 15,20 shows that the sister of Moses, Miriam, was called *nəbî'āh* (נְבִיאָה) prophetess. In addition, there were other women recognized as prophetesses in Israel. One of them is Deborah, whom Judges 4.4 calls *îššāh nəbî'āh* (אִשָּׁה נְבִיאָה)-a woman prophetess. As we read in the book of Judges, this woman was also a judge in Israel. It is quite interesting that she was even recognized as a prophetess by Jerome.[110]

Apart from the two prophetesses just mentioned (Miriam and Deborah), surprisingly, the ultra-conservative Nehemiah recognized another woman, No-adiah, as a prophetess (Neh 6,14). From this, one can say that women continued to be recognized as prophetesses even in the post-exilic period of Jewish history. Being a prophet was not simply a male job. Both men and women enjoyed this privilege. This further highlights the non-sexist character of the prophetic office.

The last instance to be considered is the case of Huldah. This woman was also recognized as a prophetess in 2Kgs 22,14 and 2Chr 34,22. As the sources show, she was a contemporary of Jeremiah, the prophet. This shows that prophetesses existed in Israel at this time alongside with great prophets like Jeremiah. Relevant evidence shows that Hilkiah the priest once consulted the prophetess Huldah in the company of some other men. *This is quite unusual, to see a priest in Israel submit to the prophetic authority of a woman.* More surprising is the fact that Jeremiah, who was a contemporary of this prophetess, was not the one consulted in this instance. Here, one sees further evidence that the prophetic ministry of women was indeed recognized in ancient Israel. It was an exalted office, even in the time of the monarchy. This may have led the prophet to be addressed as *îš hā'ĕlohîm* (הָאֱלֹהִים אִישׁ)-the man of God or the woman of God.[111]

3) Prophetesses in the New Testament

The New Testament imitated the non-sexist nature of the prophetic office in both the Old Testament and Hellenistic cultures. Hence, there is widespread evidence that it emphatically recognized the ministry of women prophets. The first instance of this is from the gospel of Luke. Here, the prophetess Anna was recognized and given a prominent role in the Lucan infancy narratives (Luke 2,36). Therefore, it is not surprising that this recognition went beyond the New Testament period. In this regard, it is interesting that Jerome also recognized Anna as a Christian prophetess.[112]

Of particular interest to us in this work is that Pauline Christianity recognized the ministry of women as prophetesses. Hence, in 1Corinthians, Paul advised these prophetesses, as well as prophets in these words:

> Any man who prays or prophesies with his head covered dishonors his head, but any woman who prays or prophesies with her head unveiled dishonors her head--it is the same as if her head were shaven (1Cor 11,4-5).

From the standpoint of this text, the only difference between the prophet and prophetess in Pauline Christianity was their dressing attire, which, of course, has to do with convention rather than with theology or religion. In other words, Paul gives a dressing code of conduct for the two groups of prophets. However, this did not make the ministry of the prophetess inferior to that of the prophet. Nor did it make the female prophet less of a prophet than the male prophet

Finally, in the Acts of the Apostles, the apostolic church also recognized the ministry of women prophets. In this regard, the four daughters of Philip the evangelist are known prophetesses in this church (Acts 21,9). It is interesting that these prophetesses functioned alongside with other eminent prophets, like Agabus (Acts 21,11). Their importance is even further highlighted by the fact that they were also known outside the New Testament. In this regard, Eusebius of Caesarea showed awareness of this particular tradition concerning the four daughters of Philip when he was writing about the death of John and Philip.[113] Besides, he knew of other prophetesses, apart from the ones mentioned above. This was what prompted him to write as follows:

> Does not all Scripture seem to you to forbid a prophet to receive gifts and money? When therefore I see the prophetess receiving gold and silver and costly garments, how can I avoid reproving her?[114]

In view of this fact that Eusebius associated these prophetesses with gold, silver and costly ornaments we can safely infer that they belonged to a noble class. All the same, we can see that the activities of Christian prophetesses went beyond the New Testament period. [115] They were not just *housekeepers* of male prophets. To the contrary, they participated in the prophetic ministry like their male counterparts.

These prophets played a "mirror-like role" in their society. They were continually pointing out the evils of their time. They acted as the "remorseful conscience" of a "remorseless society". In view of this, Abraham J. Heschel said that these prophets "challenged the injustices of their culture".[116] In a sense, they played an ethical role, trying to bring moral sanity to a morally bankrupt society. In view of this, Heschel further said:

> The prophet is an iconoclast, challenging the apparently holy, revered and awesome, beliefs cherished as certainties, institutions endowed with supreme sanctity. They exposed the scandalous pretensions, they challenged kings, priests, institutions and the temple.[117]

In the light of this ethical and moral function, one sees why the contemporaries of a prophet like Jeremiah considered him to be a thorn in their flesh.[118] Consequently, they sought to kill him.[119] This tallies with Paul, who says that the prophetic preaching brings out the secret wickedness of people which leads to the worship of the true God (1Cor 14,25). This makes the prophet the custodian of morality.

In view of this emphatic endorsement of the ministry of women from all the sources mentioned in this work, one sees that the reality of women prophets was not only peculiar to Paul and the New Testament. As we have seen, it was a feature of both apostolic and non-apostolic Christianity. It continued into the post-apostolic phase of early Christianity. This shows that we are not dealing with isolated instances in the history of the early church.

The interesting thing here is that it was not a *gender-based* ministry. Here, men and women exercised the prophetic ministry, without rancor or discrimination. As a result, there was harmony between gender and ministry in this Christianity. It was only in later church history that conflict arose between *ministry and gender* .

This mishap in church history was due to the patriarchalisation of ministry in Christianity. The consequence is that men "usurped" the right to appoint and designate officials in the church. Hence, we have a strange situation where "men crown men" in the church. Here, the old Latin adage – *vox populi, vox die-*(voice of the people, voice of God) is swept ashore. The voice of the people can now only mean the voice of men. In this way, leadership in the church becomes a "men's club" affair. The hierarchy of the church becomes "men only area", where men belong to it by divine right, but women only by human concession. For the men, it is a right. But for the women, it is only a privilege. This male supremacist situation is simply justified as part of the divine order. The subordination texts of the New Testament household codes[120] are even quoted to strengthen this argument. Hence, we see a situation where this male usurpation of power in the church was later coated with theology to give the false impression that it is the will of the Holy God, who created men and women equal.

At this juncture, we shall make a slight change, though within the same frequency range. Since we have firmly established that women participated in the prophetic ministry, whether in the Old Testament or the New Testament, we shall now go ahead to examine the prophetic ministry in the post New Testament period. In other words, this discussion goes into the world of the post New Testament church. This leads us now to examine the relevance of the *Didache* (an early Christian literature) to this discussion on women and the prophetic ministry.

4) Post-Apostolic Christianity and the Prophetic Ministry

This discussion begins with the *Didache*, an early Christian document. It spent a reasonable amount of time talking about the prophets of its day. In this regard, out of its sixteen chapters, it devoted two chapters (11 and 13) exclusively to this topic. This shows the measure of importance it accorded to this group of "ministers" in the church of the time.

Chapter 11 of this document shows how to distinguish a false prophet from a true one. This is typical of Deut 18. And chapter 13 of Didache outlines how a prophet is to be treated. This very chapter holds the key to the discussion here. It shows also what roles these prophets played in 2nd century Christianity. The relevant text reads:

> Every genuine prophet who wants to settle with you "has a right to his support." Similarly, a genuine teacher himself, just [2] like a "workman, has a right to his support." Hence take all [3] the first fruits of vintage and harvest, and of cattle and sheep, and give these first fruits to the prophets. *For they are your high priests* [emphasis mine]. [4] If, however, you have no prophet, give them to [5] the poor. If you make bread, take the first fruits and give in [6] accordance with the precept. Similarly, when you open a jar of wine or oil, take the first fruits and give them to the [7] prophets. Indeed, of money, clothes, and of all your possessions, take such first fruits as you think right, and give in accordance with the precept.[121]

This text points to the early development of the Christian priesthood. It is very pregnant for the ordination of women as priests and their recognition as ministers in different capacities in the church of God. Anybody reading this document sees how "pick and choose" works in Christianity. For instance, chapter 9 of this same document, dealing with the Eucharistic celebration, is widely quoted in Roman Catholic liturgical circles when treating the Eucharist. On the other hand, chapter 13 is glossed over in silence when treating the priesthood because this would undermine its supposed sacramentality on which the whole argument for not ordaining women hinges.

Whatever the case may be, what this document clearly tells us is that the idea of the Christian priesthood was still developing during this second century period. At this time, it was not yet defined and was not *clearly* in existence. Hence, in this community, prophets were recognized as priests. In view of this, *Didache* says, *"they are your high priests"*. Here, prophecy and priesthood merged. The prophet became also the priest of the community, *but in a non-cultic capacity, without ritual connotations.* In which case, they too were among those presiding over the Eucharist mentioned in chapter 9 of the document. *This is one indication that the celebration of the Eucharist has never been the exclusive reserve of cultic officials called priests.* At least, this is perfectly the case in the New Testament period when the Eucharist was celebrated in the *house churches.* At this time, there were evidently no Christian priests.[122] Whoever precided at the Eucharistic celebration was the priest of the moment.

Indeed, the argument that the church cannot ordain women because it is not the intention of Jesus begins to weaken here. If this priesthood is as important as it is construed to be today, why did *Didache* not know about it, as early as the 2nd century AD? And if it knew about it, why did it not say it? All that the *Didache* knew was about "bishops" and deacons.[123] On the question of the priest it recognized *only* the prophets. This continues to strengthen the argument that the Christian priesthood is a development of church history.

In view of this, let us not create our own Jesus to put words into his mouth so that our "created Jesus" can defend and protect "androcracy",[124] the rule by men. Indeed, the evidence is overwhelming that both the New Testament and early Christianity were unaware of a Christian priesthood. Certainly, Jesus did not, nor did Paul.[125] This is what the *Didache* has clearly demonstrated. In which case, the "male church" *simply does not want women in the priesthood so that its power base can be protected.* In view of this, Jesus is neatly *recruited* as the most convenient spokesperson of the authorities involved. The Jesus-argument is only a pretext, a camouflage, just to hold on to church power. It is all about *potestas* (power) in the *ekklêsia* of God.

a) Prophets as "Priests"

The language used in the *Didache* above clearly treats these prophets as "priests". In the text, these prophets have two basic rights. First of all they have right of residency. They can reside in any community should they so desire. I guess that this right results from the fact that they are treated as "high priests". This shows that later in the history of Christianity prophets became the "priests of Christians". This right of residency here marks also the beginning of settled preachers, later known as the clergy or priests.

Next, the prophet is entitled to *support* from the community. This is already the beginning of church benefice for the clergy. So the prophetic office was a precursor of the later priests of Christianity. Accordingly, the type of support that *Didache* solicits for the prophet became the prerogative of the local clergy in later church history.

b) Prophets and First Fruits

In the text above, the association between *prophets* and *first fruits* is very striking. Hence, this needs further investigation. As we know, the Old Testament used "first fruits" in two distinct ways. The first is in relation to the Lord. Several texts point this.[126] Here, the offering of the first fruits to the Lord is also called the *minhāh* (מִנְחָה)-*cereal offering*. The second is in relation to the Levitical priests. In this regard, two texts are outstanding. The first is Ezek 44,28-31, while the second is Deut 18,1-8. Let us begin with the former.

5) Ezekiel and First fruits

This prophet has a special rapport with the priesthood of his day. Hence, he is also known as a *cultic prophet*. Here, the tension that existed between some of the prophets (like Amos and Isaiah) and the priesthood disappears. This close affinity between the priesthood and the prophetic institution makes Ezekiel very relevant to this discussion. In view of this, let us review the following text from him.

> [28] And it shall be unto them [the levitical priests, the sons of Zadok] for an inheritance: I am their inheritance: and ye shall give them no possession in Israel: I am their possession. [29] They shall eat the meat offering [מִנְחָה], and the sin offering [חַטָּאת], and the trespass offering [אָשָׁם]: and every dedicated thing in Israel shall be theirs. [30] *And the first of all the firstfruits of all things, and every oblation of all, of every sort of your oblations, shall be the priest's: ye shall also give unto the priest the first of your dough* [emphasis mine], that he may cause the blessing to rest in thine house. [31] The priests shall not eat of any thing that is dead of itself, or torn, whether it be fowl or beast (KJV: Ezekiel 44,28-31).

First of all, the reader of Ezekiel sees that the whole of Ezek 44 is heavily cultic. The right attitude to worship is meticulously stressed and underlined. The way the sons of Zadok should be remunerated is also outlined. This is what is related to our discussion.

Looking at the text of *Didache*, it seems that Ezek 44 *may* have influenced the formulation there, since there is evidence that it may have been influenced by the Old Testament. Unlike some of the other prophets (like Amos, Isaiah, etc.), who were somewhat "anti-priesthood" and "anti-cult", Ezekiel is pro cult. He stresses the relationship between the priesthood and the prophetic institution. The harsh critique of cult that one sees in Amos 7,9[127] and Isaiah 1.10-17,[128] for instance, disappears completely here. Hence, one sees a common pattern between the *Didache* and Ezekiel in establishing a strong bond between the priests and prophets.

The most striking thing for us here is the mention of "first fruits". Ezekiel tells us that these are meant for the priests. And he was quite insistent on this. These *first fruits* represent the benefice or religious remuneration for the priests involved. This is exactly the role it plays in the *Didache*. In other words, the "first fruits" in the *Didache* are not to be understood in terms of the "cereal offering" of Leviticus, which was offered to the Lord. The prophets mentioned in the *Didache* were genuinely recognized as the "priests" of the community, since there were none other than them. Hence, they were given a priestly entitlement or remuneration, which is the "first fruits". This is further reinforced in Deuteronomy. Let us consider it.

6) "First fruits" in Deuteronomy

There is a wonderful striking similarity between Deut 18 and *Didache* 13. In this regard, the first thing is that both of them were concerned with *priests and prophets*. Hence, Deut 18,1-9 is about priests, while Deut 18,15-22 is about the prophets. This structure is somehow imitated in *Didache* 13. Let us place the two texts side by side for a comparative analysis.

| **Didache 13,1-7:** Every genuine prophet who wants to settle with you "has a right to his support." Similarly, a genuine teacher himself, just [2] like a "workman, has a right to his support." Hence take all [3] the first fruits of vintage and harvest, and of cattle and sheep, and give these first fruits to the prophets. For they are your high priests. [4] If; however, you have no prophet, give them to [5] the poor. If | **Deut 18,1-7** "The Levitical priests. . . shall have no inheritance among their brethren; the LORD is their inheritance, as he promised them. . . . [4] The first fruits of your grain, of your wine and of your oil, and the first of the fleece of your sheep, you shall give him. . . .[6] "And if a Levite comes from any of your |

you make bread, take the first fruits and give in [6] accordance with the precept. Similarly, when you open a jar of wine or oil, take the first fruits and give them to the [7] prophets. Indeed, of money, clothes, and of all your possessions, take such first fruits as you think right, and give in accordance with the precept.	towns out of all Israel, where he lives--and he may come when he desires—to the place which the LORD will choose, [7] then he may minister in the name of the LORD his God, like all his fellow-Levites who stand to minister there before the LORD.

As in the case of Ezekiel above, Deuteronomy also understands "first fruits" as remuneration for the Levitical priests. This is highly stressed in the text above. As I argued in the case of Ezekiel, the prophets in *Didache* seem to be modeled on the Levitical priests. Hence, in both texts, we see that a prophet, as well as a Levite, can reside in a community. Both have the right of residency in the believing community. Also the *Didache* was constantly referring to the "precepts". This seems to be a reference to the Old Testament guidelines for remunerating the Levitical priests.

The conclusion to be drawn is obvious. *There were no priests, as some of the Christian churches have it today, during the period of the Didache.* The notion of the priesthood was still evolving at the time. In a situation where there was no clear concept of the priesthood, the *Didache* developed its own idea, *loosely* modeled on the non-cultic elements of the Levitical priesthood. Hence, the prophets in the community were chosen to play this role. This position is indirectly reinforced by this other text from the *Didache*, which says:

> You must, then, elect for yourselves bishops and deacons who are a credit to the Lord, men who are gentle, generous, faithful, and well tried. For their ministry to you is identical 2 with that of the prophets and teachers. You must not, therefore, despise them, for along with the prophets and teachers they enjoy a place of honor among you.[129]

The word "bishop" in the text can be a bit misleading. This is not a bishop in terms of *ordained ministry* in the present day context. It is simply a translation of the Greek *epískopos*, which at the time meant an "overseer". However, the modern understanding of this *epískopos* has influenced this and similar translations. All the same, one sees that the *Didache* was clearly aware of the existence of these "bishops" (*epískopoi*) and deacons (*diákonoi*). On the contrary, it was unaware of priests (*hiereus*) or presbyters (*presbýteros*).

The interesting thing here is that the text *even equated these "bishops" and deacons with the prophets and teachers, showing that there is no drastic hierarchical difference between these figures at this time. Didache* says that they performed *identical* ministry. In which case, the line between them was blurred. In other words, this association shows that the *episkopoi* and *diakonoi* were *not* cultic officials at the time. This explains why these are associated with prophets and teachers in the community.

Also the omission of priests or presbyters here is not accidental. This shows very clearly that this reality was not in existence at this point in time. The conclusion to be reached here is that *we cannot be arguing that Jesus did not permit women to be admitted into a priesthood that clearly developed after him and outside the New Testament.* The priesthood is the product of church history. It is an offshoot of post-apostolic Christianity. Of course, this questions its sacramentality in those Christian churches cherishing it today. Therefore, it is wrong to exclude women from it.

The problem of ordaining women or not ordaining them, admitting them into leadership positions in the church or not admitting them is created by us in the first place. It is the unfortunate outcome of patriarchal logic. This means that the onus is on us to resolve it. With goodwill and open-mindedness on all sides we can solve it. There is no need to continue hiding under the canopy of the divine just to avoid solving it.

The Christian church has dodged this problem for a long time. It is time to come out from our hideout and confront this perennial problem. Unless we do it will continue to distract us from the ministry of leading the sheep to greener pastures. We have begged this question for a long time. Now is the time to be honest enough to call *a spade, a spade. Jesus will not deny anybody salvation simply because such a one admitted women to the top hierarchy of the church.* The time has come to do away with this power-grab in the church and concentrate on the real ministry of tending and feeding the lamb.

7) Women as "Priests"

What we have said so far has a serious implication for the ordination of women either as deacons, or priests. It has also serious consequences for their appointment as pastors and senior pastors in the churches of the Christian religion. If the priesthood is a later development of church history and tradition, as we have maintained in this work, one sees that the Jesus-argument that he did not permit the ordination of women becomes *laughable* and so *crumbles* like a deck of cards. By all reasonable accounts it is hollow and porous. An argument of this nature is simply the result of *"eisegesis"*[130] and not of *"exegesis"*.[131] It is lacuna-decked.

In this place, I am aware that the traditional Roman Catholic argument has been that the "do this in memory of me" of the institution narratives in the synoptic accounts constituted the ordination of the twelve. *This is entirely hollow and empty since the twelve were never seen performing any priestly act in the New Testament, nor were they ever addressed as priests.*[132] There is nothing in the texts of the institution narratives[133] that suggest an act of ordination. Not even in post-apostolic communities were we told that they performed cultic acts or priestly duties. Besides, the link between the commissioning of the twelve and the priesthood is non-existent. In addition, it is not contained in any extant New Testament text that it was their exclusive reserve or prerogative to preside over the Eucharist. The church was first a *house church* and women presided over the Eucharist in these house churches, as we have shown in chapter one. No designated cultic official was necessary for this act. *And gender was not a criterion for determining who should preside.* The relationship, which we have established between gender and the Eucharist, was not there in the beginning. The "genderlization" of the Eucharistic celebration in some of the Christian churches is also a product of church tradition. The New Testament does not clearly attest to this.

Indeed, a document like *Didache* purporting to have been written by the twelve apostles (or at least written in the name of the Twelve) could not have ignored such an important institution supposed to have been neatly packaged by the master. If it remembered the Eucharist, that the Lord instituted, it becomes even more obvious that the priesthood now associated with the same Eucharist *could not* and *should not* have been forgotten. The simple deduction from this is that no Christian priesthood was in existence at that time. On account of this, the *Didache* did not know of any Christian priests ordained with an exclusive cultic mandate to officiate in the name of Christianity. It could not have remembered the "bishops" and deacons in the text without at the same time remembering the priests, if there were already recognized priests then.

This means that if we want to ordain women today, *we surely can.* There is *nothing theologically* against it. *Instead, sound theology favors it.* Even the New Testament itself is not against it, as we have set out to demonstrate in this work, using examples from the early church and beyond. Also a good number of the early Christian sources did not forbid it. Of course, *they could not have proscribed a non-existent reality at the time.* Since this was not in existence, the prophets in the community of Didache received the benefits meant for priests.

As we mentioned in our analysis of prophecy above women were prophetesses in the early church and beyond. There was no gender bias in this regard. That ministry was not "genderlized". If the *Didache* recognizes prophets as "your high priests" and women were prophets, then, women were also "your high priests". For the sake of clarity, this argument can be summarized with the following logical syllogism:

Major Premise: Prophets are high priests.

Minor Premise: Women are prophets.

Conclusion: Therefore, women are also high priests.

This may not be a perfect syllogism. Nonetheless, in a syllogistic argument, such as we have here, once the premises are correct the conclusion should also be logically correct. Even though Christian doctrine is not dictated by rules of logic and syllogism, nevertheless, it is not something irrational. Rules of reason and commonsense also govern it. Hence, based on the understanding of the *Didache* about the priesthood, women too were "your high priests".[134] This is a sound logical deduction, though as I have already said theology is not always governed by rules of logic. All the same, there is no need ignoring important information such as we have here. Meanwhile, we shall now go further to examine the relevance of "Jesus the prophet" to this discussion. Here, the importance of the prophetic ministry in the New Testament will be further highlighted.

8) Jesus and the Prophetic Ministry

Why is this gospel topic relevant here? It is pertinent because it is the continuation of what we have just said above. In this regard, we begin by pointing out that *the entire messianic ministry of Jesus was anchored on the prophetic tradition and not on the priesthood of the Old Testament.* This was what essentially defined the activities of "Jesus the messiah" and "Jesus of Nazareth". In fact, it even helped to place him above the Jewish priesthood of his day. As far as the gospel evidence shows, neither the synoptics nor the gospel of John knew about "Jesus the priest". Instead, what they knew was about "Jesus the prophet". Besides, the ideal on which the New Testament ministry is based is the prophetic and shepherd's model and not the priestly one.

This has a serious implication for the ministry of women today. As we have seen above the elasticity of the prophetic model creates a high degree of openness to the ministry of women. The reason for this is that the prophetic institution, either in the Greek world, the Old Testament or the New Testament, was not an all-male affair[135]. It is all-inclusive. Hence, it did not promote gender exclusion, or gender prerogatives, *as did the Old Testament priesthood.*

Whereas Jesus the prophet emphatically embraced an all-inclusive model – the prophetic model, on the other hand, Jesus as priest would have done the direct opposite. He would have simply taken a gender-excluding model – the priesthood, which would have eternally prohibited women from participating in the ministry of the church. This would have forced him to accept a male supremacist's point of view, which was what the Old Testament priesthood radically represented. Consequently, he would not have stood out, as he did in the Jewish society of his day. Besides, his partially non-conformist approach to the Jewish traditions before him would not have been possible since he would have been taken captive by ritual norms and dietary regulations as a priest in Israel.

One, sees, why this aspect of New Testament christology is attractive to us in this work. Since Christian tradition normally knows of *Jesus the priest* and poorly knows of *Jesus the prophet*, which is an upside down situation, how can we really establish our case in this work? This is now what we intend to do. We shall now point out the prophetic credentials of Jesus.

Although later Christian traditions, based on the later apologetic theology of the letter to the Hebrews, emphatically affirm the priesthood of Jesus, *the gospels are totally unaware of such a priesthood.* Hence, they *never* told us about *Jesus the priest*. This is said because no text of the canonical gospels contains it. Instead, the gospels were constant, consistent and very generous in telling us about the frequent and widely reported confrontation between Jesus and the priests of the New Testament time. The gospel theology does not establish any friendly link between christology and the priesthood in any shape or form. It is true that Jesus may not have been against the priesthood *qua tale* (as such), yet his dislike for the priests of the day was an open secret. He showed contempt and dissatisfaction with the priests of the day. One example suffices to underline this point here.

In the Judaism of the time of Jesus one of the worst thing that anybody could have done was to compare the priests of the day with harlots with the intention of denigrating these priests. This would have been a form of sacrilege and a possible death sentence for the culprit. But Jesus did this. He fearlessly told the chief priests and the elders of the people, who came to him as he was teaching in the temple to find out by what authority he was doing it, "that the publicans and the harlots go into the kingdom of God before you" (KJV: Matt 21,31). This would have been an incomprehensible statement for a first century orthodox Jew. How could anyone prefer a "dirty harlot" to a "holy priest", according to the purity guidelines of the day?[136] This is not a sign that Jesus embraced the ideals of the priesthood of his day. He had no need to identify with it.

With this in mind one sees something quite enigmatic in the text. Here, the harlot considered to be a pariah is recognized, while the supposedly praiseworthy cultic persons (the priests) could not be proposed as a model. This becomes a harsh critique of the cultic institutions of the Old Testament. Jesus points out their deficiencies. In a sense, those considered to be sinners and anomalous persons by the orthodox Judaism of the time now qualify for the kingdom of God, while the priests of the holy covenant are seen to be lagging behind, in danger of being excluded.

Hence, between Jesus and the priests of his day there was no cordiality and no friendship. In a sense, the priests were not the friends of Jesus. In addition, Jesus had no good words for them. In this regard, he even prophesied that he would die in their hands (Matt 16,21; 17,22-23; 20,18-19). As we know, this was meticulously fulfilled for it was the same priesthood that put him to a violent death under the high priest Caiaphas as we read in Matthew (Matt 26,3.57) and John (John 18,13.14). This "cat and mouse" situation between Jesus and the priests of the day prevented the gospels from associating him with the priesthood. Instead, they distanced him from it.

On the contrary, both the disciples and the contemporaries of Jesus knew him as a *prophet*. Here, there is overwhelming and emphatic evidence in support of this. First of all, for his immediate disciples, he is the full realization of the eschatological prophet of Deuteronomy, who is to come (cf. Deut 18,15). For them he is "a prophet mighty in deed and word before God and all the people" (Luke 24,19). This shows that Jesus emerged in his society as a *great prophet*, with impeccable prophetic credentials.

In a similar way, Luke acknowledges this fact. After the raising of the widow's son at Nain, he reports, "Fear seized them all; and they glorified God, saying, 'A great prophet has arisen among us!' and 'God has visited his people'" (Luke 7,16). Here, the people recognized that God has raised a great prophet for them. They took it that this is a sure sign that God has visited his people. On account of this, they glorified God. Even during his triumphal entry into Jerusalem, this declaration becomes more intense and louder. In view of this, his exuberant Jewish followers declared: "This is the prophet Jesus from Nazareth of Galilee" (Matt 21,10-11). The crowd is right since a priest could only be a descendant of Levi or Aaron. In their minds, Jesus was not a priest but a prophet.

This emphasis on the prophetic personality of Jesus is also continued in the gospel of John. First of all, the woman of Samaria professes him as a prophet. Hence, the text tells us:

> Jesus said to her, 'You are right in saying, 'I have no husband'; [18] for you have had five husbands, and he whom you now have is not your husband; this you said truly." [19] The woman said to him, "Sir, I perceive that you are a prophet" (John 4,17-19).

Even the Samaritan community, taken to be an anomalous group by the Jews of the period, professed Jesus as a prophet. This is the testimony seen also in John 7,40-41. The text says, "when they heard these words, some of the people said, 'this is really the prophet.' Others said, 'This is the Christ.'" Here, there is something very striking – the link between the prophet and the Christ. This is the testimony of John. One sees that Jesus is not seen as a priestly messiah, but as a prophetic messiah. In other words, the Christ is also the prophet. Here, Jesus is associated with the prophetic ministry and not with the cumbersome and burdensome priestly one, overloaded with endless rituals and delicate dietary regulations.

Further, the text of the confession of Peter helps to underline this prophetic dimension of Jesus. Hence, people were guessing that he could be Elijah or John the Baptist or any of the other prophets (Matt 16,13-14).[137] This reveals the minds of the contemporaries of Jesus who saw him as a prophet and not as a priest.

The prophetic character of Jesus is even seen in some of his sayings which are based on prophetic imageries. For instance, in Matt 10.41, he said: "He who receives a prophet because he is a prophet shall receive a prophet's reward". In a similar way, Jesus tells his contemporaries that a prophet has no honor in his own country (Matt 13,55; Mark 6,4; John 4,44). Even Jesus became the defender of the prophets by accusing his countrymen of murdering the prophets. Hence, he accused his contemporaries saying, "thus you witness against yourselves, that you are sons of those who murdered the prophets" (Matt 23,31).

Not only did the contemporaries of Jesus profess him as a prophet there is evidence also that Jesus saw himself this way. Hence, in Luke 13, we read:

> [31] The same day there came certain of the Pharisees, saying unto him, Get thee out, and depart hence: for Herod will kill thee. [32] And

he said unto them, Go ye, and tell that fox, Behold, I cast out devils, and I do cures to day and to morrow, and the third day I shall be perfected. [33] Nevertheless I must walk to day, and to morrow, and the day following: for it cannot be that a prophet perish out of Jerusalem. [34] O Jerusalem, Jerusalem, which killest the prophets, and stonest them that are sent unto thee; how often would I have gathered thy children together, as a hen doth gather her brood under her wings, and ye would not!

If the historical Jesus was a priest, his disciples did not reveal this to us. Beyond the theologoumenon of Hebrews, we don't know any other thing about the priesthood of Jesus, what more of the priesthood of his followers.

9) The Consequences of the Prophetic Ministry of Jesus

In his capacity as a prophet, Jesus performed actions which no other priest of his day would have performed for fear of ritual dirt or contamination. In this regard, we see him raising the dead to life, be it in the case of Jairus' daughter (Mk 5,35-43), or the widow's son at Nain (Luke 7,11-17), or Lazarus his friend (John 11,17-44). This is in the tradition of the prophet Elisha who brought the son of the Shunammite woman to life (2Kg 4,32-37; 2Kg 13,21). If the historical Jesus were a priest, he would not have come in contact with the dead in view of this legal provision in the book of Numbers:

[1] And the Lord spake unto Moses, saying, [2] Command the children of Israel, that they put out of the camp every leper, and every one that hath an issue, and whosoever is defiled by the dead: [3] Both male and female shall ye put out, without the camp shall ye put them; that they defile not their camps, in the midst whereof I dwell. [4] And the children of Israel did so, and put them out without the camp: as the Lord spake unto Moses, so did the children of Israel (KJV: Num 5,1-4. See also, Lev 21,1-3; Num 6).

Also typical of Elisha (2Kg 4,42-44) we see Jesus multiplying loaves of bread for the multitude, first for the five thousand (Mk 6,35-34) and then for the four thousand (Mk 8, 1-9). He also healed the sick (Matt 8,14-15). His cure of lepers (Luke 17,11-18) is comparable to the cure of Naaman the leper by Elisha (2Kg 5,8-14). This act carries ritual pollution or contamination. In view of this, no priest could have attempted doing it.[138]

This prophetic dimension of the ministry of Jesus is further seen in the text of Luke 4,18-19, which says:

The Spirit of the Lord is upon me, because he has anointed me to bring glad tidings to the poor. He has sent me to proclaim liberty to captives and recovery of sight to the blind, to let the oppressed go free,[19] and to proclaim a year acceptable to the Lord. (Luke 4,18-19).

This text is taken from Trito-Isaiah[139], which can also be called the *book of consolation*. However, in a typical prophetic style, Jesus adopted and adapted it. Here, he is given the prophetic anointing by the *rûach YHWH* (Spirit of God). This defines the terms of his ministry. His anointing did not usher him into the cult to draw a line of separation between him and the people. Instead, it brought him into a radical solidarity with humanity. He had no need to undergo the traditional priestly consecration, which separated the priests of the Old Testament covenant from the people. Unlike the anointing of these priests, which separated them from the people and dedicated them exclusively to a cult, Jesus was anointed to operate outside the cult and to encounter the people. His shrine was, wherever there were people.[140]

Here, there is both a puzzle and an enigma. Whereas the priest is anointed to encounter God, Jesus is anointed to encounter people. His altar becomes wherever human beings are. He is anointed in the Spirit to deliver people from oppressive situations. In this way, Christianity becomes a religion of liberation from hostile elements, which could be spiritual or worldly. The woman is not forbidden from doing this.

The anointing of Jesus by the Spirit is also aimed at lifting man and woman from the conditions of poverty. Every bodily ailment is hostile and so should be eliminated. As people anointed by the *rûach Yahweh* (Spirit of God) we should become the prophets of consolation, the prophets of hope, and not the prophets of doom or despair. The good news brings glad tidings. *This is why men and women must be disciples of Jesus in every respect.*

If the New Testament did not talk about any woman priest or the priesthood of women it is because there was no Christian priesthood in existence at the time. On the other hand, there was a prophetic ministry. Hence, the New Testament talked about women in this regard. In other words, if the New Testament recognized women prophets, based on the prophetic foundation of Jesus, it is wrong to argue against the ministry of women in the church today. Since the cornerstone of Christian ministry is *prophetic* and not priestly, the yardstick for knowing the mind of the master about women should be this prophetic signpost and not the priestly tradition which clearly developed outside the sacred canon. This should be the theological principle needed when discussing the ministry of women in the church.

Whereas the Christian prophetic ministry has overwhelming New Testament and unchallenged support, the Christian priesthood does not enjoy this. At best, it is a *derived ministry*. This means that there is no real theological obstacle towards ordaining women priests. As a result, they cannot be *justifiably* excluded from it under the pretext that the Lord did not permit them to be priests or leaders in the church. This is an anachronistic argument. However, since women were already prophetesses, which was the core of ministry in the New Testament period, the consequence is that we cannot disqualify them from any church ministry today.

10) Conclusion

Finally, the information that we have from *Didache* shows that the question of the ordination of women is not a "heaven-made" one, needing only a divine solution. Instead, it is "man-made". *Therefore, let us solve it because it is our own making.* It is the product of church history, the accident of patriarchal evolution in Christianity. *This is not a christological question, but an ecclesiastical one.* It is on the same level with the celibate institution, which was dogmatized at the Council of Trent in the Middle Ages.

In contemporary times, there is a feeling that the church cannot simply continue to be like a fixed mountain, absolutely unready to move. It can no longer be acting like the "unmoved mover" in the theodicy of Thomas Aquinas. The time has come to review the facts of church history and tradition and see how much they are at odds with evidence from the New Testament history and theology. This type of thinking has led to the spontaneous formation of the *charismatic movement* to challenge the present situation in which men exclusively control and manage the destiny of Christians. They do this because God, who is our Holy and Almighty Father, cannot have preferences in his "divine family". The οἰκεῖος τῆς πίστεως (*oikeíos tês písteôs*) *household of faith* (cf. Gal 6,10) belongs to all of us on *equal terms*. Here, both the *principles of equality* and *equal protection* apply. Since the institutional church is resistant to change, insulated from new ideas, this movement challenges a deeply entrenched status quo. In a sense, then, this movement is an attempt to "pull the rug" from the feet of the hierarchy. This explains why it is resented in some places by some church officials in the third world countries where it is operational.

Indeed, the New Testament made frantic efforts to incorporate both men and women in the ministry of the church. As we saw in the first chapter above dealing with the fellow workers of Paul, there were high profile women in the community of Paul. In which case, they are in agreement that God cannot be seen to be gender-affiliated, favoring only one sex. It is a fundamental mistake to present God as if he were a gender profiler. After all, the benefits of the kingdom are available to all, regardless of gender or race. In effect, this signals to the institution-alized churches that the era of unquestionable openness has arrived. The age of male-monopoly is gone. The epoch of unchallenged dogmas is equally over. Women are also created in the image and likeness of God. The New Testament tells us that God is the "God of equal op-portunity". It is ludicrous that while the secular state is seriously talk-ing about equal opportunity, justice and fairness for all, religious authorities, all over the world, keep resisting them. Here, the world seems to be far ahead of us, beckoning on us to follow in its footsteps. What an irony! And what a pity!

At this juncture, it is relevant to make a few remarks about the text of 1Cor 14,33b-35. Since this is at odds with the ideals of Pauline Christianity, as regards the ministry of women in the church, it is my intention to try to clarify the puzzle, which the text creates. This leads us to the next chapter.

Chapter 4
Gender and Ministry in 1Cor 14,33b-35

Why have I included this chapter in this book since the text to be analyzed is decidedly anti women? The reason is simple. 1Cor 14,33b-35 and 1Tim 2,11-15 have always been used by male activists to show that Paul himself was against the ministry of women in the church. As the reader will soon see, there is a clash between gender and ministry in this text. It is in view of this that I wish to straighten the records.

Accordingly, this chapter is divided into two. The first deals with general matters, trying to determine the authorship of 1Cor 14,33b-35. It is very important to resolve this problem so that the obstacle on the road to full ministry positions for women can be removed once and for all. The second section deals with exegetical details focusing on the text itself. Let us now begin with the first part of the study.

A) General Investigation

1) Introduction: The text of 1Cor 14,33b-35 introduces the reader to the reality of deutero-Pauline Christianity. This version of Christianity was operated in the name of Paul and on his behalf. Nonetheless, the text in question creates a dilemma for the student of Paul because it runs contrary to the Pauline principle of non-discrimination which we have seen so far. The argument for the equality of man and woman, which Paul has hitherto advanced, is now in danger of collapse. And his "no male, no female" slogan in Gal 3,28 is about to be canceled out. As the reader will soon see 1Cor 14,33b-35 challenges the ministry of women in Pauline Christianity and even in the church today. Here, there is a *de iure* (by law) excision of women from participation in leadership ministry in the church. This becomes all the more worrisome because 1Corinthians is unanimously accepted as an authentic Pauline letter and the text in question is found within this uncontested corpus.

Indeed, 1Cor 14,33b-35 raises some fundamental questions in Pauline exegesis. How can we explain the fact that Paul, who preached the equality of man and woman in Gal 3.28, now preaches a radical subordination of the woman to the man? And how can one also explain this irreconcilable position between allowing women to be prophets in the church in 1Cor 11,5 and commanding them to be silent in the same church? Since prophets are supposed to speak in the church for the building up of the church, is this not a clear fallacy? How can Paul the rhetorician be caught up in this type of open contradiction? How can one explain the fact that Paul, who never talked about the subordination of women in any of the seven letters attributed to him *by scholarly consensus*, now brings it to a head without prior notice? Nothing whatsoever prepared the student of Paul for this apparent sharp U-turn. How can the gag order in 1Cor 14,33b-35, which effectively muzzled women in the church, be explained? This points to the reader that we have now arrived at an *unfortunate* ecclesiological juncture-the *prohibition* of women from teaching in the *ekklêsia* of God, though Paul allowed them to do this as prophetesses in the charismatic communities. But who is to blame for this?

The answer to this question lies in the fact that the extreme wing of deutero-Pauline Christianity seems to be at work here. Hence, 1Cor 14,33b-35 points to an interpolation theory.[141] In this regard, Craig S. Keener appears to be very cautions. He seems to steer a middle course. While not embracing this interpolation theory, he also leaves the possibility that its proponents are correct. Hence, he said:

> Although I think that this passage is Pauline, *I concede that some text critics far more capable than myself* [emphasis mine] believe that it is a non-Pauline addition. I can only say that, if they are right, we may conclude quickly that Paul does not oppose women speaking in church. Because if Paul did not write it, this text clearly supplies no evidence for his position. I continue with this chapter, however, in the event that many of my readers, like myself, believe that these words are part of Paul's original letter to the Corinthians and must be understood in that context.[142]

Here, let us digress a little bit. In what we have just quoted, Keener has exhibited unusual humility rarely seen in published works. For me he has demonstrated the mark of the *homo sapiens*. Rarely one comes by authors who say it loudly that they are not so sure, leaving the possibility that some others may know more than themselves. This is worth emulating by today's pastors, ministers and preachers of the good news. This advice has in mind especially the TV and flamboyant evangelists of our day who have become "omniscient preachers", "knowing" the A-Z of the bible and so needing nobody to direct them on biblical matters. Here, is a well-reputed scholar, with numerous publications, an authority on Paul, who concedes that he is not omniscient, unlike many of our modern day preachers, who give their listeners the false impression that they know everything in the bible, when they may be preaching ignorance as the word of the Lord. They falsely make themselves bible encyclopedias. They can preach from Genesis to Revelation as "experts". They fail to recognize their limitations. And they rarely read what professional interpreters say about the bible because according to them, the Holy Spirit, who cannot teach them to read the bible either in Hebrew or Greek, the original languages, nevertheless teaches them everything in the translation of the bible. They forget that this same Holy Spirit can also teach other Christians thereby making their position irrelevant.

The outcome of this unfortunate situation is that today we have many "junk-preachers", who use their half-baked theological knowledge or no theology at all, to confuse and mislead Christians. Hence, it is not surprising that we have so much "*theological junks*" circulating around in the name of preaching. Regrettably, a good number of these "self-styled pastors and preachers" do not have any formal theological education. Some of them are comparable to people without formal education in law but going to the Supreme Court to represent clients before the learned judges. This shows the irony involved.[143]

Therefore, it is not surprising that today we have so many "junk preachers", even on our TV screens, who are parading as pastors. The mark of a good pastor, for some, has become the ability to shout as loud as one can, all in the name of preaching, quoting loosely connected and sometimes unconnected texts. Pastors of unaffiliated mushroom churches are also guilty in this respect. They parade themselves as biblical experts. I wish that we could learn from the honesty of Craig Keener, who is Professor of New Testament at the Eastern Seminary in Pennsylvania.

Despite the uncertainty of Keener,[144] the interpolation theory has the upper hand. In view of this, David G. Horrell said, "of all the suggested interpolations in 1Corinthians, this is the one most frequently accepted as such".[145] In other words, we are introduced to a non-

Pauline text in a Pauline corpus. In the light of the similarities between 1Cor 14,33b-35 and 1Tim 2.11-15, these two texts will now be presented side by side for a critical scrutiny.

2) Text and Translation

Text: 1Cor 14,33b-35	1Tim 2,11-15: γυνὴ ἐν Ἡσυχίᾳ μαν-
ὡς ἐν πάσαις ταις ἐκκλησιαις των ἁγίων [34] αἱ γυναικες ἐν ταις ἐκκλησίαις σιγάτωσαν οὐ γὰρ ἐπιτρέπεται αὐταις λαλειν, ἀλλὰ ὑποτασσέσθωσαν καθὼς καὶ ὁ νόμος λέγει	θανέτω ἐν πάσῃ ὑποταγῇ [12] διδάσκειν δὲ γυναικὶ οὐκ ἐπιτρέπω οὐδὲ αὐθεντειν ἀνδρός, ἀλλ᾽ εἶναι ἐν ἡσυχίᾳ. [13] Αδὰμ γὰρ πρωτος ἐπλάσθη εἶτα Εὔα. [14] καὶ ᾽Αδὰμ οὐκ ἠπατήθη, ἡ δὲ γυνὴ ἐξαπατηθεισα ἐν παραβάσει γέγονεν·
[35] εἰ δέ τι μαθειν θέλουσιν, ἐν οἴκῳ τοὺς ἰδίους ἄνδρας ἐπερωτάτωσαν αἰσχρόν γάρ ἐστιν γυναικὶ λαλειν ἐν ἐκκλησίᾳ	[15] σωθήσεται δὲ διὰ της τεκνογονιάς, ἐὰν μείνωσιν ἐν πίστει καὶ ἀγάπῃ καὶ ἁγιασμῷ μετὰ σωφροσύνης
1Cor 14,33b-35: Translation	1Tim 2,11-15: Translation
[33β] As in all the churches of the saints [34] let the women in all the churches keep silence; For it is not permitted to them to speak, they should be submissive, even as the law says;	[11] Let the woman learn in silence in all submissiveness; [12] So I do not permit any woman either to teach or to domineer man, but to be in silence. [13] For Adam was formed first, then Eve.
[35] If there is anything they want to know, let them ask their husbands at home; for it is disgraceful for a woman to speak in the church.	[14] And Adam was not deceived, but the woman was deceived and [consequently] became a transgressor. [15] Yet she will be saved through childbearing, if she remains in faith and love and holiness with sobriety.

The reader sees that the contents of both texts are basically the same. Both texts are guided by the same goal – the silence of women in all the churches. First of all, they are directed against women. Secondly, these women are *forbidden* to do something in the *ekklêsía* (ἐκκλησία) of God. Accordingly, both texts do not permit them to teach in the church. Worse still, women are ordered to be *silent* and to be *submissive* in the church. As the reader can see, the language used is very tough. Hence, both authors are uncompromising in their hostile reaction against women *speaking* or *teaching* in the church. The early Christian communities associated with this text could not entrust the faith of Christianity into the hands of women. Of course, this goes against the mandate given to them by the post-resurrection Jesus and by Paul himself.

Finally, in both traditions, the subordination of women reaches its irreversible turning point or crescendo. Here, the question of ordination for women is *emphatically* ruled out. In its place, subordination is unconditionally offered. In the light of these similarities, one question faces us now: Is the text of 1Cor 14,33b-35 Pauline or not? How do we know? And how can these similarities be adequately explained?

3) Resolving the Problem[146]

These two texts really present a textual critical problem to the professional interpreter of the bible. Since we have argued that Paul was not against the ministry of women in the church, why do we suddenly find such hostile and anti-feminine statements in a letter (1Corinthians) coming from him? Does the exegete now not find himself or herself boxed into a corner? Is he or she not in a dilemma or possibly on a theological crossroad? Is there no impasse? How can one resolve this *apparent* contradiction in Paul, without *explaining away* the problem just to uphold the thesis that Paul favored ministry roles for women in the church? Is it simply enough to say that 1Cor 14,33b-35 is an interpolation? This is now the task before us. So let us try to solve this apparent exegetical puzzle.

a) The Literary and Textual Critical Approach

The first thing which any Greek reader of the New Testament notices is that the text of 1Cor 14,33b-35 is found in a somewhat awkward place. This becomes clearer when it is seen in the overall context of the Pauline discussion on the charismatic gifts (1Cor 12-14) in which it is found. One sees that there is both a literary and contextual problem. Hence, we ask, is this text Pauline or not? We do not intend to take up all the details of the arguments here.[147] But our response will be measured and commensurate.

With this in mind, the first thing that I wish to point out is that the manuscripts are themselves *confused* about the authenticity of 1Cor 14,33b-35 as a Pauline text. Hence, they were not even sure where to fit it. Already, this points to the problematic nature of 1Cor 14,33b-35 from the earliest beginning of manuscript transmission. Accordingly, we have three different sets of manuscript evidence:

Evidence 1: The following sample manuscripts retain the text of 1Cor 34-35 where it is now, that is, coming after 1Cor 14,33 as one finds in the *Revised Standard Version* and some other translations. These manuscripts are p[46], ℵ, A, B, K, Y and several others.

Evidence 2: Some other manuscripts place this 1Cor 34-35 after 1Cor 14.40, that is, at the end of 1Cor 14. These include such Western witnesses as D, F, G, 8, 8* and many others. Here, the controversial text is made to be an appendix to the discussion on charisms.

Evidence 3: This is a unique witness. Hence, in the *codex Fuldensis*, these verses were inserted at the margin after 14,33.[148] In other words, this very manuscript was totally confused, unsure of what to do with the text of 1Cor 14,33-35. The fact that it was placed in the margin means that the scribe or scribes responsible for this very manuscript did not recognize it as an authentic Pauline text. Possibly, they considered it to be an interpolation or an editorial appendix of former scribes. Hence, they removed it from the main Pauline text.

Based on this textual information David G. Horrell says, "in the case of 1Cor 34-35 the textual tradition clearly shows some sort of break and so allows that the case for interpolation should be carefully considered."[149] This is precisely what we are doing in this work. The evidence from textual transmission enables us to argue in favor of a non-Pauline origin. In view of this, David G. Horrell concludes, "the hypothesis that 1Cor 14.34f was added in the margin at a time very early in the textual history of 1 Corinthians, but some years after Paul wrote the letters, offers the most plausible explanation of all the available evidence."[150] This helps to build a strong case against Pauline authorship of the *obnoxious* and anti feminist text.

As we have seen from the manuscript evidence the text of 1Cor 14,33-35 began to raise problems as early as the textual transmission of 1Corinthians. The question, which we ask today about its Pauline authenticity, was already asked from the earliest possible time. Doubts existed, as it still exists in our own time about its Pauline authorship. In effect, then, we see that even the ancient scribes were not so sure of what to do with this very unit. Some of them were hesitant to include it in the main body of the Pauline letter. This begins to alert us that Paul is the spurious author of the text in question.

But how can one explain the confusion surrounding the authorship of this text? The reason for this may be twofold. In the first place, the fact that it is found within the context of a charismatic discussion makes it all the more *suspicious*. Secondly, its inconsistency with the Pauline attitude towards women, *for those who accept the seven-letter theory of Paul*, may be another reason for the lack of consensus among the manuscripts. So from a purely manuscript tradition, the Pauline authorship of 1Cor 14.33-35 is *suspect* and *questionable*.

b) The Internal Evidence

The next thing we intend to do now is to make an internal examination of 1Cor 14,33b-35. Does contextual evidence support its Pauline authorship? In other words, what is the context in which it is found? First of all, it is situated within the context of the discussion on the charismatic gifts. The language of the *dubious text* is completely at odds with the overall language of 1Cor 12-14, which set the operational modalities for the charismatic church. Anyone reading it sees that 1Cor 14,33b-35 suddenly breaks up the logic and sequence of the discussion and abruptly introduces a topic completely outside the universe of discourse. This is a curious digression.

Besides, it contradicts the overall approach in the letter. This is maintained because, in 1Cor 11.5, Paul allows women to prophesy in the Corinthian church. In which case, he did not impose silence on them.[151] Paul was out to re-unite the divided Corinthians (1Cor 1,10-17). As a result, his language was love-oriented, appealing to all to work harmoniously to build up the church. He could not have introduced gender-conflict or discrimination as an instrument of peace and tranquillity in the divided Corinthian church.

Next, it has also to be pointed out that the introductory part of the text of 1Cor 33b-35 does not reflect the reality in the Pauline churches, as seen in the seven-letter theory. In 1Cor 14.33b-34, the deutero-Pauline author began by saying: *as in all the churches of the saints* (ὡς ἐν πάσαις ταις ἐκκλησίαις των ἁγίων). Here, he makes it clear that this prohibition against women speaking in the church exists in all the churches known to him. *This is a practice not seen in the Pauline churches.* Instead, it is a feature of deutero-Pauline Christianity. The churches, which the author has in mind, are seemingly those of the Pastoral Epistles, as the text of 1Tim 2,11-15 highly suggests. Otherwise, this practice is not attested elsewhere in the seven letters accepted to be Pauline. In effect, this points towards a different authorship of the spurious text in question.

Indeed, if one removes 1Cor 33b-35 (and perhaps including also 1Cor 14,36) there is a perfect link with the rest of the discussion. This suggests, but not in itself conclusive, that 1Cor 14,33b-35 is an editorial insertion by somebody at home with the tradition of the Pastoral Epistles. Such a person possibly felt that Paul has gone too far in granting too many concessions to women. He therefore made this corrective remark to try to set the clock "right" from his own perspective. In effect, the person sought to apply the brakes. So this text appears to be *reactionary*.

Based on the manuscript evidence above and the internal evidence which we have presented, I ascribe to the solution found in the *codex Fuldensis* above, where 1Cor 14,33b-35 was simply placed at the margin after 14,33. In this case, I would label this text as deutero-Pauline.[152] It works against all that we know of Paul in the seven-letter theory. It has an unambiguous affinity with the Christianity of the pastoral letters.

It is quite curious that some feminists reject this conclusion on the non-Pauline nature of the text in question.[153] They think that it is a Pauline text. However, interpretative interests should be neatly distinguished from the question of authorship here. Granted that the text is offensive, it does not by this very fact make it Pauline. In this regard, I agree with David G. Horrell that "the decision to regard 1Cor 14.34f as a post-Pauline interpolation must be based on substantial grounds and not merely on their unpalatability."[154] It seems to me that Schüssler Fiorenza has based her argument on this unpalatability, instead of on substantial grounds. Since we do not want to argue against the non-Pauline authorship of this text just for its sake, we shall now go forward to show that the authorship of the text in question is from another New Testament tradition altogether.

4) Comparing 1Cor 14,33b-35 and 1Tim 2,11-15

A close examination of the text of 1Cor 14,33b-35 and that of 1Tim 2,11-12 (already presented above) shows an obvious similarity in *world-view, style, vocabulary,* and *emphasis.* In view of this, let us make a comparative evaluation of the two.

a) Both texts are very insistent and unambiguous on the question of the silence of the woman in the Christian assembly. This makes it a "text of terror".[155] For both authors, the Christian church is a place where only men could be active participants, with the women members only passively in attendance. Hence, this Christian church is presented here as an ideal *patriarchal assembly*, with no matriarchal importance. This is a typical synagogue or temple situation in biblical times. Hence, for these authors, women are to participate as "dumb" people, saying or uttering nothing in the *ekklêsia* of God. They are simply to attend only as the "yes members" of Christianity.

How far has this picture changed today? Has not the negative ecclesiology in question influenced the practice in many Christian communities throughout the ages? Does the Christian assembly today not still gag and stifle these women, making them only listeners? How often are they heard? Are they ever there when very important church decisions are made? What is their ranking on the hierarchical scale? Even when they are also celibates, like their male counterparts, does it make any difference? That this subordinating ecclesiology is so cherished even today, as coming from God is sad and regrettable. The women in the community of Timothy and some others have no authority to teach. In our own communities today, do they? Yet the slogan from Paul was *no male, no female*, and we pretend as if this is not part of the Holy Scripture. Is this not the game of pick and choose?

Anyway, as can be seen from the texts above, the Greek reader notices that both of them used the negation of the same verb-*epitrepó* (to allow or permit someone)-to refuse women the permission to teach in the church. Similarly, they used the same word group to insist on the subordination or total submissiveness of the woman. The first is ὑπο- τάσσω (*hypotásó*), a verbal form meaning to subordinate, and the second is ὑποταγή (*hypotagê*), a nominal form, meaning subordination. This is typical of the household codes of the New Testament.[156] Summarily, these similarities are presented as follows in the table below.

1) οὐ γὰρ ἐπιτρέπεται αὐταις λαλειν (1Cor 14,34)	1) διδάσκειν δὲ γυναικὶ οὐκ ἐπι- τρέπω οὐδὲ αὐθεντειν ἀνδρός (1Tim 2,12)
2) ἀλλὰ ὑποτασσέσθωσαν καθὼς καὶ ὁ νόμος λέγει (1Cor 14,34)	2) μανθανέτω ἐν πάσῃ ὑποταγη (1Tim 2,12)
1) They are not permitted to speak.	1) I do not permit any woman either to teach or have authority over the man.
2) But they are to be totally submissive as the law says.	2) Let them learn in all submissiveness.

These different formulations are strikingly similar. The two traditions have very close affinity to one another. As one can see, undiluted and undeniable silence was imposed on women, using a similar formula. They were also refused the permission to teach. Hence, they make these women to be the "*muzzled women of Christianity*".

b) Both texts made a common appeal to scripture (the account of the fall) in proposing their subordinating ecclesiology. However, whereas 1Tim 2 mentions the text of scripture concerned, 1Cor 14,33a-35 only says that the law (meaning also scripture) said so-καθὼς καὶ ὁ νόμος λέγει.

c) The radical and extreme subordination which one sees in Eph 5,21-33 is again repeated in these two traditions. However, there is a difference between the two. Whereas Ephesians stopped with a *family code*, the two authors above enacted an *ecclesiastical law*, which disfavors women. Hence, these women are now in a position of double deficit – in the family and in the *ekklêsia*.

Finally, the stand taken in this work, when this literary similarity, text critical evidence and all other arguments are assembled together, is that 1Cor 14,33b-35 offers *no convincing reason* to make this author believe that it belongs to Paul. Consequently, based on all the available evidence my own final conclusion, along with some other exegetes, is that it belongs to the same tradition or to a similar tradition with 1Tim 2. This conclusion is in line with Murphy-O'Connor who summarized his similar position as follows:

> These verses are not a Corinthian slogan, as some have argued. . . but a post-Pauline interpolation. . . Not only is the appeal to the law (possibly Gen 3:6) un-Pauline, but the verses contradict 11:5. The injunctions reflect the misogyny of 1 Tim 2:11-14 and probably stem from the same circle.[157]

This conclusion is sound and convincing in the light of the arguments above. As far as the text under analysis is concerned, I think that we have the case of *pseudonymity* here. Somebody (perhaps, a fundamentalist Jewish Christian disciple of Paul) has written in the name of Paul in order to try to reduce the influence of his liberally proclaimed freedom and equality of all Christians, irrespective of gender.

Here, a segment of the early church stamps the subordination of women and forestalls their ordination. From now onwards, this becomes official church policy and practice, which as we shall soon see, Roman Catholicism has espoused. Today, this early church practice is part of what propels the Christian churches that deny active role for women in the ministry, including ordination. Easy and ready-made answers are sought here by men who are reluctant and afraid to cede church authority to women or share it with them. In this place, Paul and his revolution are neatly packaged and kept in the archives of history.

Indeed, 1Cor 34-35 shows how the men who shaped the New Testament "usurped" divine powers and imposed a ban on women neither to speak nor to teach in the church, thereby giving the impression that New Testament Christianity upholds *the inequality of the sexes*. The unfortunate thing about this prohibition is that it is done under the umbrella of Holy Scripture – the word of God. In so doing the false idea is given that this is also the revelation of God to be accepted and enforced by all. Of course, Paul disagrees with this and recognized women prophets in his churches, accepted them as his fellow workers, deacons and apostles. With this, let us now go into the details of the exegesis of the controversial text in question.

B) Exegetical Analysis of 1Cor 14,33b-35[158]

This text begins with the introductory phrase in 14,33b: as in all the churches of the saints (ὡς ἐν πάσαις ταις ἐκκλησίαις των ἁγίων). With it the author notifies his readers that there is an already existing practice *in all the churches known to him*. He gave this important signal with the use of the Greek particle ὡς (*hôs*), which simply means "as". So what he is about to say is not a new thing. It is an old custom in what he calls the "churches of the saints" (ἐκκλησίαις των ἁγίων). He now proceeds to tell us what this practice is all about.

1) Let the Women in the Churches keep Silent

The author now tells us what the practice is by commanding that women should keep silent in the churches (αἱ γυναικες ἐν ταις ἐκκλησίαις σιγάτωσαν). With this ecclesiastical injunction this author carries his own subordination of women from the home into the church.[159] Accordingly, he precludes women from the ministry of the church. Here, these women are to become "tongue-tied" Christians. They should participate like silent and bereaved mourners, not saying anything. As a result of this, they have been deprived of initiatives. From now on, men are the only ones who should speak in the church and who could legislate for them. They should only be *silent worshippers in Christianity,* contributing nothing to official church teaching. In effect they have absolutely no say in dogmatic or doctrinal formulations, making no serious contribution towards church policies, *though they are capable of doing these.*

The seriousness of this prohibition lies in the fact that it is in all the churches of the writer. This was what led Tertullian to say, "A woman may not speak, nor baptize, or 'offer' [the Eucharist], nor claim the right to any masculine function, still less to the priestly office."[160] Here, one sees the tension between gender and ministry. Besides, gender conflict is introduced into Christianity, thereby giving rise to the present day gender struggle in the church. This is in sharp contrast to the charismatic church where this was not the case.

2) The Relevance of the Greek Verb σιγάω

The Greek imperative form used to effect this ban on women is *sigátôsan* (σιγάτωσαν), which is from the verb *sigaô* (σιγάω). It is used in the intransitive sense and has the following meanings: to keep silent, to say nothing, to stop speaking, to become silent.[161] From this lexical meaning the reader sees that the author chose his word very carefully and left no room for any ambiguity. He knew what he wanted to say and was very precise about it. Absolute silence is imposed on these women, all in God's name. Hence, they become the "*mute members*" of the Christian church. With this the author has effectively gagged them. They have become muzzled in deutero-Pauline Christianity. Now they are in a secondary situation, something that persists till today. Hence, equality is *absolutely* ruled out, though Paul himself guaranteed this, as we have seen in the chapters above. In view of this, it is no longer possible for women to be deacons, priests, pastors and bishops in many of the Christian churches today. Unfortunately, the bias of this author has become the revelation of God and women must now pay dearly because of this.

Regrettably, some of the Christian churches, including the Roman Catholic Church, live under the shackles of this teaching on subordination. The "official Roman Catholic Church" thinks that women is not and cannot be equal with men. As a result, these women qualify only for inferior roles in this church. They can only participate in a *subordinating capacity*, taking the back benches in the church.[162] Hence, leadership positions are never for them. In view of this, *masculine sacraments* are created and firmly put in place to make sure that this subordinating policy is firmly maintained in God's name. In the end, this has led to decreeing away the possibility of ordaining women as priests in the Roman Catholic church, as we shall soon see in this work.

However, as will also be shown, it is equally a source of comfort and consolation that some courageous Christian churches have broken ranks with tradition to ordain women. These churches involved have taken some hits from critics who scorn them for daring to say that men are equal with women in all things, including ritual leadership. We shall dedicate more time to this. At this juncture, the next thing that the author of 1Cor 33-35 does is to reinforce his religious ban on women by means of the Greek word ἐπιτρέπω.

3) The Meaning of the Greek Verb ἐπιτρέπω

With further insistence the author maintains that women are not permitted to speak (οὐ γὰρ ἐπιτρέπεται αὐταις λαλειν). Here, the author shows that he means what he is saying. He does not mince words. When he says that *these women should keep silent in the church,* there is no joke about it. This is seen in the use of this verb *epitrépetai* (a passive form) from *epitrépô* (ἐπιτρέπω).

Ordinarily, this verb *epitrépô* means to allow, permit, order or instruct. When used with the infinitive, as we have it above, it means to permit or allow.[163] However, it was *negated* in our context. The construction is *ou gàr epitrépetai* (οὐ γὰρ ἐπιτρέπεται), which means *it is not permitted*. So these women are neither permitted nor allowed to speak in the church. This is bad ecclesiology. It has provided some people today with the platform for prohibiting women from teaching in the church. Also, it has put "ammunition" in patriarchal hands, thereby making it much easier for women to be placed on the firing line. This explains why these women are still forbidden to preach in many Christian churches, though they had the divine privilege of being the first preachers of the resurrection on which depends the fate of Christianity. Finally, from what these women should not do, the author goes forward to tell us what they should do. This is the next thing in the text.

4) Let the Women be Submissive

As far as he is concerned, *they should simply be totally submissive (ἀλλὰ ὑποτασσέσθωσαν).* The use of this word ἀλλὰ (but) plays a contrasting role here. In the context of this discussion, we translate it as "on the contrary" to bring out this contrast. The author is contrasting what these women should not do (teaching) with what they should do (submissiveness). On the one hand, they are not to speak in the church. On the other hand, they are to be totally submissive. Both are extremes, which help to create second class Christians. As one can see, *instead of ordination, they are offered only subordination.* The author is simply doing this because of the biological gender of those involved. Hence, we see "gender profiling" in force.

These women have to be subjugated in this way for the simple reason that they are women. So, for this author, it is virtuous for the woman to keep silent in the church and to be subordinated to the man. Simply, she has to accept the authority of the man *in all things.* Even today she has to sit down in silence and await council decisions and synodal declarations. All she needs to do is to wait for the men to conclude either the Council or the Synod so that she can nod her head and say "Yes Lord". Whenever she does not do this, she is not considered to be a "good" Christian. Anyway, the author of the text under analysis now camouflages himself further with Holy Scripture in order to justify his discriminatory statements against women in the church of Christ. Unfortunately, contemporary Christians copy this false principle.

5) Authority of Scripture Invoked

Now the author seeks to reinforce his ban on women once more. Hence, he invokes the authority of scripture by saying καθὼς καὶ ὁ νόμος λέγει (just as the law says). As we already know, the Pentateuch[164] is technically referred to as the *law* or the *torah*. This is what the author means. However, he did not give us the particular text he has in mind. If I may speculate, based on the corresponding tradition in 1Tim 2.13, the text of the law he has in mind is *probably* the Yahwist account of the creation in Gen 2,4b-25 or possibly Gen 3,6. Reading the text of Ephesians one sees that its author equally knew this particular Yahwist account of creation. He even quoted directly from it (Eph 5,31). The reader sees that the Yahwist sowed a *dangerous* seed of subordination, without possibly intending this. However, later generations now use his narrative as a weapon against women. He is used to maintain male-domination over the woman.

6) Let Women ask their Husbands at Home

Now the deutero-Pauline writer goes on to make his final remarks about women. He is left with one more question to battle with. In view of the ecclesiastical embargo now placed on women, how will they get matters clarified should they have a question? The author answers in 1Cor 14,35 by saying that if there is anything they want to know, they should ask their husbands at home (εἰ δέ τι μαθειν θέλουσιν, ἐν οἴκῳ τοὺς ἰδίους ἄνδρας ἐπερωτάτωσαν). As far as the author is concerned the reason why they have to ask their husbands at home is that *it is disgraceful for a woman to speak in the church* (αἰσχρόν γάρ ἐστιν γυναικὶ λαλειν ἐν ἐκκλησίᾳ). *Here, the author sealed his doctrine of subordination.* The only place where women can now open their mouths is in their homes. Only, then, could they put their questions to their husbands and not to any other person. But he did not care to address the question of women without husbands. Whom shall they ask their own questions? Or are they to remain "dumb" forever, saying nothing and asking nothing? Even if the author did not foresee the possibility of celibacy and celibate communities, it would have been naive to think that, at every given time, every woman must be married and so has a husband to ask questions.

One sees early *Christian fundamentalism* at work, which shapes the direction of the next chapter. There is no doubt that an early Christian fundamentalist is writing.[165] Unfortunately and sadly, his mentality has heavily shaped church history and ecclesiology in relation to women. There is no doubt that the embargo placed on women today in our churches is part of this fundamentalist agenda, put in place over 2000 years ago, by a segment of the early church. This is always reformulated and re-invigorated to the exclusion of authentic Pauline teachings that we have seen in this work. Every generation repackages it to its taste and liking. Now and then it is given new clothing and new face, but with the same content. The time has come, not only to challenge it, but also to resist this rigorous fundamentalism retained and enforced in God's name. *Indeed, it is time to get Martha out of the kitchen.* This is the main point of this book.

7) The Meaning of αἰσχρόν

Finally, the author concludes his teaching on subordination by repeating his stated position that it is not good for women to speak in the church. For him, this is *aischrón* (αἰσχρόν), an adjective from *aischrós* (αἰσχρός), which means disgraceful, shameful, ugly, or base.[166] Here, we see that this author was totally uncompromising. He was in no mood to dilute his statements. For him it is a shameful, base, ugly and disgraceful thing for women to speak in the church of God. He sees it to be such a repulsive thing for a woman to speak in the *ekklêsia*. For this author, it is something outrageous, scandalous, reprehensible, appalling, dishonorable, discreditable and dreadful. He sees it as something nasty, unattractive and shocking.

Indeed, it is unbelievable that one could write in this way in the name of God and in his church. Here, one sees a language of dislike, an unparalleled misogyny, labeled as "the word of God". This is the case of gender profiling par excellence. One begins to wonder why such inciting texts were not expunged from the New Testament canon. It would have been better for this information to exist in the writings of the New Testament *pseudepigrapha*[167] than in a body of writing accepted to be inspired by Christians. *This teaches us that something is not necessarily inspired because it is in the bible.*[168]

8) Final Critical Remarks

Summarily, as we have already seen, on account of the hard-line attitude of the author of 1Cor 14,33b-35, women are absolutely forbidden to speak in the church. Secondly, they are ordered to be submissive. This is the way the author has defined the place of women in the "churches of the saints". With this he has brought the tension between gender and ministry to a head. He has now put women in a second class position, which they still occupy till today. They have been prohibited from speaking in the church and banished from ecclesiastical offices. Effectively, this disqualifies them from the ministry of the Christian church. The simple reason for this is because, through no fault of theirs, they are women. From now on, their voices are no longer meant to be heard. They are now caged, muzzled and gagged. This is total strangulation. These women are now stifled and throttled. In the end, they are securely locked up. In view of this, *the present work is about lifting this gag order in the* ἐκκλησία τοῦ θεοῦ *(ekklêsia tou theou) church of God.*

In 1Cor 14,33a-35 we see the beginning of the suppression of women in Christianity. But will the critical woman reading the text of 1Cor 14,33b-35 be happy? When this is proclaimed in liturgical assemblies as *the word of God,* will she willingly and happily respond, "Thanks be to God"? Will it be "thanks be to God" for humiliating her or for subordinating her perpetually to men? Will it be "thanks be to God" for putting her in this terrible deficit situation?

From now onwards, some Christian synods will meet but without these women. Ecumenical councils will be convoked without them. Whenever and wherever there is any of these gatherings, often times, they are only present as cooks, waiters at table, and the like. It is theirs to be house cleaners, housekeepers and dry cleaners for the men supposed to be preoccupied with the serious task of theologizing. For these women, they are simply there to serve men, while men are the only ones expected to offer ritual intercessions on their behalf to a God presented as pro male. Church decisions are made without these women. Theologically, these women are being suffocated, *even in our own time.* They have now been permanently silenced, prevented from speaking out.

Some of the present day church leaders even continue to use church power to issue decrees aimed at maintaining this regrettable status quo *in perpetuity.* Whenever women want to challenge this, church decrees are used to decree them back into the status quo. Since they neither have the dogmatic hammer, nor in any position to use it, they are in a very beggarly and weak position, impotent to mount any effective challenge. As a result, they have only to wait to say "amen" to the decisions of church councils. Hence, the woman becomes an "amen-saying-Christian" par excellence, a "head-nodding" creature in the church of men. The limited progress already made by some women does not change this sad reality. This situation is depressing for the woman, hence the urgent need to intensify and coordinate efforts in the various women liberation movements throughout the world.

As we noted at the beginning of this chapter, the subordination of women in 1Cor 14,33-35 and 1Timothy assumed an extreme dimension representing a *fundamentalist* position. What makes this position very worrisome is that it was put forward in the name of the church and in the name of Christianity, thus giving this teaching official ecclesiastical status. This becomes like an injunction handed out by an ecclesiastical "Supreme Court". Hence, it has been enforced, in one way or the other, throughout the history of Christianity. In these traditions we see the beginning of "church veto". Here, women have been vetoed out of ecclesiastical office. An ecclesiastical ban has been imposed on them.

This has a serious and drastic consequence for women, past and present. The reason for this is that they have been outlawed from performing certain functions in the church. They are now effectively under *church interdict*. They are disallowed, restricted, effectively blocked, obstructed and prevented from teaching in the church. This means that they are barred, banned and forbidden from holding ecclesiastical offices. Ordination is no longer for them, though subordination is readily offered to them. The unfortunate thing is that this prohibition and proscription is now assuming a permanent place. *Hence, to talk about the teaching authority of the church today, is to talk about the men who are controlling the destiny of women.* These women have been deprived of the authority to teach. For them to go against this now is to engage in illegality. *This is terrible!* And to hold a contrary view is to be unorthodox, even to be viewed with heretical suspicion.

The Christianity represented by these New Testament communities can hardly be for women. This is not the brand of Christianity which the 21st century woman wishes for herself. This type of Christianity is *divisive* and *discriminatory*. Instead of a congregation in Jesus Christ, it entrenches a "sacred segregation" in the name of Jesus. It creates a male oligarchy, a male ruling clique, determined to cling on to power no matter what it takes. A Christianity that teaches and institutionalizes inequality between man and woman can hardly be the ideal Christianity that Jesus intended for his followers. *This can hardly be the real Christianity in which women had the singular privilege of being the first preachers of the resurrection.* It does not represent the true Christianity of Paul. *To disown, ignore or downplay this fact is to show disregard for sacred tradition.*

Since 1Cor 14,33-35 is presented in misogynist terms, our critique of it is in every sense undiluted and unmitigated. It is in every respect anti-feminine. Sadly, together with 1Tim 2,11-15, it has laid down very firmly the foundation of an unfortunate and regrettable situation, which women suffer, even today in many of the Christian churches. These texts applied a typical temple or synagogue mentality in which the woman was supposed to be purely passive and quiet, ever preoccupied with her menstrual flow, which made her a pollutant. The men of the Old Testament used it to veil her away from worship and from public life. Accordingly, in the synagogues these women were assigned special places behind a screen,[169] from where they acted like silent "ritual spectators".

Indeed, our authors were working within a tradition of this kind inherited from their Jewish past. Will a critical woman ever forgive them? Can any woman conscious of the women liberation movement read this also as *the word of God?* By no means! Indeed, the position of 1Cor 14,33-35 is completely at odds with Paul and his liberating Christianity, as this work has been demonstrating.

9) 1Cor 14,33-35 and Gender Profiling[170]

The way 1Cor 14,33-35 has treated women has led us to this aspect of the discussion. It is important that Christians should no longer repeat the blunders of church history and tradition. In the past, the misuse and misapplication of the bible has brought tears and sorrows to humanity.[171] In this way, the *good news* was turned into "bad news". Accordingly, was it not the bible that the church of the time used to condemn the Italian scientist Galileo Galilei that he was contradicting the truth of scripture? Was the authority of scripture not invoked to support the brutal slave trade against blacks, which led to the depopulation and brain drain in Black Africa? Did the medieval inquisitors not think that they had biblical support to kill under the terms of the inquisition?[172] Was this not killing in the name of God? Is it supported by the commandment *thou shalt not kill?* Did the *South African Dutch Reformed Church,* of recent memory, not use the bible to support the apartheid policy in South Africa? Is it not the bible that some use to support that Africans and blacks everywhere are cursed, citing the case of the biblical Ham in the narratives Genesis? Is it not the bible that was used to help fan anti-Jewish sentiments in the past? *And now it is also the same bible that is being used to profile women in the church in the name of God.* This is becoming another blunder of history.

The mistakes of history should caution us against this latest mistake. Just like these past blunders, just mentioned above, harmed humanity, brought misery and untold hardship to the world, sometimes with horrific and unimaginable consequences, we are also harming women with our intransigence in respect of their place in the church today. *The more they are profiled, the more their wound deepens, and the more we encourage secular or other religious societies to do the same.* We may not even use words to do this. But action, it is said, speaks louder than words. This is to say that we could even become accessories to crimes against women and against the womanhood without even intending it. So the example of 1Cor 14,33-35 is not worth imitating by Christians of all ranks and file. It should be discarded altogether in the 21st century. Paul himself was unaware of this, as we have meticulously shown in this work. Hence, he did not recommend such a discriminatory practice in his Christianity. With this in mind what, then, does *profiling* mean in the context of this work?

The term *profiling* is a very common word in a place like the United States of America. Here, one can talk about various forms of it. Among the commonest ones are *secret profiling, racial profiling,* or *gender profiling.* In all these cases, profiling involves discrimination based on prejudice or biased judgment. The profiled group or individual is singled out based on an assumption. This contradicts the principle of *justice and fairness* or the legal doctrine of equal protection. It shuns equal opportunity for all. Hence, the individual is distrusted *a priori* (in advance) simply because he or she belongs to a "disfavored" class or group. This makes one to preclude the profiled group or person from getting certain benefits. In this case, the merits and demerits of a case are not the basis for action. Here, one judges before the facts and sometimes without the facts. Oftentimes, the facts having a bearing on the situation are simply ignored. Bias becomes the prevailing norm and the rule of law is *quietly* and *carefully* ignored.

In view of this, if a decision is made against a person based on race, color or ethnic background this is called racial profiling. Similarly, if a woman is precluded from performing certain functions in the society, on account of her gender, this is called *gender profiling.* Here, the woman is discriminated against simply because she is a woman. Without being responsible for it, her feminine gender becomes a liability and so counts against her. This puts her in a deficit situation. On account of this, she is ignored in making certain appointments or in apportioning some responsibilities. She is judged in advance of being either incapable or unworthy of discharging the function involved because she is a woman. This bias is not because of merit, but because of gender. Hence, *competence is compromised with gender bias.* Sometimes, mediocrity is even preferred to a competent woman.

This is also a problem for Christianity today. The woman is precluded from certain ministry positions in the church. There is no other reason for this regrettable act than that *she is a woman*. Why can't a woman be a priest, senior pastor, or a bishop? As we have seen in our analysis of 1Cor 14,33-35 the answer is because she is a woman. Why can't she be a deaconess? The answer is the same. And why can't she be the leader of a church in many of the Christian churches? It is also the same answer. Is this not gender profiling? Has 1Cor 14,33b-35 (and the like) not entrenched this type of impartiality against women? One sees that we have to be extremely cautious and careful with using texts like this. Their negative effects on womanhood are too much to be comprehended.

It is unchristian to protect one's power base at the expense of the majority. Minority rule in South Africa, under the then apartheid government was universally condemned as evil. One of the problems of this apartheid system was that the black majority was excluded from the leadership of their nation simply because they are blacks. In the same way, women are excluded from the leadership of their church simply because they are women. If the problem in South Africa hinged on racism, the problem in the Christian church hinges on sexism. And if the skin color of the black folks was a liability for them, the gender of women is now their own liability in the οἰκεῖος τῆς πίστεως (*oikeíos tês písteôs*) *household of faith* (cf. Gal 6,10). What a pity!

In view of this comparison, it is unfortunate that many Christians do not know that by excluding women from the leadership of the church it is a *form of religious apartheid*. The reason for this is that it is *institutional segregation*, which was what defined apartheid in South Africa. In addition, in the Christian church, we have *minority rule* because women are almost always the majority in all our Christian churches. Even in some of these churches men are becoming an "endangered specie".

Besides, by using these "apartheid texts" or "terror texts" found in the bible to show that men have the divine right to rule, harm upon harm has been inflicted on women. People commit acts of violence against women based on the same principle. Rape and sexual crimes are committed against them based on this same principle. Domestic violence is perpetuated against them based on this same "right-to-rule" and "right-to-dominate."

Indeed, it is time for all governments and churches throughout the world to consider the objections raised in this book very seriously. The onus, to change this situation, falls on us as Christians more than the rest of the world. The reason for this is that secular society and many governments around the globe are taking steps to fight this evil. This explains why it is even more baffling that some Christian churches "enthrone" and cherish gender profiling in the church. What the secular society is making effort to discard, the Christian church is making serious effort to embrace and to perpetually institutionalize. Here, the world leads a moral crusade and the Christian church is being urged to follow from behind. What a reversal of role!

As the facts show, the present day women liberation movement arose out of a feeling of this type of institutional discrimination. This created an inferior class, a group of second class Christians in the οἰ- ʹκεῖος τῆς πίστεως (oikeíos tês písteôs) household of faith (cf. Gal 6,10). Hence, women became subordinate and lower creatures in the ἐκκλησία του θεου (church of God). As a result, they were not considered competent to rule or become church leaders. As we have shown in the preceding chapters above, Christians forget that neither the charismatic church nor the apostolic church in Acts countenanced this type of discrimination. They neither recognized nor promoted gender profiling. To have done it otherwise, would have made God a gender profiler. Fortunately, *he is not.*

We are happy that Paul shunned this, thereby saving the Holy Spirit the embarrassment of being seen as the patron of men or the author of gender profiling. Although, there was tension in the Corinthian church between rival groups of charismatics, yet this was not a gender struggle. The question never arose as to whether women should or should not be allowed to exercise certain ministry positions in the church. This was not a problem in the community and there was no need to raise it.

Even though these ministry positions or *charismata* are diverse, as the body-imagery of Paul shows, none is reserved for any one particular gender. Indeed, in the charismatic community, the Holy Spirit had no need to profile any gender in order to apportion these gifts. This means that the Holy Spirit, who distributes these gifts, is not and cannot be a *gender profiler.* Therefore, let us not recruit him to discriminate on our behalf. It is unfair to use him to explain away the gender profiling which has persistently remained a characteristic feature of the Christian church. The Holy Spirit plays neither partiality nor favoritism. Let us not make him the author of gender struggles.

All the same, Paul recognizes distinctions and various roles. In view of this, he said, "the body does not consist of one member but of many" (1Cor 12,4). However, this has no gender characteristics. With the use of the body-imagery he illustrated the importance of a united church community. Hence, he addressed the quarreling Corinthians as follows:

> [15] If the foot should say, "Because I am not a hand, I do not belong to the body," that would not make it any less a part of the body. [16] And if the ear should say, "Because I am not an eye, I do not belong to the body," that would not make it any less a part of the body (1Cor 12,15-16).

All the various charisms or ministry positions, as Paul said elsewhere, are from the same Spirit. So irrespective of which one you have, you cannot isolate yourself from the main body, the church. Neither the prophets, nor the pneumatics should behave this way. Even Paul justifies the differences in the charisms in the following words.

> [17] If the whole body were an eye, where would be the hearing? If the whole body were an ear, where would be the sense of smell? [18] But as it is, God arranged the organs in the body, each one of them, *as he chose* [*kathôs êthelsen*]. [19] If all were a single organ, where would the body be? (1Cor 12,17-19).

The non-discriminatory policy of the Pauline charismatic church is seen very clearly in this text. God's plan is not influenced by any human forces. No human power or authority can counsel him. God has no human advisor. This reminds us of the earlier statement of Paul that the Spirit "apportions to each one individually as he wills" (1Cor 12,11). Here, it is all about the *will* and *choice* of the Holy God (ἅγιος θεός). It cannot be interpreted that part of his divine will is to discriminate against women. Fortunately, *God is the author of non-discrimination*.

Consequently, the present day discrimination against women is *depraved* and *ungodly*, even when a text like 1Cor 14,33b-35 is used to support it. The fact that there is a ritual and liturgical institutionalization of this bad policy does not justify it. Tradition is man-made and not God-made.[173] If Christians of past centuries ignored Paul and excised women from playing important roles in the church it is not justified for us to continue with such a *bad and detestable tradition*.

Indeed, Paul points out to his church community that the existence of the various charisms calls for interdependence. There is a connecting link between all of them. The Christian should not forget that a symbiotic relationship exists. Hence, he says, "as it is, there are many parts, yet one body" (1Cor 12,20). Here, he also introduces us to the principle of "unity in diversity". The ability of a living body to operate well depends on the effectiveness of all its parts. If there is any sick part, the whole body becomes sick.

In which case, if we weaken the position of women in this one body called the church, this body becomes weakened also. This becomes the sick part of the body. Unless it is healed, there will be a certain degree of malfunction in the body. In other words, every Christian member counts no matter how insignificantly perceived. Hence, Paul continues in these words:

[21] And the eye cannot say unto the hand, I have no need of thee: nor again the head to the feet, I have no need of you. [22] Nay, much more those members of the body, which seem to be more feeble, are necessary: [23] And those members of the body, which we think to be less honourable, upon these we bestow more abundant honour; and our uncomely parts have more abundant comeliness. [24] For our comely parts have no need: but God hath tempered the body together, having given more abundant honour to that part which lacked: [25] That there should be no schism in the body; but that the members should have the same care one for another (KJV: 1Cor 12,21-25).

Paul proposes ideal guidelines for his church and for the church today. As one can see, this is cohesive in nature, intended to create a universal sisterhood and brotherhood. With this he aims at the solidarity of his Christians. Oneness and unity are recommended characteristics for this church. The diversity of charisms means that his Christians have to agree among themselves to make it work. Fellowship should be a priced jewel for them. In the Christian community the norm should be agreement and not disagreement, unity and not disunity, peace and not pieces, accord and not discord, association and not dissociation, congregation and not segregation, communication and not excommunication, benediction and not malediction, *ordination and not subordination*. In view of this, a synthesis of all the charisms becomes desirable and worthwhile. One sees that an integrated Christianity is the goal of the charismatic church.

If this is the case, are we really integrated when we discriminate against women under whatever pretext and with whichever text of the bible? Are we not re-enacting the Old Testament temple segregation, which barred women from entering certain parts of the temple of God?[174] Indeed, no one should be disregarded, disrespected, or looked down with disdain. No one should be humiliated because of one's gender. It is in this spirit that Paul says, "if one member suffers, all suffer together; if one member is honored, all rejoice together" (1Cor 12,26). In the context of this book, this means that when one woman suffers discrimination in the church of God, all of us should be suffering with her. And when one woman is elevated in the church, all of us should equally rejoice. This becomes an encouragement to join in the women liberation struggle so that every member may be honored to the glory of God Almighty.

Finally, even though the deutero-Pauline churches practiced gender profiling in allotting ministry positions, it has to be reiterated that the Pauline charismatic community did not know of any "gender-affiliated Spirit". The problem today is that man has thwarted his will in his name and on his behalf. Hence, the ideal of Paul is now kept walking on its head. This is why there are hues and cries today in the women liberation movements for this anomaly to be rectified. In a sense, *this liberation movement becomes an open cry for justice in the church and in our world* today. It is not simply a question of gender struggle or merely a feminist agitation. It is a movement for egalitarianism, justice and equity both in the church and in our world. *Since this movement is about justice, it becomes also an ethical movement.* To be at odds with this, is to confront the ethical, or to be in conflict with what is moral. Also to be against it, is to be against what is morally correct. What would ethics or morality be without justice? In a sense, then, *the women liberation movement is a moral struggle.* At this juncture, in the light of this tension between *gender and ministry* seen in this chapter, it is now important to bring the gospels into the "witness box" to testify on behalf of women. This is what our next inquiry intends to do.

Chapter 5
The Gospels and the Ministry of Women

The tension between *gender and ministry*, which we saw in the last chapter, has led to this present topic. As we saw, the female gender was made to be incompatible with the ministry of the church. This has provided ammunition for the opponents of the ministry of women in the church today. Often times, this is the only scripture they know and so use it to whip women into silence in the church. In view of this, it is important to argue on the other side of the debate, so that the reader can contrast the two positions in order to make a personal decision. This process can only but lead to the truth *for those earnestly seeking it*. We intend to use the information contained in this chapter to supplement the position of Paul in respect of the ministry of women in the church. Since this work is dealing with the early Church it is important to have this discussion here.

As the reader may recall, in the last chapter, we saw a negative patriarchal attitude towards the ministry of women. This present chapter will show that it was simply one-sided. It is to counterbalance the one-sidedness of the arguments that I wish now to present, in a nutshell, the main points of the gospel favoring full ministry positions for women. This has to be concise since this work is not simply about the ministry of women in the gospels. Notwithstanding, we wish also to bring in Jesus to take the witness stand on behalf of women. This is why this chapter is considered very important.

Before we do the analysis involved, I wish to point out that our study of the relationship between the gospels and the ministry of women will build largely on circumstantial evidence. In a forensic setting, as we know, this can lead to conviction. One does not necessarily need to find the "smoking gun". It is the weight and profundity of the circumstantial evidence that matters.

Similarly, in our own situation, we will try to acquit women from their patriarchal conviction using a mountain of circumstantial evidence in this chapter. Bur is this approach legitimate? Isn't it shaky to build a theology of the ministry of women in the church using mainly circumstantial evidence? The answer is an emphatic and unambiguous no. The reason for this is that those who use the Jesus-argument to reject the ministry of women in the church do so equally on circumstantial grounds. This is maintained because *there is no where in the gospels where Jesus explicitly said that only men should be leaders in the church, or that women are forbidden from ordained ministry.* No gospel text expressly said that only men should be pastors and teachers in the church. All that has been done is to interpret the acts of Jesus to mean that he does not permit women to operate in ordained capacity or to occupy senior ministry positions in the church. In other words, the prohibition of women from full ministry participation is largely the product of church hermeneutics and tradition. Otherwise, Jesus did not *explicitly* forbid them from playing ministry roles in the church.

With this in mind, it is fair game to adopt the same methodology based on circumstantial evidence to show that the gospels actually supports the ministry of women in the church instead of forbidding it. Let us now begin with the first element of the discussion centering on the role of Mary in the history of salvation.

1) The Infancy Narratives[175]

The gospel evidence shows that women were at the center of the *Heilsgeschichte*[176] (salvation history). Unambiguously, they played pivotal roles in the saving events of the New Testament. For instance, they alone were privileged to conceive and give birth to the Messiah. In this regard, they had the rare privilege of being the living "tabernacle" of the Most High. In which case, women began to be *active* in the story from the first moment of the New Testament salvation history.

Whereas in the Old Testament they were kept in the background, in the New Testament they were kept in the forefront. Whereas in the Old Testament they were passive, in the New Testament they were active. Further, in the New Testament, when contrasted with Joseph, the "husband" of Mary, one can say that there is a reversal of roles here. Whereas Mary, representing the woman race, is presented as playing an active role, on the other hand, Joseph played only a *passive role.* Whereas Mary played a visible role, his was invisible. Joseph is seen more as a character of the evangelists, while Mary played an unambiguous historical role.

Further, as can be seen from the pages of the New Testament this Joseph is more of a narrative ingredient needed to tell the story. His role is comparable to the silent role of Adam in the scene of the fall in Gen 3. In a similar way, the New Testament Joseph had to operate behind the scene. Here, he assumed the role of women in the Old Testament who had to operate from behind a curtain. The narrators simply assigned him a silent role. Possibly, he was only a narrative figure. This is said because he was rarely seen doing or heard saying anything.

On the contrary, the historicity of Mary is not in doubt. She could be heard speaking and performing actions. In the Jewish context of the tradition, in which the woman was rarely heard, the New Testament becomes quite striking here. Mary is seen playing the traditional male role, by being the spokesperson, speaking on behalf of Joseph and herself. She was the one doing all the talking, and Joseph doing the listening. In this regard, her prominence is well highlighted. One sees, in the story, that women are now projected as important players. In the New Testament, they were not taking the backstage that they have been forced to take today. Here, they were not playing only a secondary role.

All these put together give one the impression that Joseph was merely a shadow, perhaps the creation of the New Testament narrators. It is likely that he was a *figmentum mentis* (figment of the mind) that was made a necessary ingredient needed to fill the gaps in the infancy narratives. While he was passive, Mary was active. Here, there is a reversal of role in the salvation history. *The woman assumes the active position, while the man plays only a hidden and obscure role.* How can this be an argument against the ordination of women or ministry roles for them?

There is no gainsaying that Mary has a very exalted position. Even angelic beings respected and revered her. In this regard, when Zechariah (the priest), doubted the angelic message that his wife Elisabeth was to conceive in her old age (Lk 1.18), he was immediately struck with dumbness (Lk 1,19-20). But when Mary doubted that she would be the mother of the messiah (Lk 1.34), the angel could only try to persuade her until she accepted the will of the Lord (Lk 1,35-38). This shows an elevation of women in the New Testament, something not seen in the Old Testament. Besides, it is also striking in the New Testament that a woman was respected more than the priest Zechariah. This is an upside down situation. Here, the New Testament makes the

Old Testament to walk on its head. Women are now used to challenge the ministry of the priest in Israel, something that no orthodox 1st century Jew would have countenanced. This new role supports ministry roles for them at all level.

We have to argue further that if the messiah of the world was humble enough to be carried in a woman's womb how could this support the argument that Jesus wants them now to be excluded from certain ministry positions in the church? Since ministry is about doing the work of the Lord, in this sense, was Mary not the *first minister of the Lord*? Is it right, then, for us today to continue to prevent women from continuing to serve the Lord in the ministry forms available? Indeed, Christian ministry is in urgent need of reform.

2) The true Followers of Jesus

The facts from sacred scripture show that women were faithful to Jesus *till the very end*. They neither ran away nor abandoned him in his difficult times. In every respect, they were his trusted companions. They were not haphazard in following Jesus. On the contrary, the male disciples were following Jesus principally because he was preaching about a kingdom. In their ignorance they thought that this kingdom was a political one. I have maintained this because a political reward was even promised them. Hence, Luke says, "That ye may eat and drink at my table in my kingdom, and sit on thrones judging the twelve tribes of Israel" (KJV: Luke 22,30). One sees that it is all about authority here. Unlike these male followers who could not complete the *via crucis* (the way of the cross), women continued to journey with Jesus throughout the passion events down to the moment of resurrection. This helps to explain why the male disciples did not know that the "cross-phase" of the struggle was over and that the moment of glorification, the resurrection, had arrived. Hence, in the passion narratives, the high point of the ministry of Jesus in the Gospels, the *consistency of women* is sharply contrasted with the *inconsistency of the male disciples of Jesus*. In other words, as far as the narratives of the passion show, *consistency* becomes another name for women, while *inconsistency* is another name for men. The synoptic gospels contrasted this irony in the table below.

| About men:
Mk 14,50
Καὶ ἀφέντες αὐτὸν ἔφυγον πάντες.
And abandoning him, *they all ran away*
Matt 26,56:
Τότε οἱ μαθηταὶ πάντες ἀφέντες αὐτὸν ἔφυγον.
Then all the disciples abandoned him and *ran away.* | About women: Luke 23,49
Εἱστήκεισαν δὲ πάντες οἱ γνωστοὶ αὐτῷ ἀπὸ μακρόθεν καὶ γυναικες αἱ συνακολουθουσαι αὐτῷ ἀπὸ της Γαλιλαίας ὁρωσαι ταυτα.
And all his acquaintances and all the women who had *followed* him from Galilee were standing at a distance to see these things".
KJV: Mk 15,40-41: There were also women looking on afar off: among whom was Mary Magdalene, and Mary the mother of James the less and of Joses, and Salome; (Who also, when he was in Galilee, followed him, and ministered unto him;) and many other women which came up with him unto Jerusalem.
KJV: Lk 23,27-28: And there followed him a great company of people, and of women, which also bewailed and lamented him. But Jesus turning unto them said, Daughters of Jerusalem, weep not for me, but weep for yourselves, and for your children. |

As one can see, the old adage holds well here: *a friend in need is a friend indeed*. Accordingly, the passion event becomes the moment of truth, when Jesus knew his *real* friends. The men, who were apparently following him with zeal, proved to be *cosmetic*. They seemed to be just jostling for positions.[177] They were seeking for power, which is still the reality today in the Christian churches. Apparently, faith in the man Jesus was not their ultimate motivation.[178] They seemed to have a hidden political agenda, which became threatened by the shattering events of the passion. Hence, in this moment of need, they failed to pass the litmus test of faith. This was understandable since there was no more power to grab or wield. The promise of sitting on thrones and judging the twelve tribes of Israel (Matt 19,28) now seems to be mere utopia. Hence, there was no more reason to continue journeying with Jesus. The result was that *all his disciples abandoned him and fled*, like runaway slaves in antiquity. As if to anticipate this anti-climax situation, in John's gospel, Jesus asked these disciples: "Will ye also go away" (KJV: John 6,67)? One sees that this was indeed a prophetic question. Even though Simon Peter replied, "Lord, to whom shall we go? thou hast the words of eternal life" (KJV: John 6,68). yet he was the first to deny his master. As far as these disciples are concerned, we see a list of broken words, promises not kept.

As the table above shows, both Matthew and Mark are very *damning* in their testimony about *all the disciples of Jesus*, which includes the twelve. The formulations about the disciples are more or less the same, retaining key words, which describe the role of men in the passion narratives. For Matthew the grammatical subject of the sentence above is *hoi mathêtaì pántes* (οἱ μαθηταὶ πάντες) *all the disciples*. They were the ones who abandoned their master and took to their heels when the time of his disguised glorification arrived.

Like Matthew, Mark also targets *all the disciples*, as can be seen above. His use of πάντες (all) refers to the *mathêtáis autous* (μαθητάις αὐτους), his disciples in Mark 14.32, who were with Jesus in the garden of Gethsemane when the arrest took place. In which case, the phrase in Mark should also read: *all his disciples*. These men were presented to be *moral cowards*, who could not see their master through to the end. When the *Heilsgeschichte* (salvation history) reached its crescendo, they lost morale, *something that the women did not quite do*. Yet this is an argument against ministry roles for them and their ordination as priests and deacons. What an irony!

Notwithstanding, the fact is that at the greatest moment of need, Jesus' trusted disciples fled and abandoned him to his ultimate fate and destiny. In our table above, this indictment was shown by the use of the Greek word ἔφυγον (*éphygon*) they fled, in both Matthew and Mark. This verbal form is from φεύγω (*pheúgô*), meaning to *flee* or *runaway*. Here, Matthew and Mark present to us the picture of "runaway disciples". Like a defeated army, these disciples could only flee, abandoning their master to his captors, losing hope that the ultimate battle is lost, thus making the war to be over. In a sense, they thought that the opponents of Jesus have won the "war". Consequently, they took to their heels to hide for fear of the Jewish opponents of Jesus (John 20,19). This is both a retreat from battle and a concession of defeat. But women did not descend to this level. *They followed Jesus from afar*, notwithstanding the risks to their lives.

Of course, since the male disciples were thinking in terms of the "kings of this world", which Jesus warned them against (Mk 10.42), with a captured and subdued "commander-in-chief", they could only run for their own lives. Hence, none was there to give a helping hand to his Lord and master. Even from their rank and file too emerged the betrayer (Matt 26,14.47), the one who nailed the coffin of the messiah.

The consequence of the abandonment of Jesus by his disciples was that he now needed a conscript to help him carry his cross. The one who was *conscripted* to do this job was someone outside the circle of his disciples. He was one Simon, a Cyrenian, the father of Alexander and Rufus. We are told that he was a passer-by, coming out of the country. This was the one called upon to carry his cross (Mk 15,21). In which case, when the heat was turned on, the male disciples tuned off, leaving women and outsiders to carry on with the ministry of the cross. So when it is tough, women are called in. They move to the vanguard. But when it is "soft," men take over and tower above.

One can, then, say that during the passion there was a "ministry vacuum" resulting from the fleeing of the male disciples. They vacated their positions and their posts, and simply went into hiding. Now women and outsiders took over the vacated functions. However, we have to note that even when men assisted Jesus in the passion events, as in the case of Simon of Cyrene, they acted only as conscripts. It was not a volitive act, as in the case of the women who were freely following Jesus on their own accord. Is this also an argument against ministry positions for women in the church today?

Indeed, during the passion events, the hour of glorification, men became unwilling and even hostile partners of Jesus. Here, the sacred sources show the apparent incompatibility between the "ministry of the cross" and the "male followers of Jesus", who ran away, instead of following him till the very end. On the other hand, women were shown as being courageous enough to identify with this cross, even in the most difficult circumstances. Whereas these women were shown to have affinity with the cross, on the other hand, this was not the case with the men in the story. They were seemingly distanced from this cross. Also, whereas women showed affection to the crucified, the men showed disaffection for him.

This can even be seen in the disappointment that Peter had in Matt 16.21, when Jesus prophesied that he was going to die in Jerusalem in the hands of the elders, the chief priest and the scribes. Peter quickly challenged Jesus, saying, "Be it far from thee, Lord: this shall not be unto thee" (Matt 16,22). Of course, Jesus knew that he was ignorant about the real nature of his messianic mission. Hence, Jesus replied him in these harsh words, "Get thee behind me, Satan: thou art an offence unto me: for thou savourest not the things that be of God, but those that be of men (KJV: Matt 16,23)". As we can see, he called him *satanas*, which in the context means an opponent or adversary and not the Satan found in most of the translations of Matt 16,23

Any way, during the passion events, the glorious moment is over. So these disciples had no need to identify with a fallen hero. This explains why they even went to the extent of denying him publicly, when he needed them most (cf. Matt 26,74; Mk 14,68; Lk 22,60 and John 18,27).[179] And ultimately, they betrayed him (Matt 26,14.25).

The interesting thing here is that the betrayer was introduced as one of the twelve in these words: "Then one of the twelve, called Judas Iscariot, went unto the chief priests, And said unto them, What will ye give me, and I will deliver him unto you? And they covenanted with him for thirty pieces of silver" (KJV: Matt 26,14-15). The unfortunate thing here, for the first time, is that there is a rapport between the priesthood of the time and a member of the twelve. Both are now united to do violence, to destroy Jesus, to silence him once and for all. Their cooperation was not to further the work of the kingdom, but to commit a crime, to shut down the kingdom. While the women followed from afar, the men simply fled from the scene.

For the women there was an eruption of emotions and concern for Jesus, but for men there was a disruption. Luke noticed this difference in these words: "And there followed him a great company of people, and of women, which also bewailed and lamented him" (KJV: Lk 23,27). Even though Luke added a great number of people, yet Jesus didn't seem to have noticed them. Hence, in his response to this wailing, he said: "Daughters of Jerusalem, weep not for me, but weep for yourselves, and for your children" (KJV: Lk 23,28). This means that the evangelist probably added "the people", which is anonymous, to mitigate the negative effect the testimony might have on the male disciples. Other wise, those who were wailing were the women and those addressed by Jesus were also these women. As the sources show, Luke exalts women in the passion narratives. He presents them as following Jesus, despite the odds.

In this place, the word *synakolouthousai* (συνακολουθουσαι) used in the text above, from *synakolouthéó* (συνακολουθέω), becomes relevant. It means to follow, accompany, and follow as a disciple. It was used for a total of about *three times* in the gospels, with different meanings. The first instance is found in relation to Peter, James and John, the brother of James. The occasion was when Jesus went to heal the daughter of Jairus, the ruler of the synagogue. In this instance, Mark tells us that Jesus did not allow any other person to *accompany* him except the names just mentioned (Mk 5,37). The form of the verb used to describe this company is *synakolouthêsai* (συνακολουθησαι). Here, it means either to follow or to accompany.

The other two instances are already seen in the table above. They are found in Matthew and Luke in connection with the passion narrative. Both of them are in relation to women. Here, the verb means to *follow as a disciple.* The women were not just accompanying Jesus, they were following him as disciples. This makes them the "arch-disciples" of Jesus in the passion struggle. Isn't this ministry testimony *par excellence*?

In the light of all three instances of the use of this verb *synakolouthéō*, the reader sees that the verb was used in relation to both men and women, *but in different contexts.* Whereas the word was used to describe the male disciples accompanying Jesus on a "miracle expedition", it was used to describe the action of the women who were following Jesus during the passion. Here, we see two different situations and two standards of discipleship.

In the light of what has been said so far, one sees that these women displayed a disproportionate amount of courage in following Jesus in the *via crucis*, given their low status in Israel at the time. Notwithstanding, they were presented as watching from a distance (ἀπὸ μακρόθεν). However, what is important is that they were bold enough to witness what happened. They were within a "seeing distance". This means that they did not disappear from the scene, like the men did. Unlike men, they were *eyewitnesses* to the passion events. Unfortunately, however, when the time for telling the glorious story came these women were simply relegated to the background by power-seeking men. Does it, then, surprise anyone that no document of the New Testament canon was written by a woman, though men ran away during the passion events they were narrating?

When everything is summed up we see that women were actively present both at the beginning of salvation history and at the end of this same process. The greatest irony of this story is that even the men, who fled, later came back to become the only recognized gospel evangelists. Whatever women wrote was simply designated as *apocrypha* or *pseudepigrapha*. Of course, those who decided what the New Testament canon should be were only men. The female witnesses were simply ignored and sometimes silenced. Today, they are no longer remembered. Roman Catholicism and some other conservative churches no longer want them even to tell the story during liturgical celebrations, as preachers of the word. They are muzzled and decreed into silence.

However, the most interesting thing for this discussion is that true discipleship is defined during the passion. For Luke to be a disciple is to be a follower of Jesus. Those who have met this criterion are women. Hence, Luke avoided any ambiguity by saying, "all the women followers" (πάντες γυναικες αἱ συνακολουθουσαι) were standing from afar (ἀπὸ μακρόθεν) to witness what happened (ὁρωσαι ταυτα). The important thing is that this following which began in Galilee (ἀπὸ της Γαλιλαίας) continued during this hour of need. *Hence, these women passed the litmus test.* Their journey terminated, not only at the foot of the cross, but at the empty tomb, which began the resurrection story. Courageously, they reached the place of messianic triumph, where the journey also terminated in violence. The extent of their involvement made Jesus to console them, telling them to weep for him no more (Lk 23,28). These women were full of grief. They were really touched by what happened. *Is this the role of second class Christians in the church?* And how could this constitute an argument against women ordination or senior ministry roles for them?

Nonetheless, one sees that the *real* disciples of Jesus were women who never abandoned him in his greatest hour of need because they were not power-conscious. They proved to be the "disciples in need". Therefore, they turned out to be the true disciples. On the other hand, the male disciples needed assurance of what their concrete reward for following Jesus would be in return. They seem to be operating on the principles of a theological "trade by barter". Of course, the idea of a coming kingdom, which they mistook to have geographical boundaries like the *Hasmonean Kingdom* of Jewish history, may have misled them (cf. Mk 10,35-40). This probably shaped their mentality and attitude towards Jesus.

In this regard, Peter asked, "Behold, we have forsaken all, and followed thee; what shall we have therefore (KJV: Matt 19,27)? Peter needed a practical assurance of what their reward for following Jesus would be. Everything needed to be worked out in advance. So he had to bargain with Jesus. As a result, the Matthean Jesus gave a reply which suggested an idea of a political kingdom. Probably, he knew what the disciples were itching to get and simply told them what the wanted to hear. Hence, he replied Peter, "Verily I say unto you, That ye which have followed me, in the regeneration when the Son of man shall sit in the throne of his glory, ye also shall sit upon twelve thrones, judging the twelve tribes of Israel (KJV: Matt 19,28). Here, we see the promise of a political reward and not even a spiritual one. Spirituality is not the issue here. This answer seems to have satisfied the inquirers.

On the contrary, women were not preoccupied with this type of assurance and so needed to ask no question to know what their ultimate reward would be. As far as they were concerned, *Jesus is Lord!* (John 11,24.27). This was all that matters. Hence, they followed him unconditionally, *even unto death.* However, with the male disciples, it was not so. They were following Jesus based on what he was willing to give back in return. They seemed to have believed in the principle of "give and take". Their commitment to Jesus was not unconditional. The authority-seeking men were seemingly interested in a political messiah,[180] and so were simply scrambling for position,[181] including who would be at his right and left (cf. Mk 10,35-40). The disappointment of the two disciples on the road to Emmaus (Luke 24,19-21)[182] represents the attitude of the male disciples towards the Jesus event.

As we have already stated above, in the paschal mystery, while the men fled (according to Matthew and Mark), the women "saw these things" (according to Luke). Hence, Luke makes women to be , while in Matthew and Mark the men became the "runaway disciples". However, from the backdoor they came back to seize church power, thereby dethroning and displacing women. Hence, we see a "religious coup" against women. This is wrong. It should be rectified in this 21st century. Indeed, it is in view of this that I am writing this book on the ministry of women in the church of God.

Further, the role of men in the whole passion events leaves nothing good to write home about. In this regard, the one who denied Jesus (Peter) was a helmsman in the community of the disciples, those crucifying Jesus were men, those fleeing from him were the very men he chose, and one of the twelve men he chose (Judas) betrayed him. Ironically, this same Judas was the one who offered him the *kiss of death*, which effectively signed his death warrant and sent him to the place of crucifixion. This *kiss* is contrasted with another recorded one involving a woman in the table below.

3) Judas and the Kiss of Death

The Kiss of Judas	The Kiss of the Lucan Woman
[47] And while he yet spake, lo, Judas, one of the twelve, came, and with him a great multitude with swords and staves, from the chief priests and elders of the people. [48] Now he that betrayed him gave them a sign, saying, Whomsoever I shall kiss, that same is he: hold him fast. [49] And forthwith he came to Jesus, and said, Hail, master; and kissed him (KJV: Matt 26,47-49).	[37] And, behold, a woman in the city, which was a sinner, when she knew that Jesus sat at meat in the Pharisee's house, brought an alabaster box of ointment, [38]. . . and kissed his feet, and anointed them with the ointment. . . .[45] Thou gavest me no kiss: but this woman since the time I came in hath not ceased to kiss my feet. . . .[47] Wherefore I say unto thee, Her sins, which are many, are forgiven; for she loved much: but to whom little is forgiven, the same loveth little. [48] And he said unto her, Thy sins are forgiven. . . . (KJV: Luke 7,37-48).
But Jesus said unto him, Judas, betrayest thou the Son of man with a kiss? (KJV: Luke 22,48)	And he said to the woman, Thy faith hath saved thee; go in peace (KJV: Luke 7,50).

These texts summarize the respective attitudes of the different categories of the disciples of Jesus. The interesting thing in the text is that the betrayer is known not only as Judas, but also as "one of the twelve" (εἷς των δώδεκα). This puts his kiss in its *horrible context*. Whereas Judas offered Jesus the *kiss of death*, the woman of the city in Luke 7 offered him the *kiss of love*, the *kiss of life*.[183]

With a kiss Judas signed and sealed the arrest warrant of Jesus, which led to his ultimate capital punishment. His kiss opened the violent way for Jesus. But with the woman, the story is reversed. She offered a kiss of reverence, which recognized Jesus as Lord and Master. *Whereas Judas neatly packaged betrayal with a kiss, the woman wrapped genuine love with a kiss.* Conclusively, Judas showed disaffection, while this woman showed affection. Is this also an argument against ministry roles for women in the church?

The reaction of Jesus to these two "kisses" highlights the differences in their contents. In both instances, Luke packaged it excellently well. Hence, Jesus reacted to the falsehood of the chosen apostle with this pathetic question in Luke 22,48: Ἰούδα, φιλήματι τὸν υἱὸν του ανθρόπου παραδίδως; (O Judas, is it by means of a kiss that you are betraying the son of man?). Here, *kiss* becomes the instrument of betrayal. And the reaction of Jesus highlighted this as well in his use of the vocative case. In Hellenistic Greek, this grammatical case shows emotion. Hence, the emotion involved in the question Jesus asked his trusted disciple could not be hidden. This shows that he was touched by the deceit of his chosen apostle.

On the other hand, the reaction to the woman was completely different. Here, love was genuine and so it achieved much. Hence, Jesus pronounced forgiveness on her. Secondly, Jesus identified this kiss as an act of faith, as seen in Luke 7,50 above. Whereas in the case of Judas faithlessness is underlined, in the case of this woman faith is emphasized. So we have a faithless male disciple versus a faithful female disciple.[184] Judas did not pass the litmus test. On the contrary, the woman did. This had two consequences for the woman. First of all, it brought her salvation. Hence, Jesus could authoritatively say: Ἡ πίστις σου σέσωκέν σε – *your faith has saved you*. Secondly, she was dismissed in the peace of the Lord-πορεύου εἰς εἰρήνην-(*go in peace*). Don't we have yet sufficient reasons in favor of the ministry of women in the church? Let us now consider the much-used traditional argument involving the twelve.

4) The Ministry of Women and the Twelve Apostles

The argument of the "twelve apostles" has been a safe haven for those denying women senior ministry roles in the church today. The traditional argument has always been that denying women these ministry roles is carrying out the mind of Jesus whom they maintain chose only men to be apostles. Hence, this ministry denial is said to be doing what Jesus did. I have discussed the demerits of this patriarchal argument in chapter two above, while discussion the place of women apostles in the early church. There I pointed out the differences between Jewish Christianity, where the notion of the twelve apostles was strong and Hellenistic Christianity, where the number of apostles was indeterminate. That chapter is a direct response to this sort of argument marshaled out here. In any case, we shall go further to bring in more limitations to this patriarchal reading of scripture.

For the sake of the discussion here, it has to be repeated once more that there is no single extant evidence to show that any of the apostles or disciples of Jesus was a priest or was addressed as such. None was seen performing any cultic function. Whenever they came in contact with cultic places, like the temple, it was in connection with the Judaism of the day. If Jesus appointed non-cultic officials and we are appointing cultic officials today, is this doing exactly what Jesus did? Or is it another interpretation of the Jesus-event? One can only adduce circumstantial evidence to establish a Christian priesthood. If we can do this, then, we can also use the same principle to establish the ministry of women in the church today. In any case, the reader sees that the argument of the twelve is only a convenient one intended to help support the power base of the male ruling class in the church.

On another note, let us be very slow with the argument that the "Palestinian Jesus" chose only "twelve men" to be apostles. This additional caution is offered here because some of the twelve apostles of the Palestinian Christian tradition were *merely* names, without any verifiable historical quantification. In this regard, Jude is merely a narrative voice only heard in the farewell discourse in John 14,22. Apart from the fact that his name appeared in the list containing the names of the twelve he is not mentioned again, though one insignificant letter with pseudepigrapha leaning is pseudonymously ascribed to him. The obscurity of this particular apostle is further highlighted by the textual confusion surrounding his real name, which no one seems to know with certainty. In this regard, different gospels and different manuscript traditions know him by different names, suggesting a somewhat anonymous figure. Hence, he is known as follows in these manuscripts of Matthew's gospel in the table below.[185]

Name	Translation	Manuscripts
Θαδδαιος	Thaddeus	א, B, , etc. C*
Θαδδαιος ὁ ἐπικληθεὶς Λεββαιος	Thaddeus who is called Lebbeus	13, 346, 543, 826, 828
Λεββαιος ὁ ἐπικληθεὶς Θαδδαιος	Lebbeus who is called Thaddeus	C², K, L, W, X, etc.
Λεββεδαιος?	Lebbedeus? (questionable)	Only in: eth
Λεββαιος	Lebbeus	D, Origen[lat]

As one can see, Matthew did not even know how this very apostle is correctly called. The name is uncertain, suggesting anonymity or even a dubious origin. It was so early to forget such an important character supposedly chosen by Jesus as a pillar of faith. The modern reader is baffled that Matthew is not sure whether this apostle is Thaddeus, Lebbeus, or the questionable Lebbedeus.[186] We see a guesswork going on here.

This same confusion exists also in Mk 3,18. Here, the manuscripts (א, A, B, C) know this name as Θαδδαιον (Thaddeus); Δαδδαιον (Daddeus) by K; Ταδδαιον (Taddeus) by Δ*; and Λεββαιον <(Lebbeus) by D. One sees that Mark is equally as confused as Matthew. Is the name Thaddeus, or Daddeus, or Taddeus, or Lebbeus? No one seems to be sure?

Luke adds to this confusion by introducing another name altogether. So he deviates completely from the Matthean and Marcan traditions on this point. He is quite unaware that this figure has already been named *Lebbeus* and *Thaddeus* in the other traditions. For him the name of the apostle in question is ᾿Ιούδαν ᾿Ιακώβου[187] <Judas [son] of James> (Luke 6,16). In other words, his name is also Judas, but not Judas Iscariot. John knows this apostle also by this name (John 14,22). So Luke knows of two apostles with the same name-Judas. This uncertainty does not augur well for a historical case for this unknown apostle. With only a name to work with, no sound historical arguments can be made in favor of this obscure figure.

As for Andrew, the brother of Peter, he is also mentioned merely as a name in connection with others. Twice, he was presented as an "unheard voice".[188] Otherwise, the only time he is heard saying something is in the feeding narrative in John.[189] In addition, he is never seen doing any ministry or performing any action, giving the impression that he too was a character of the evangelists. Like Jude, he existed largely in name. At best he was presented as an inactive disciple.

Similarly, Bartholomew existed *only* as a name, found only in the list of the twelve and nowhere else in the gospels. This was also the predicament of Matthew, the tax collector. He existed only in the list of names. So also is with Simon the zealot. They all existed as biblical shadows on the pages of Holy Scripture. In this sense, they appear to be narrative ingredients needed to tell the Jesus-story, as it relates to his public ministry. The members of the twelve whom we can really talk about are Peter, James and John (the two sons of Zebedee) and Judas Iscariot. On the contrary, we have eminent women disciples of Jesus of whom so much is known. Among them were Mary Magdalene (the "darling" of the community of the beloved disciple), Mary, Martha, etc.

This analysis helps to underline the fact that *it is impossible to do exactly what Jesus did.* Those using the "twelve" as an argument know this too. Hence, they explain away the idea of choosing only many people today to be priests and bishops by saying that it is the college of bishops succeeding the college of "apostles". *This is already an interpretation and not doing what the master did.* In other words, it is not correct to say that not ordaining women is what Jesus did. It is the outcome of biblical interpretation and tradition.

If we want, we can also interpret the facts to support the ministry of women. In this case, the argument will be as follows: Although the Palestinian tradition talks so much about Jesus commissioning twelve men, yet the post-resurrection Jesus commissioned women to be announcers of the good news. This indicates his acceptance of them to be ministers in his church, *at all levels.* When he commissioned them after the resurrection to be his *commissioned messengers* to the twelve, this has an elevated position, even higher than the priesthood. This would be a fair interpretation of the mind of the risen Lord. After all, this risen Lord had to deal with the Eleven and not with the Twelve, since Judas was no longer reckoned as an apostle at this point.

5) Women as the first Post-Resurrection Evangelists

In the light of what has been said above, the reader sees that it was no coincidence that women were the only ones privileged to discover the empty tomb (Matt 28,1-6; Mk 16,2-5; Lk 24,2; John 20,1) in all the gospel accounts. As we know, it was from this that the resurrection story began (Matt 28,6; Mk 16,6b). In addition, these women were the first to see the risen Lord (Matt 28,9-10: John 20,14-16) *face to face*. They were also the first to be *commissioned* either by an angel (Matt 28,7; Mk 16.7) or by the risen Lord himself to announce the resurrection to the world (Matt 28,9; John 20,17). The women, full of courage, went to look for the crucified in the place of the dead (Luke 24,5). Their faith was not yet lost, unlike the men who betrayed themselves by saying, after he has risen, "we had hoped that he was the one to redeem Israel" (Lk 24,21). The restoration of the kingdom of Israel was of vital importance to them (cf. Acts 1,6). They followed Jesus in this hope, which appears now to have been miserably shattered.

On account of the incontrovertible mandate given to the women, they were the first to proclaim that "he is risen" (Matt 28,8; Lk 24,9-11; John 20,18), on which the faith of Christianity stands. It was on their lips that the world first learnt about this word-ηγέρθη (*êgérthê*) – *he is risen*. They brought this reassuring message to a distressed world, to the disciples that were still mourning the resurrected, as still dead. Armed with the divine or angelic mandate, they brought courage to the male disciples in scattered hideouts. Is this also an argument against the ordination of women or ministry roles for them?

Indeed, the New Testament salvation history began with women and ended with women. They were there at the beginning and at the end. *In a sense, post-resurrection Christianity was founded on the faith and perseverance of women.* In view of this, if the church of the pre-resurrection community was built on Peter, the church of post-resurrection Christianity was built on the faith and courage of women.

With this in mind, it is inconceivable, if Jesus were to be here today, that he would ban these women from the exercise of priestly or diaconal ministry, when they were the first ones he commissioned to be the preachers of the resurrection. In this sense, they were the first post-resurrection evangelists,[190] commissioned by the risen Lord himself. In this instance, they were "preachers to the preachers", including now the Eleven.[191] They proclaimed the glad tidings of the resurrection to the Eleven and others. Certainly, they had an elevated and unique position in the post-resurrection assembly. *Here, these women formed the sacred link between Jesus and the disciples*, including the Eleven. The medium of communication between Jesus and these disciples was women. They functioned as the mouthpiece of the risen Lord. They acted as a "conduit pipe" from Jesus to the disciples. In other words, *in the post-resurrection situation, the position of women further changed.*

Unfortunately, today, these women have been relegated to the background by power obsession. This is a false application of the biblical principle, "the last will be first, and the first last" (Matt 20,16). The only consolation prize deemed fit for them now is to carve out a place for them in religious orders, in the case of Roman Catholicism, just to contain them and to give them less sensitive roles in the church. Alternatively, they are made to take the back seat in the churches, saying nothing, or to be wives of pastors and bishops, where this applies, or to be *concubines* and mistresses of so-called celibate priests.

In the case of religious nuns, the convent situation is like giving a dog a piece of bone to keep it busy and quiet so that grumbling can stop. Hence, this situation restrains these women from meddling with church structures and the authority to decide. Here, they become sedated, behaving like the "opium-drinkers" of Karl Marx. In this way, the "religious house" becomes the "house of sedation". It becomes a place where these women are adequately tranquilized into a harmless sleep. The outcome is hypnotized Christians, thoroughly brainwashed and indoctrinated. This weakens the resolve of these women to oppose an oppressive and unjust situation in the church.

This leads us to the next chapter to see the attitude of Roman Catholicism towards the ministry of women in the church. In a sense, we are about to see the ordination and the subordination of women in Roman Catholicism. The next chapter deals with these issues.

Chapter 6
Roman Catholicism and the Ministry of Women Today

It is now time to see how different church traditions have evaluated and implemented the various New Testament attitudes towards the ministry of women as presented in the preceding chapters. As has already been seen, Paul definitely favored the ministry of women in the church at all levels, while deutero-Pauline Christianity resented and even rejected it. Today, Christendom is divided along these lines. Accordingly, one group says "yes" to the ministry of women at all levels, while the other flatly says "no" to this. Hence, in 21st century Christianity, we find ourselves in this "yes and no" situation. It is the "no-aspect" of this situation that we wish to consider now.

1) Preliminary Remarks

In the discussion to follow, we shall see how later generation of Christians ignored a holistic approach towards biblical hermeneutics. Here, "pick and choose" becomes the *espoused* exegetical norm. By this I mean that people select biblical texts thought to support their position. They so emphasize it to the point of interpreting the text in question out of context. Other texts, which seem to contradict such a position, are ignored, downplayed or outrightly forgotten. Here, unbiased objective reading and interpretation of scripture are sacrificed on the altar of selfishness and denominational doctrines. Sometimes, biblical theology is *defaced* in order to maintain sectionalism among the churches. *The distinctive mark of each church becomes its own subjective reading of scripture.* The various church denominations are guilty of this, without exception. One sees an unfortunate hermeneutic situation in 21st century Christianity. Unfortunately, the ministry of women has been caught up in this crossfire.

In view of this subjective approach to biblical hermeneutics, different attitudes towards the ministry of women in the church today have resulted in two opposing camps, with irreconcilable positions. Accordingly, the pro-Pauline groups adopt his position and have gone ahead to ordain women deacons, priests and bishops. This progressive situation is represented by Anglicanism.[192] On the other hand, the pro deutero-Pauline groups emphatically reject the ministry of women in the church, especially in ordained capacity. Roman Catholicism champions this particular view. Here, we see the liberals versus the conservatives – a reenactment of the New Testament situation. As a result, the liberal wing of Christianity has pitched itself with the conservative wing. Unfortunately, women are the ones on the firing line. This confirms the old adage that when two elephants fight, the grass suffers. Hence, they have been caught in a "theological crossfire". This battle continues to rage on. And there is no sign of immediate truce.

Here, the drama at Antioch is played out, once more, in our own day. As Paul told us in Gal 2,11-14, the conservatives, (represented by Peter and the circumcision party) and liberals (represented by Paul) clashed over dietary rules in the Syrian Antioch. This led the conservatives to withdraw from table fellowship from the Gentiles, thought to measure below the Jewish dietary standards. However, Paul saw no problem in eating with the Gentile Christians.

On the contrary, Peter wasn't so sure. So he withdrew from table fellowship from the Gentiles in order to appease his Jewish-Christian conservative constituency. In view of this, Paul reacted angrily and charged the conservatives with *hypocrisy*. Similarly, at various junctures in the history of Christianity, this clash has been relived and reenacted. The various attitudes towards the ministry of women help to reopen this divide at Antioch.

In the raging controversy over the ministry of women in the church today, the question now is: Who plays the role of Peter? And who plays the role of Paul? I leave you, the reader, to answer this question after reading this book.

However, in this chapter, it will be the turn of the conservatives "to go on trial". With this in mind, the searchlight will be focused on Roman Catholicism and the ordination of women in the church today. Before we do the analysis involved we wish to address two important questions here. First of all, why is the searchlight on Roman Catholicism here? And secondly, why is this issue of ordination very important? Let us begin with the first question.

2) Roman Catholicism

This church denomination is the "giant of giants" in Christendom. It is like a "religious colossus". Whether one accepts it or not, it is to the Christian world what the United States of America is to the secular world. If the United Nations, for instance, were to pass a resolution without the US on board, it would have no backbone. Similarly, if Christendom adopts a position without the Roman Catholic Church, something will still be regarded as missing, even if one pretends that this would not be the case.

Apart from its numerical strength (with over 700 million followers worldwide and over 60 million alone here in the US), the Roman Catholic Church is the biggest religious Christian denomination. Besides, it is the oldest institution with the oldest tradition in the world. Possibly, it has also the best bureaucratic apparatus, which has evolved over several centuries of bureaucratic experience and experiments. In addition, it has a United Nations recognized diplomatic status, with diplomatic missions around the world.

This has a consequence. Sometimes, when the Vatican, the center of power in Roman Catholicism, takes a position, it has a type of domino effect. For instance, if the world were to wake up tomorrow to hear that the Vatican has announced that women are to be admitted to ordination without further delay, this would significantly weaken the position and resolve of those churches still opposing full ministry position for women. Secondly, those criticizing the churches, who have already recognized full ministry positions for women, might be significantly weakened in their resolve. They will have less ammunition to continue the fight.

Indeed, the Roman Catholic Church may be widely attacked and criticized, yet its position in the world carries a lot of weight. One loose example is the Gibbson's movie, "The Passion of the Christ", which is arousing some misgivings in some Jewish quarters. In view of this, some of the Jewish leaders want the Vatican to make a statement about it. This underlines the importance of the Vatican in world affairs. In view of this, I have decided to concentrate on its position in relation to the ordination of women.

3) Ordination and Leadership

The next thing now is to answer the second question we asked above: why is this issue of ordination very important? The answer is simple: An evangelical Christian, with no ritual tradition, will not understand this problem well. However, in Roman Catholicism and those denominations with ordained ministry, this is the only gateway to full ministry position. In these churches, one cannot be a pastor, bishop, or even a deacon without ordination. In other words, to prevent women from receiving ordination is to shut them out from ritual leadership in this church. The result is that the world is given the false impression that women cannot be ritual intercessors before God, or that they cannot offer ritual prayers to God on behalf of men, or that their ritual offering cannot be acceptable to God. Above all, with the ban on women ordination *they cannot be members of the ruling hierarchy*. So this is what has locked women out of church leadership in these churches. In other words, it has kept Martha *permanently* in the kitchen. But the contention in this work is that it is time to get her out of this kitchen so that she can also participate fully in the ministry of the church. It is only in this way that this church can truly be the λαός θεου (*laós theou*) "people of God" of 1Pet 2,10 and not the " church of men" that it seems to be now.

4) The "No Male, No Ordination" Slogan

As we already know, Roman Catholicism champions the "no ordained ministerial role for women" slogan. Here, we shall see how the ministry of women is understood in this church tradition today. Of course, as I have continued to point out, this is not the only church denomination opposing full ministry position for women. There are also some of the evangelical churches, who are in this category. However, the Roman Catholic church stands out clearly among these conservative Christian denominations that are *bluntly* refusing to ordain women in their churches. They refuse to give them *meaningful* ministry roles, like senior pastors or ordain them bishops.[193]

On this question of full ministry roles for women, we see that Roman Catholicism and some of the evangelical churches are strange "bedfellows". Together, they are insisting that women should not be leaders in the Christian church. In other words, they insist that "no male, no church leadership" or "no male, no ordination" in the church. With this in mind, the world is told in very clear terms that men are born to rule in the ἐκκλησία του θεου (*ekklêsía tou theou*) church of

God. This is their non-negotiable birthright. Hence, any talk of sharing power with women in the church evokes sharp criticism. Manufactured theology is used to defend this. These churches are still holding tenaciously to that ancient relic called *the tradition of the church*.

It is important to remember here that the Pharisees, in the days of Jesus, did a similar thing with their own traditions thought to be the immutable word of God. The controversy with Jesus in respect of this came to a head in Mk 7, where Jesus was accused of breaking the law. Jesus turned the argument against them by maintaining that they were only keeping "the tradition of men" (Mk 7,8) to the detriment of the *commandment of God* (Mk 7,9.13). In view of this, he accused them of teaching for doctrine the commandments of men (Mk 7,7).

Indeed, in our own situation it is not impossible that we may be caught up in a similar situation by disproportionately insisting on this so-called "tradition of the church". Like the Pharisees, we may even be setting aside the *commandment of God* in favor of our own human traditions, while still thinking that we are doing the holy will of God. This means that we have to be very cautious in thinking that our refusal of full ministry position for women is from God.

As the facts will soon reveal, the rejection of female leadership in the church is basically a re-statement and re-enactment of the *rejected* ecclesiology of 1Cor 33-35 and other similar ones. As we saw in chapter four above, this type of ecclesiology ignores the reality of the ministry of women in the New Testament and beyond. In view of this, to talk about the ministry of women in Catholicism becomes almost a contradiction in terms since what is recognized and endorsed is the ministry of men.

Here, consciously or unconsciously, Roman Catholicism is in un-qualified agreement with the philosopher Plato that "ruling and not serving is proper to man".[194] In view of this principle, *women should serve, but men should rule.* – a re-enactment of the Genesis curse-בָּךְ־ וְהוּא יִמְשָׁל-*and he shall rule over you* (Gen 3,16). This means that women will have to be subordinated in the church in perpetuity. *This is a somewhat apartheid situation in the church.*

In view of this, if minority rule in the apartheid South Africa was bad, minority rule in the church, worse still by a few men, is equally bad. It cannot be wrong in secular society and be right in the οἰκέιος τῆς πίστεως (*oikeíos tês písteôs)-household of faith*, even if in a recycled form or under a different trademark. Indeed, apartheid is a system of government based on racial segregation. Similarly, the sacrament of ordination creates a system of church administration based on gender segregation. The reader sees that the things compare very well.

In the light of this, it is our intention now to examine some of the arguments advanced in favor of this unfortunate tradition which excludes women from the *sacrament of holy orders* through which the priesthood and the diaconate are conferred on men only. Unfortunately, when the apostle says, "no male, no female", on the contrary, Catholicism preaches "no male, no ordination". And when "white-only-area" has been abolished, both in the United States of America and South Africa, we still have "men-only-area" in the church. What an irony! What a pity! If certain forms of ministry are reserved exclusively for men, this becomes "men-only-area" in the context of the discussion.

5) Shattered Hopes

The beginning of the pontificate of the Catholic Pontiff, John Paul II, ushered in high hopes in the Catholic world. His election as Pope marked a sharp departure from the tradition of the "Holy Spirit" of Catholicism to appoint only Italian popes. People hoped that his pontificate would really usher in the *aggiornamento* (modernization) that Pope John XXXIII dreamt of, when he was convoking the *Second Ecumenical Council of the Vatican*, popularly known as Vatican II. The thoughts of many were, coming from communist Poland, that this would enable John Paul II to do a radical restructuring of the Catholic Church in the spirit of Pope John XXIII. As a result, there was euphoria. People were understandably upbeat since the church was already suffocating. The feeling then was that it was time to let in some fresh air in order to refresh the system.

But pundits were wrong because hopes began, at the early years of his pontificate, to fade. With one encyclical after another, John Paul II began to role back from the progress made at Vatican II. In stead, of going forward from Vatican II, he began to inch back towards the *First Council of the Vatican* (1870), known as Vatican 1. To solidify the gains made by the conservatives, the Pope appointed Cardinal Joseph Ratzinger from Germany, former bishop of Munich, to head the prestigious and most influential office – the *Sacred Congregation for the Doctrine of Faith and Morals.*

Hopes were shortly raised. First of all, Ratzinger was a former professor of theology in Germany before his episcopal elevation. As "Professor Ratzinger", he was moderately progressive. Secondly, coming from Germany, it was hoped that he would bring in some bit of "German liberalism". Again pundits got it completely wrong. Ratzinger made a sharp "U-turn" that stunned even his admirers.[195] In effect, with document after document his office began to tighten the nooks around Catholic theologians. Some of them were either terrorized into submission or summoned to Rome for not towing the official line. Worse still, no one dare publish anything in support of the ordination of women in the church. This became the "Area 51"[196] of Roman Catholicism.

Gradually, theologians across the spectrum began to be disillusioned. They started realizing that the other name for John Paul II is "traditionalism". Accordingly, he began to soft-pedal and even to backpedal from what is achieved in the *Second Ecumenical Council of the Vatican* (Vatican II). In the end, *the liberals lost woefully*, while the conservatives totally won. This is how the *aggiornamento* (modernization) of Pope John XXIII began to exist only in church dictionaries. Unfortunately, the hope that women will ever be ordained priests in Catholicism was dashed and shattered. Elsewhere, in my *Biblical Exegesis and Inculturation in Africa in the third Millennium*, I have summarized this papal predicament in connection with another published topic in these words:

> The first observation to be made here is that this Pope specifically uses the word *inculturation*. However, he uses it in a way which tended to cover up or to blur the central issues involved in inculturation theology. Certainly, he goes one step forward in his recognition of the term inculturation. But the issue at stake is not about a terminological endorsement. This explains why evidence from his *Redemptoris Missio* also shows a certain "theological back-pedaling" in relation to the ideals of *Gaudium et Spes* and Paul VI, as outlined above. Here the emphases begin somewhat to change in a one-sided direction. The mutual respect and benefit which both *Gaudium et Spes* and Paul VI created between the church and culture seems to be downplayed or glossed over.[197]

This was written in the year 2000. Today, this analysis has not changed. The situation is even worsening. The "nooks" are becoming tighter and tighter just to silence dissenting voices. We have a Pontiff who seems to go one step forward, four steps backwards. This is not the best of times for Catholic scholarship. Regrettably, the liberals have been subdued. Only a few voices are heard fighting for women today. Those afraid of losing their leadership positions have decided to be silent to avoid stirring up the hornet's nest or waking up a hungry tiger from sleep. This regrettable situation exists because there are no more prophets and prophetesses in our own day. Unfortunately, prophetic pastors are in short supply, while the prophetic ministry has been downgraded to the ministry of the seer.

6) Ordination and Gender

The law books of Roman Catholics, called the canon law, undoubtedly helped to seal the fate of women. It dampened their spirits, despite the high hopes leading to its promulgation in the Catholic Church by John Paul II in 1983. In the end, many were disappointed.[198] The changes, which people thought would be made to the obsolete code of 1917, turned out to be like changing a hard cover book to a paper back edition. In other words, it was cosmetic, resisting the bold and courageous reforms of the *Second Vatican Council*. In view of this, activists of the women liberation movement were dumbfounded since none of their aspirations were met by the new codex. Instead, their hands were tied behind their back.

In this "new" code, the *discriminatory* relationship between *ordination and gender* is unmistakably underlined. And the tension between female gender and ritual leadership is equally highlighted. Accordingly, this code *insensitively* said, "Only a baptized man can validly receive sacred ordination" (cc. 1024).[199] By means of this legal provision, whatever is female is now at odds with this sacred function. Sex and gender become an issue here. Hence, we see a situation of *gender and danger*. Consequently, there is a ritual segregation put in place in the name of Jesus.

As can be seen from the text of the canon law above, a baptized man is simply a male human being. This means that God confers the validity of "sacred ordination" *only* on the male members of this church. In other words, God has been made to appear to be the author of gender discrimination in the church *de iure* (by law). He is presented as sanctioning it, at least, in the cultic sphere where men are the only ones who can make ritual intercessions and function as ritual officials.

In view of this, the Vatican document *Liturgiae Instaurationes,*[200] said: "In accordance with the rules governing this matter, women may: a) Proclaim the scripture readings, *with the exception of the gospel* [emphasis mine]" (LI,7). Once more there is something considered to be a male prerogative. But is this not a terrible misrepresentation of God? Does this not falsely mask him with misogyny?

The implication of this legal provision is that God is made to examine the biological sexes or gender of the church members before giving them the gift of "sacred ordination" or the charism of leadership. Here, he is made to be a gynecologist. But has this God such a time? Isn't it naive to contemplate this? Is he really gender-conscious in terms of the distribution of ministry roles in the church? This is a classic case of anthropomorphism in the church, presenting God as if he were a human being. Here, the "other worldly" is presented in terms of "this worldly", thereby secularizing the Transcendence. It amounts to the "domestication of God" such that he becomes a manageable and controllable household item.

Fortunately, however, God does not worry about sex and gender, as we do in the church today. *He does not favor any gender.* If he can appoint women to be leaders in secular society, he can also appoint them to be leaders in the church since all authorities come from God (cf. Rom 13,1-3). As we saw in the preceding chapters, the God who appointed Deborah to be judge in Israel also called her to be a prophetess. There is no gender discrimination here.

7) Ordination and Ostracism

The discussion on love in 1Cor 13 by the apostle Paul should give us some food for thought in relation to the ministry of women in the church today. It raises some questions for church officials who are still resisting the ordination of women as priests and deacons, or their appointment as pastors and to other leadership positions in the church.

Indeed, how can such an intransigent church reconcile itself with the position of Paul on love? Can intransigence and love go hand in hand? Is it correct for a church that claims to profess love to ostracize or antagonize any segment of the congregation, even in the name of God? Does the refusal of sacred ordination to women not constitute ostracizing them in Christianity?

When these women are interdicted or prohibited from exercising the office of the priesthood simply because they are women, is this not ostracism? When a ban is placed on them because of their sex, is this not ostracism? This puts a halt on them from being leaders in the church. It downgrades them in the hierarchical church and leaves them with no higher ambitions in this church. Hence, limits are set for them, as in the temple liturgy, which banned Jewish women from entering the "holy of holies", the supposed place of divine presence.

These questions are asked because to prevent women from being ordained in the church or to exercise some forms of ministry is certainly to ostracize them by male consensus. This is maintained because to ostracize (from the Greek word *ostrakizein*) is to exclude somebody from society or a particular group, either formally or informally.[201] In other words, it means exclusion by general consent. This precludes those excluded from common privileges and even social acceptance. In this case, the formal exclusion of women from the clerical group in the Christian church becomes ostracism *par excellence*.

In other words, to proscribe or outlaw women from being priests, deacons or pastors, as the canon law has done, is nothing but ostracizing them in the *household of faith*. As a result, they are made incapable of performing certain actions *because of their gender*. Here, we have made the gender of women an issue. Hence, an obstacle is put on their way. We see how the male oligarchy of Christianity has made being *female* to be incompatible with the exercise of sacred rites. Once more, gender and ministry are at the odds. As a result, women are prevented from being ritual officials in this church.

This gender-based ministry is completely unfortunate. Today, in our world, secular powers should not discriminate against women. But the church can do this, since it is a justifiable thing to do an injustice of this nature in the name of God. Shall we say, "Amen"? Far be it! It is quite unfortunate that when the church of Paul offered women "ordination" later generations offer them subordination. Yet we try to justify this, as if it were from God. Indeed, *the making of this problem is ours.* This means that we can unmake it, *if and when we want.*

In our own day, when these women are disallowed from performing priestly or diaconal functions, from ritual intercessions, this is certainly ostracizing them. In this way, the priesthood becomes an "untouchable" for them, a theological "hot iron" which only men are deemed strong enough to touch. In other words, it becomes the "forbidden fruit" for women. Hence, to "eat" it stigmatizes, discredits and dishonors them. Of course, this helps to create antagonism in the Christian assembly. The activities of the women liberation movement are a pointer to this. In the opinion of this author, *it is time to get Martha out of the kitchen.*[202] Let us stop hiding under ancient relics and obsolete church traditions.

As a matter of fact, it has become very urgent to do this because in many Christian denominations, whereas men qualify to be ordained and to be senior pastors, women are simply *proscribed*. For men it is "prescription", but for women it is "proscription". The sacrament of *holy orders* is now ironically made to be the "sacrament of holy disorders". In this way, the "sacrament of reparation" is made to be the "sacrament of separation" between the sexes. The "sacrament of unity" becomes the "sacrament of disunity". In effect, man has willed it to become the "sacrament of unequal opportunity", which runs against the Pauline principle of equal opportunity for all.

Hence, the present form of this sacrament of ordination makes the church operating it the "church of gender profilers", the "church of unequal opportunity". This militates against the interest of women all over the world. On account of this, the womenfolk rightly frown at it. This explains why the example of Paul and the *house churches* is proposed here as the ideal. The *charismata* of Pauline Christianity are based on the principle of "non-discrimination" and "non-gender profiling". This ostracizing situation in which the woman finds herself today only leads her to more subordination in the secular society. This downgrading situation was not seen in the New Testament house churches, where women housed some of them and were part of the church leadership in such churches.

8) Ordination and the Nuns of Catholicism

The traditional theological perspective of Roman Catholicism recognizes seven sacraments.[203] Unfortunately, the *vita religiosa*-"religious life"-(convent life), which women dominate, is not one of them. Catholic men can *possibly* get all these seven sacraments.[204] But this is not the case with women since they are barred from receiving the "holy orders", the sacrament of ordination. Consequently, convent life is not recognized as a clerical state, even though these women (nuns) also embrace the same celibate life with the Catholic clergy.

Although the hierarchy claims also to have vowed this celibacy, the practice shows that it is more often than not "celibacy without continence", "celibacy without celibacy". Archbishop Emmanuel Milingo of the Roman Catholic Church, who briefly wedded the South Korean, Maria Sung, has neatly packaged this reality for the world to read. Accordingly, the *Los Angeles Times* of August 25th, 2001, commenting on this, writes as follows:

> Defending his marriage, Milingo asserted last month in a statement that the celibacy rule had failed its purpose of strengthening the Catholic clergy's spiritual purity. Instead, he said, the priesthood is "riddled" with "secret affairs and marriages, raping of nuns, illegitimate children, rampant homosexuality, pedophilia and illicit sex.[205]

This is a 71 year old Roman Catholic Archbishop speaking. Though a church used to *cover-up*[206] in order to maintain the logic of a *failed celibate institution* will not be happy reading this bitter truth in the press. Notwithstanding, *it is a solid fact no sane person will attempt denying or defending*. It is so obvious that it can only be mildly described as an "open secret".

Indeed, celibacy has become the empty shell of church history, *the relic of a bye-gone age*, even when Catholic fundamentalism tenaciously holds onto it and defends it. The sexual scandal in the Catholic

Church in America, which broke in January 2002 in the Archdiocese of Boston, is an eloquent testimony to this.

All the same, *the facts show that nuns, in convents, are comparatively more faithful than priests in observing the celibate rules or norms of chastity.* Despite this, celibacy is tenaciously held, just as the ordination of women is flatly rejected. This has become a catholic window dressing.[207]

Although these women appear to be more faithful than men in keeping the celibate vow, yet they are only confined to the seclusiveness and quietude of convents. Their life, though not accepted as a sacrament, is still described as the *vita religiosa* (religious life) and the "way of perfection". This is cleverly tagged in such a way that these women would not become easily disillusioned and disenchanted with a monotonous way of life, which offers them little in this world but paradise *only in the world to come.* In view of this, entry into this type of life is described as "entry into the perfect life". However, the ruling hierarchy of the church does not aspire to it. This shows that we are dealing with an obvious embellishment. The aim is just to calm down the womenfolk, even though everything is religiously colored just to sedate them. Hence, these women are made to be holding an empty shell *jealously* and *with all seriousness.*

In view of this, vows are produced for the nuns in convents to take and keep.[208] One of these is the so-called vow of *obedience.* Essentially, this means obedience to constituted ecclesiastical authorities, who are presented to these women as the "deputies of God" or his lieutenant governors.[209] In view of this, radical submission to these religious authorities becomes the excellent mark of a "good nun". To be critical of them is to become a renegade nun, a pariah. This is taken to be the sign of a "bad nun" or even the lack of vocation. It is seen as a violation of one's vow of obedience. Hence, instead of *ordination,* a *radical subordination* is put in place for these women as an alternative religious value. This acts as a perfect tranquilizer. In this way, the vow of obedience becomes the instrument of subtle enforcement and subordination. This becomes the "sacred charm" needed to keep these women under perfect submission, securely locked up in convents, neatly wrapped and decorated in religious habits in those places still retaining them. This acts like a consolation price for these nuns. In a sense, they are made to hold an empty shell, embellished in such a way that it is mistaken for gold.

Under this situation, this religious dress, nicely made for these women, becomes the symbol of their disguised oppression and alienation from society and real life. Heaven is made to be their "life insurance company", while the ruling hierarchy enjoys all the pleasures that there are in our world. In addition, they wield all the power in the church. For this hierarchy paradise begins on earth, whereas for these "holy women" begins after. That is the only time the God of the nuns can reward them.

Threats of hell and eternal damnation are constantly used to block their escape route and to intimidate them into further submission. This frightens many of them away from escaping from their oppressive and repressive conditions. The theology of the cross is truncated and used to justify their superficial suffering. They become trapped, bottled up and road-blocked. They are now afraid of calling a *spade a spade* since they have been indoctrinated and brainwashed into believing that to do otherwise would be questioning the holy will of God. Unfortunately, this "whitewash" remains largely intact. But what we see today is a situation where these women are *inside, but still out*[210] on account of the "theological sedatives" given to them.

Sadly enough, the "pious" forgets that all is almost gimmick, partially aimed at excluding women from ruling in the church and taking their legitimate positions in the assembly of the faithful. The whole convent saga can be said to be a sedating-concession aimed at preventing women from fighting for their legitimate rights in the church. As long as they are there, they are under control. This means that they cannot openly be women activists. They are effectively muzzled and gagged like the women of 1Cor 14,33-35 seen in chapter 4 above. Hence, they cannot challenge the injustice against them. Only an insignificant minority can brave it to go against the status quo and possibly risk expulsion from the convent. The vast majority suffers in a "holy silence" without a courageous spokesperson.

Worse still, these women cannot participate in open demonstrations to challenge their human degradation by men, who have staged a "sacred coup" that has resulted in the usurpation of divine powers. They are simply there, confined to chapels and other places of prayers, firmly kept away from the "center of gravity" in the church. They are excluded from the politics and governance of the *ekklêsia* of God. The best honor accorded to a good number of them is to be the cooks and household keepers of priests and bishops and to serve as unnecessary embellishments during colorful religious ceremonies. In this way, one sees that these women have been sufficiently distracted from agitating to be ordained priests as well. For the time being, the strategy seems to be working.

9) Bringing Martha out of the Kitchen

Has the time not come for Roman Catholicism to let Martha out of the kitchen? How long is she still expected to be there? Fortunately, Anglicanism has taken a courageous and commendable step in this direction. On the contrary, with the greatest thinkable emphasis the Pope of Roman Catholicism continues to resist this laudable move. Hence, *these women can serve in the kitchen of priests and bishops but not at the altar of the priesthood.* Notwithstanding, this unfortunate situation, the women piously nod their heads in submission to the holy will of the Pope and his lieutenants, thereby accepting their sedation. Has the time not come when women shall take their destiny into their own hands and challenge their oppressors and oppressive conditions?

It is important for women to bear in mind that it is to achieve this state of stupor that this "theological tranquilizer" called "the state of perfection" is offered to them. In this way, they are adequately neutralized and hypnotized, since everything is carefully done in the name of God and Christianity, thereby arousing less suspicion. The promise of heaven to these nuns of Christianity becomes an act of "theological hypnotism" aimed at preventing women from ever rising from their dogmatic slumber. This is an effective check put in place to keep them at bay. It becomes an effective means of "religious containment". Indeed, it helps to prevent them from revolting and demonstrating in the church since to do otherwise would be seen as revolting against God, and not man. Hence, the woman is left with no further ambitions in life in the church, though his male counterpart persistently has. The reward of heaven does not hinder him from "fighting on". He struggles and aims at higher positions in the church. He even studies for it. On the other hand, the promise of heaven is used to calm down these women who are now so afraid to challenge the status quo for fear of challenging God. This serves as effective deterrent in the church.

Indeed, in the Roman Catholic tradition and those Christian churches resisting women in senior ministry positions, this obstinacy on the part of the ruling "seniors" of Christianity helps to create *artificial* scarcity of church leaders. This has an immediate outcome-the enhancement of the chances of leadership positions in the church for any member of the male class willing to become a church leader. Of course, this has to be so since the Holy Spirit of these churches recognizes only the male sex for leadership positions. This gives the false impression of a God that is overtly obsessed with gender.

But are we to be simply deceived into believing that the Holy Spirit is now a "holy gynecologist" interested in determining the sex of individuals before allotting positions to them in the church? If the Spirit were to do this, at the level of the church, why would he not repeat it at the secular level? This means that if the Spirit does not profile in the secular state and at the secular level, also he does not profile anyone in the church. Men are the ones profiling women in order to protect their power base. However, they hide under the canopy of the Holy Spirit, using his emblem and seal of authority. This gives the world the blasphemous impression that the Holy Spirit of Christianity is a gender profiler, *which he is not*. This mistaken impression should be rectified in this 21st century. But we are the ones to do it. At this juncture, let us now focus attention on some of the Vatican documents expressly forbidding the ordination of women.

10) John Paul II and the *Ordinatio Sacerdotalis*

This is a papal document issued on the 22nd of May 1994 by the Roman Catholic Pontiff, John Paul II. As the historical facts show, it was written two years after the Church of England voted earlier in 1992 to ratify the decision of the Lambeth Conference of 1988 to ordain women priests in the Anglican Communion. This puts the document *Ordinatio Sacerdotalis* in its reactionary context.

The Pope felt that the momentum generated by the Anglican decision to ordain women had to be slowed down or even contained. It was important for him to be swift and decisive in restating an *archaic* position. The outcome is this document, which has effectively set the clock of hope back for women all over the world.

a) Ordination and Subordination

The English translation of *Ordinatio Sacerdotalis* is titled: *On Reserving Priestly Ordination to Men Alone*.[211] This caption has already said it all. Without even reading it, the reader already knows what the conclusions of the document would be and, of course, what the arguments would equally be. The caption of the document is already a thesis to be radically defended. It was not out to find the truth, but to defend a position. It sought to maintain the status quo. In other words, it was an *apologia*. Consequently, the language is highly apologetic. *Ab initio* (from the beginning), it is out to define the relationship between gender and ordination. The document highlighted the differences between ordination and subordination. For the man it is ordination. But for the woman it is all about subordination.

This document was hurriedly issued in 1994, when the debate about the priestly ordination of women was getting hotter and hotter following the decision of the Church of England. Hence, it was written as a response to this debate on the ordination of women. The Pope was getting increasingly impatient that theologians of all walks of life and thinkers across the religious spectrum were cornering the Vatican on this matter. He was increasingly becoming uncomfortable with the discussions tilting almost always in favor of the ordination of women, especially since after the decision of the Church of England in 1992. The response was this attempt in the *Ordinatio Sacerdotalis* to decree theologians into silence. As a result, the Pope issued this document to entrench his well-known personal opposition to the ordination of women, even though some German and American Catholic bishops and other Catholics elsewhere are firmly in favor of this.

If the Pope had wanted the intervention of the Holy Spirit on the matter to discern the holy will of God, what he would have done would have been to emulate the example of the Anglican Communion. Accordingly, he should have called for a synod of Roman Catholics throughout the world to discuss and debate the matter since it is of universal importance. However, *he did not do this*. Instead, he worked on the archaic principle of *Papa locuta est, causa finita est* – the Pope has spoken, the matter is over.

Aware of what the likely outcome of such a synod would have been, he cleverly avoided an apparent defeat. Instead, he decided to issue a "decree" in the form of this document just to state the position of the Vatican on the matter. Unfortunately, for liberal Catholics, this is now *imposed* as the "Catholic position".[212] In view of this, in a *solemnly* and *carefully* worded statement, the Pope concluded this *Ordinatio Sacerdotalis* in these solemn words:

> Wherefore, in order that all doubt may be removed regarding a matter of great importance, a matter which pertains to the Church's divine constitution itself, in virtue of my ministry of confirming the brethren (cf. Lk 22:32) *I declare that the Church has no authority whatsoever to confer priestly ordination on women and that this judgment is to be definitively held by all the Church's faithful* [emphasis mine].

Indeed, the Pope has spoken. The fate of womanhood has been sealed by one man alone. This is typical of one presiding over a huge patriarchal institution like a "colossus". If this Roman Pontiff thought that this topic would become cold with his statement, he now knows that he was *wrong*. Instead, he has poured gas into a raging fire, which cannot douse it. Ever since, then, the debate has become even hotter and more intense, thereby galvanizing unprecedented opposition to the

Vatican position. *And it will not go away.* Many more people are involved in the discussion now than before.[213] *The Spirit of God cannot be decreed into silence in this way.* This is the mistake of past church history. There is no need repeating it in this 21st century because *it certainly will not work as it did in the past.*

I hope that the Pope also knows that no one has the monopoly of the Spirit, or does he? The Spirit is not discerned simply through unilateral decisions. This means that all the other people, keeping this debate on the ordination and ministry of women alive, possess this Spirit as well. He can also work through them. Shutting the door on theological discussions will not work out this time. The Spirit can no longer be made to operate in a pipeline, as Catholicism did in the past and still does. *The time for decreeing the faithful into sheepish submission is simply over.* The 21st century is no longer a time for blind compliance or obedience to papal and church declarations. Courage has taken over the place of past timidity in the church. The 21st century Christians have been delivered from the false fear of hell misused in the past to whip people back into narrow lines. Today, we know that the Spirit of God blows where he wills. And he has no counselor. Or is the Pope one? Isaiah was right, then, when he asked:

> Who hath directed the Spirit of the Lord, or being his counsellor hath taught him? With whom took he counsel, and who instructed him, and taught him in the path of judgment, and taught him knowledge, and shewed to him the way of understanding? (KJV: Isaiah 40,13-14)

This shows that no one has the monopoly of the Holy Spirit. Indeed, Popes and religious leaders of all religions have made mistakes in the past. From my standpoint, this papal document under scrutiny may turn out to be one such *mistake*. History will vindicate this author. It is not good for a "dying man" to behave as if future generations would have no initiatives at all to decide what is good for them. This is where the Pope went too far in his *Ordinatio Sacerdotalis.* Here, one sees a *wild* and *arbitrary* use of power. If he does not support the ordination of women, he is entitled to it. But he should not have issued his opinion in the name of Catholicism, worse still giving his opinion the outlook of a church dogma, by inserting the phrase – "to be definitively held by all the Church's faithful", as if this is a matter for salvation.[214] From his point of view, this means that all Catholics are expected to believe the words of this document, even though the issue at stake is not about doctrine but about *ministry* and *administration* in the church.

Consequently, it is a mistake to think that the discussion about the ordination of women is a matter of belief. As I have just said, it is not *doctrinal*. This shows that it is simply an abuse of church power to give one the false impression that the *Ordinatio Sacerdotalis* is making a doctrinal formulation, *when it is not*. There are many Catholic bishops all over the world, who would vote in favor of the ordination of women, should it ever be put to a *free* vote. The United States of America is an example. The Federal Republic of Germany is another. This means that the Pope represents only one side of the argument. However, he uses power to try to suppress the views of his "opponents". This is totalitarian in style, even though it is not a new phenomenon in Catholicism.

Of course, power is might. Now, he has his document. This is the effect of absolute monarchical rule in Roman Catholicism. When this one man sneezes, the Catholic Church sneezes. *But the argument continues, no matter what*. No human authority can stop this current in favor of the ordination of women and other ministry positions for them. Legitimate agitation should be considered *and not legislated out*. Tolerance, and not intolerance, should characterize 21st century Christianity. Open-mindedness should be the norm and not a stiff-neck attitude. It should be peace and not belligerence.

b) The Congregation for the Doctrine of Faith

This Papal teaching of 1994, the *Ordinatio Sacerdotalis*, was already pre-empted by the Roman Catholic *Congregation for the Doctrine of the Faith and Morals* Headed by Cardinal Joseph Ratzinger. On October 15, 1976, it said that the church "does not consider herself authorized to admit women to priestly ordination."[215] One sees a consistency in the position of the Vatican elite designed to make sure that women are *never* ordained priests, whether there is sufficient evidence for it or not. While this may not be characterized as misogynist, though for some it is, it certainly expresses a lukewarm attitude towards women. *This is not right.*

In view of this, the correct formulation of the statement above should be that a tiny section of the "male church" *does not want* to admit women to the priestly ordination because the priesthood is the divine prerogative of men. However, should we ever put the problem in its correct biblical context and perspective, as we have tried to do in this book, the proponents of women ordination will win the argument. But when we put the question in the context of tradition, the patriarchal church wins. Unfortunately, it is this patriarchal setting that is causing the confusion, though a superficial exegesis of scripture is used to coat the problem, thereby presenting a false biblical picture.

With both statements from the *Ordinatio Sacerdotalis* and the Vatican Congregation a theological barricade is now firmly put in place to ward off attacks against male-domination in the church of God. In this way, "androcracy"[216] is now made to be the divine plan of the Almighty. Consequently, the myth of Gen 3,16 is re-enacted and rein-vigorated: וְהוּא יִמְשָׁל־בָּךְ-*and he shall rule over you*. This means that women have no more right whatsoever to rule in the ἐκκλησία τοῦ θεοῦ (*ekklêsía tou theou*) church of God. *Subordination is therefore firmly entrenched as the ideal for women, while the right of ordination is reserved for men, who are now considered to have the birthright to rule over women in perpetuity.* This papal attitude cannot withstand the test of time in the 21st century. Resistance to it is growing and will never abate.

Indeed, this hard-line attitude towards the ordination of women is a highly worrisome development. It is pointless praying for the unity of Christendom but mounting new roadblocks on the way to Christian unity. This is simply an exercise in futility. Unfortunately, we do not give the Holy Spirit the chance to work, as he desires. Instead, man is now deputizing for him. And whenever his intervention is sought, we simply want him to do so on our own terms and only in our own church denomination. This is what is keeping him at a distance from us.

Does it really serve the course of Christianity to be *erecting* new stonewalls, when none of the old is yet removed? The "wound", which the first ecumenical council of the Vatican (Vatican I) that took place in 1870 inflicted on Christendom, has not yet healed. This "wound" was due to the fact that the council Fathers, faced with the dwindling authority of the Pope, who was losing his papal city-states at the time, hurriedly defined the dogma of *papal primacy* and *infallibility of the Pope*. This was intended to leave him with some form of authority. Ever since, then, these two *unnecessary* dogmatic definitions have remained insurmountable difficulties in Christendom.

The same "infallible authority" that authorized the so-called "holy crusades"[217] in the Holy Land, presided over the worst barbarism of Middle Ages' Europe called the *inquisition*, is once more at work in respect of the ordination of women. *The inquisitor is back, though in another form.* He now operates as a "gender profiler". Christians of all churches and denominations must not let this succeed. It has to be challenged in the most vigorous way. Other church denominations should defy this, especially those who are still dilly-dallying on this point. It is better to obey God than to obey men.

Indeed, this action of the Pope is like killing a fly with a sledge-hammer. The age of dogmas is gone. The 21st century is no longer a time for it. This Polish Pope has done what the *Second Vatican Council* wisely refused to do, that is, to define new dogmas. In the end, with his dogmatic style formulation, the women liberation movement has been apparently ambushed. In this way, the fate of women has been sealed by one man.

Unfortunately, this was done in the name of God and on behalf of many Christians across the globe. Darkness now falls over the world of the woman. Intransigence is now perpetrated and perpetuated. The woman must now be only an "amen-saying" member of the church, as long as this ban is still in force. May 22nd 1994, the day of the *Ordinatio Sacerdotalis*, becomes a black day for women all over the world. The women liberation movement should celebrate it in *sackcloth and ashes*. Statements like the ones in the *Ordinatio Sacerdotalis* should no longer be tolerated in 21st century Christianity. Women cannot be legislated out of church office in this way. It cannot be that their lot is simply to be "ordained" cooks in the church, while only the men are ordained priests and deacons. *This cannot be the holy will of God.* Once more, let Martha come out of the kitchen. She has stayed there enough. The time has come for a reversal of roles in the church.

As we may recall, the Pope said, "the church has no authority. . . ." This is the theology of "pick and choose", which sometimes characterizes Christendom as a whole. If the church today has no authority to ordain women as priests, does it then mean that this same church had authority from God to sponsor the deadly crusades planned and executed in the name of God? Does it mean that the Church had authority to condemn the great Italian scientist Galileo Galilei and others to death for stating scientific facts, for speaking scientific truth? Does it mean that the church had authority to implement the atrocious and barbaric inquisition against harmless people whose only guilt was that they were expressing their legitimate religious views, though today this same church now talks about freedom of religion?

This church wants freedom of religious expression, in a place like China, but represses freedom of the same religious expression within. So there should be freedom *ad extra* (externally) but not *ad intra* (internally). What an irony! Whenever this freedom of expression is allowed, it has simply to be conformity to laid down mode of thought. Otherwise, freedom of expression becomes simply "heresy". Not to conform or concur merits one the title of a renegade or religious dissident. This was why many great Christians of the past were simply put to a brutal and violent death in the period of the inquisition. The luckiest ones were only excommunicated from the church then erroneously thought to be heaven itself.

Indeed, if women have no right to govern in the church of God, this creates a dangerous precedence for 21st century politics in the world. Secular authorities could simply use this paradigm to justify their clinging onto power, especially in fragile democracies and non-democratic regimes all over the world. Catholic totalitarianism could even be invoked as a divine paradigm of power by secular authorities. Besides, it would be absurd to have a situation where God allows women to be political leaders in the secular state, but denies them to be leaders in the "household of faith". This would be ludicrous and against the belief of the charismatic church. Luckily, this was not the case. Paul affirmed that all authority comes from God (cf. Rom 13,1-2), including secular and religious authority. This means that if a woman can be a secular leader, with mandate from God, she can also be a religious leader, with the same mandate from the Almighty. This was what God did in the Old Testament by raising women leaders like Deborah.

As I have intensively argued above, it is not to be forgotten that the whole concept of the priesthood is the product of history, if not the accident of history.[218] A Christian ministerial priesthood was *unknown* in the New Testament period. The priesthood only started with the concept of the πρεσβύτερος (*presbýteros*) elder and the ἐπίσκοπος (*epískopos*) overseer, which emanated in the apostolic period. Originally, these had nothing to do with the priesthood. Also none of them was a cultic terminology. Besides, the New Testament itself *never* used the word for priest ἱερεύς (*hiereús*) and its cognates for any New Testament church official. Even the gospel evidence presents Jesus as a prophet, as we have seen in chapter 3 above. They did not know him as a priest. It is only the epistle to the Hebrews that theologized him into the priesthood. Hence, this becomes a *theologoumenon* of Hebrews. Even, at this, Jesus is the only one called αρχιερεύς (*archhiereús*) high priest by this author, who insisted that Jesus offered the *necessary* and *only* required sacrifice ἐφάπαξ (*ephápax*) once and for all".

In the light of this analysis, I wish to recall these words from the address of Pope Paul VI to the women gathered for the national meeting of the "Centro Italiano Femminile" on the 6th of December 1976. The relevant text says:

Within Christianity, more than in any other religion, and since its very beginning, women have had a special dignity, of which the New Testament shows us many important aspects. . . it is evident that women are meant to form part of the living and working structure of Christianity in so prominent a manner that perhaps not all their potentialities have yet been made clear.[219]

But how can women "form part of the living and working structure of Christianity" if they are excluded from the heart of ministry in Catholicism, the priesthood? To exclude them would be irreconcilable with this address.

11) Concluding Thoughts

At this juncture, some final observations will have to be made. In the first place, it is important to point out here that if women did not take the initiatives to begin the women liberation movement, which helped to change their subordination in England and the United Sates of America, change would have been much slower to come. People would have thought that they were perhaps comfortable with the oppressive and unjust situation perpetuated by the state against them. As a result, franchise for women would have delayed. The disenfranchisement of women would have lasted much longer. We shall return to this topic in chapter 9 below.

The fact that women activists were in the vanguard of the "protest movements" of the 19th century helped to bring the injustices against women into sharper focus. The level of consciousness raised turned it into national debates, thereby forcing it to become a political issue. Women, in all the Christian churches are called upon in this work to do the same. They should borrow a leaf from their counterparts in the women liberation movements and seize the initiative to force change. If they rest on their oars and wait patiently for this change to come on its own, then they must dig in for eternity. They could equally plant a bottle waiting for it to germinate before they could act. Not to do something is a tacit support for the status quo. And not to say something may be construed for a "yes".

Next, it is in vain to wait for a church that is deeply embedded in patriarchal structures, tightly controlled by men, to relinquish power to women. After all, this will be suicidal for some of the men involved. It may even amount to signing their death sentence. Because of this, women have to protest louder and louder so that the example of the Anglican Communion, which we shall see in the next chapter, may become universal. They should not be afraid. The only thing they can lose is their chains or shackles. The fetters binding them have to be broken.

Women *should* and *must* wake up from their dogmatic slumber and demand equality with men in the church. They have a responsibility towards themselves to do this. Hence, they are called upon to ignore the "opium", which men offer them to daze them. Henceforth, the Pauline charismatic church should be their ecclesiological signpost. They should aim at imitating the models of those women, who were leaders in the various house churches of the New Testament.

In this regard, they should look up to Phoebe-the deaconess, Julia-the apostle, Prisca the church leader, the four daughters of Philip-the prophetesses of the apostolic church, and so on. With this in mind, we shall now go over to the next chapter dealing with the response of the Anglican Communion This will show the reverse side of the coin.

Chapter 7
The Anglican Church and the Ministry of Women Today

This chapter is a confirmation that every coin has two sides. As we can see in this work, two mainstream churches represent the two sides of the controversy on the ministry of women in the church today. The position of the Roman Catholic Church has already been seen in chapter 6 above. Now it is time to see the other side of the coin in this chapter. On the one hand, the Roman Catholic Church thinks that it has enough biblical reasons not to recognize the ministry of women in ordained capacity in the church today. On the other hand, the Anglican Church thinks that it has sufficient biblical reasons to recognize the same ministry. While Roman Catholicism slams door on women on biblical grounds, the Anglican Church opens it widely for them on the authority of the same Holy Scripture. As we saw in chapter 6 above, Roman Catholicism upholds the gag order on women by the deutero-Pauline communities. Now, on the contrary, we shall see that the Anglican Church has embraced women in the ministry. In other words, it is convinced that there is no theological obstacle or biblical hindrance towards full and unhindered ministry roles for women in the church today. Here, we see two churches, two traditions, and two interpretations, all in respect of the same reality.

So the reader sees that Rome and Canterbury now present us with a "tale of two cities".[220] Who is right, who is wrong? Isn't it the same Holy Spirit that is operating in these churches? The truth of Holy Scripture has now been made to depend on whose newspaper you are reading. Yet the Holy Spirit is recruited to preside over this open contradiction in Christendom. Accordingly, this chapter enables us to see how two Christian churches have implemented scripture in a contradictory way. Who is right? I have provided enough evidence for you, the reader, in this work so that you may decide and take your own stand on the matter.

There is no gainsaying that the Anglican Church counterbalanced the hard-line attitude of the Roman Catholic Church on the issue of the ordination of women. It replaced its inflexibility with flexibility and its intolerance with tolerance. Hence, based on the findings in this book, Anglicanism opened itself to the voice and prompting of the Spirit. It recognized that to continue to bury itself deep into past *human traditions* might mean insulating and isolating itself from the voice of the Spirit. Consequently, it came to the conclusion that the Spirit defies these traditions and acts *when he wills, where he wills and how he wills*. He cannot be taken captive by traditions of any sort or by the absolute power wielded by one man in Roman Catholicism.

Indeed, if we believe that this Spirit continues to intervene in history, it is naive to think that he cannot change or alter a past tradition to serve the church of the 21st century better than it did in the past. This was the thinking that guided the Anglican Church to do something about an obsolete tradition barring women from becoming priests and leaders in the ἐκκλησία του θεου (*ekklêsia tou theou*) church of God. In view of this, the Lambeth Conference,[221] the deliberative organ of this Church, was called into action.

1) The Lambeth Conference of 1988

There is no gainsaying that the Anglican Communion displayed a lot of courage and wisdom on the issue of women's ordination. It displayed extraordinary maturity in handling this delicate problem. The decision to this effect was by no means easy. And when the hour came in 1988, *the year of destiny for women*, it was quite tensed. Questions reflecting this anxiety were asked. One of them was, what would happen, and what would be the likely consequences should an "untouchable topic" like the ordination of women be eventually touched? This was the anxiety leading up to the epoch-making event of 1988.

However, history was finally made in this 1988 when the Lambeth Conference mustered courage and finally approved the ordination of women to the priesthood. In a sense, the ice was broken and the unthinkable happened. By this very fact, past church history has been revised, rewritten and *possibly corrected*. The courage displayed by the Conference participants is comparable to the one that motivated Jesus in Mk 7,1-20 to challenge the *tradition of the elders* (παράδοσις των πρεσβυτέρων) of his day, alternatively called the *tradition of men* (παράδοσις των ἀνθρώπων).[222] Thanks to Anglicanism, the fact of a woman priest or deacon or bishop is no longer a taboo in our society today. It has broken the ice.

The recommendation to this effect was made earlier in the Lambeth Conference of 1978. This is an indication that the decision to ordain women was not taken in a hurry. There was a difference of ten years before the actual decision was made. One sees that there was a careful deliberation before the final vote was taken. The gravity of the matter was carefully weighed. Hence, the decision was not done in a hurry. The Holy Spirit was prayerfully invoked to guide this important discussion and decision. At the end, this Spirit showed himself not to be a gender profiler that Roman Catholicism has apparently shown him to be by insisting on a male only ministry.

Prior to the Lambeth's landmark decision of 1988 only a few of the member churches of the Anglican Communion were ordaining women as priests, but not as bishops. But after the Lambeth Conference of 1988 many began to ordain women, even as bishops. The climax of this process is that, for the first time in history, the voice of women were clearly heard in official capacity in a Lambeth Conference. Accordingly, women bishops participated in the Lambeth Conference of 1998, which took place from July 18th to August 9th 1998.[223]

Obviously, this decision to ordain women was a potentially divisive topic for Anglicanism. At the time, the world was not short of *prophets of doom*, prophesying the demise of Anglicanism should women be admitted to the priesthood. For these false prophets, the apocalyptic fire was about to erupt, capable of engulfing all of the Anglican Church. They foresaw a "theological volcano" ready to explode to cover the Anglican Church with a ball of unquenchable fire.

Turmoil was foreseen. Schisms were predicted. It was thought that national churches would be breaking away in reaction to any admission of women to the priesthood of the church. Some warned against the real possibility of opening not just a "can of worms", but a "tin of dangerous snakes". Others rumored that the faithful would leave the Anglican Communion in large numbers and join those churches resisting the ordination of women. The prospect of many Protestant pastors joining the Catholic tradition or similar ones was considered a real possibility. Skeptics thought that these predictions were like predicting the eclipse of the sun, which is always done with certainty. In this way, sadism replaced the euphoria that should have greeted the advent of the ordination of women.

Of course, the mouthpiece of this oracle of doom was the male oligarchy nervous of losing hold on church power. The relevance of the Holy Spirit was ignored. In fact, he was even forgotten. It could not be imagined that he too had some say in what was to take place. Here, Rabbi Gamaliel became wiser than our contemporaries. They forgot his famous words, full of the wisdom of the Holy Spirit. In this regard, when Gamaliel's contemporaries were confronted with this deliberative question, to let the disciples of Jesus free or not, he cautioned in these words:

> And now I say unto you, Refrain from these men, and let them alone: for if this counsel or this work be of men, it will come to nought: But if it be of God, ye cannot overthrow it; lest haply ye be found even to fight against God (KJV: Acts 5,38-39).

Yes, indeed, we may be fighting God under the guise of defending him, something that the biblical Jews wanted to do in the apostolic times, except for the intervention of Gamaliel. Christians forget this too often. The ordination of women could be one such example. We can make of our objections known, while at the same time allowing the Spirit to take care of the matter. According to Gamaliel, if it is God's, it will surely stand. Bit if it is not God's, it will collapse.

Anyway, notwithstanding all the false predictions, at the end of the day, to the greater glory of God, everything turned out to be false propaganda, mere wishful thinking. So contrary to all the false prophecies, like the false "prophets" of the much-orchestrated Y2K or millennium bug supposed to herald the dawn of the third millennium in cataclysmic fashion, this transition took place without the predicted dire consequences coming true. In like manner, the opposition to the decision to ordain women turned out to be largely symbolic, without substance. All the prophecies against the ordination of women turned out to be false. Today, the ordination of women in the Anglican Communion is an irreversible reality and there are women priests in our midst.

Under the influence of the Holy Spirit, the Lambeth Conference abolished *sexual discrimination* perpetuated in God's name and on his behalf. In its place, it boldly put *equal opportunity* in place. The equality of man and woman has been emphatically reinstated.

It is true that there is a residual opposition led by the conservative wing of Protestantism, yet there is calm now. A practical sign of this is, whereas about 518 bishops attended the Lambeth Conference in 1988, about 800 attended in 1998.[224] This has further silenced and astonished the critics of Lambeth '88. Besides, the foretold "apocalypse" did not take place, because God is on the part of this church. Whereas this decision to ordain women was taken on behalf of God, the decision not to ordain them is taken on behalf of the Christian oligarchy, the ruling clique unwilling to relinquish power in the church.

2) The Role of the Church of England

This church can be said to be the "center of gravity" of the Anglican Communion. Understandably, it did not rush to implement the decision of the Lambeth Conference to ordain women, which it supported. One of the reasons for this delay, as we know, was that the Lambeth Conference has no enforcement powers. This means that whatever it decides has really no binding effect on the member churches. However, for any of its decisions to be binding the synod of each church is required to adopt it through whatever means it chooses. This gives a partial explanation for the delay in the official implementation of the Lambeth decision in the Church of England.

Nonetheless, it is also quite obvious that the Church of England faced a dilemma: *To be with Rome or not to be.* At the time, there was a sustained pressure from the Vatican authorities urging this church not to go ahead with what was being proposed in respect of women. However, faced with choosing between "an empty unity of the churches" and responding to the genuine prompting of the Holy Spirit, in 1992, the synod of the Church of England finally approved the decision of the Lambeth Conference to ordain women priests and consecrate them bishops. All is now history. Since, then, the Anglican Church has not become less church because women participate *fully* in Christian worship. This is in imitation of Paul who did not discriminate between his fellow workers.

Indeed, the Anglican experiment in ordaining women to the priesthood deserves to be praised. There is no doubt that it is a wise and courageous step taken on our behalf and truly in the name of God. It is a challenge to male hegemony in the ἐκκλησία του θεου (*ekklēsía tou theou*) Church of God. The current discussion on the ordination of women warns us against the false illusion of the unity of the churches contemplated by the Vatican authorities. As far as this author is concerned, the present status quo is healthy for Christianity, where no one person holds absolute sway over all of Christendom. Otherwise, the issue of the ordination of women would have been stifled forever by the Vatican oligarchy.

3) Opposition from Rome

As was expected, this dignified and laudable move on the part of the Anglican Communion met with stiff and insurmountable opposition from the Vatican authorities in Rome. The discussion to ordain women to the priesthood was already going on during the Pontificate of Pope Paul VI. At that time the Archbishop of Canterbury, Donald Coggan, wrote to this Catholic Pontiff about the Anglican proposal to ordain women priests. The relevant part of the letter reads:

> It is with this in mind that we write now to inform Your Holiness of the slow but steady growth of a consensus of opinion within the Anglican Communion that there are no fundamental objections in principle to the ordination of women to the priesthood. At the same time we are aware that action on this matter could be an obstacle to further progress along the path of unity Christ wills for his Church. The central authorities of the Anglican Communion have therefore called for common counsel on this matter, as has the General Synod of the Church of England.[225]

This letter was written on the 9th of July 1975. The available historical data shows that it was written about three years before the Lambeth Conference formally recommended the ordination of women in 1978. As the Archbishop said, he is right in saying that there are no *fundamental objections* to the ordination of women either to the diaconate, the priesthood, or their consecration as bishops. This is what this book has been demonstrating so far. Biblical evidence supports the move. Only a "jaundiced exegesis" thwarts this.

4) Pope Paul VI and the Anglican Communion

This letter from the Archbishop of Canterbury did not go unanswered. Accordingly, typical of the Catholic patriarchal institution, that same year, on the 30th of November 1975, Pope Paul VI replied Archbishop Coggan, reminding him of the deeply entrenched position of theVatican in these words:

> It is not admissible to ordain women to the priesthood, for very fundamental reasons. These reasons include: the example recorded in the Sacred Scriptures of Christ choosing his Apostles only from among men; the constant practice of the Church, which has imitated Christ in choosing only men; and her living teaching authority which has consistently held that the exclusion of women from the priesthood is in accordance with God's plan for his Church.[226]

These are only convenient arguments aimed at keeping inherited patriarchal structures firmly in place and ensuring that the Catholic oligarchy is in tact. The arguments are fundamentally flawed and hollow, as the evidence from Paul and the gospels show. From the standpoint of this author they are shallow. As a result, they cannot really pass the litmus test if the Vatican officials were to permit an open theological debate on this matter. They know this very well. This is why they are afraid of such a situation. The only way to play it safe is to degree theologians into silence. Anyway, for the purposes of clarity, let us itemize the three main arguments above.

a) Christ chose his apostles only from among men.

b) The constant practice of the "patriarchal Church" has imitated Christ in choosing only men.

c) The living teaching authority of the church, *which is male*-the *magisterium*, has consistently held that the exclusion of women from the priesthood is in accordance with God's plan for his Church. We shall now consider each segment of the argument.

The first argument, which Paul VI made above, is biblically *hollow* and *fundamentally* flawed. This critique becomes more intense in the light of the evidence from Pauline Christianity and the gospel arguments presented in chapter 5 above. Here, we see the influence of a *biased patriarchal* reading of the New Testament. This is said because the reality of Hellenistic Christianity cannot be ignored. As we have clearly demonstrated earlier in this work in chapter 2 above the notion of *apostle* went beyond the number twelve, especially in Hellenistic Christianity and beyond. Certainly, this type of Christianity knew more than twelve apostles. Besides, it recognized being an apostle as a charismatic gift of the church.

As a matter of fact, biblical reality shows that there are unambiguously Palestinian, as well as Hellenistic traditions. These are the two sides of the biblical coin. If Peter represents Jewish Christianity, Paul emphatically represents Hellenistic Christianity. The Acts of the Apostles points out these two complimentary realities by devoting almost equal amount of time to these two sides of Christianity. Indeed, biblical facts show that the Palestinian community sometimes saw things differently from the Hellenistic community.[227] This is understandable since both had different cultural backgrounds, one Semitic and the other Greek, making use of different categories of thought.

In the first element in the papal arguments above, for the church of today to do what Jesus did in the Palestinian circles by choosing "twelve men" as apostles, the following steps have to be meticulously followed. First of all, Jesus did not choose from the elite and sophisticated of the day. He chose simple fishermen and the like, people with questionable integrity. He chose the outcasts of society, the marginalized, people who possibly had questionable moral characters. In this regard, the call of the tax collector (publican), Matthew, fits into this. This is because the tax collectors of the day were always grouped with sinners. Hence, the gospels always talked about *tax collectors or publicans and sinners*. Below is a list of instances where this combination featured in the gospels.

Mt:9:10 (Mk:2:15): And it came to pass, as Jesus sat at meat in the house, behold, many *publicans and sinners* came and sat down with him and his disciples. (KJV)
Mt:9:11 (Mk:2:16): And when the Pharisees saw it, they said unto his disciples, Why eateth your Master with *publicans and sinners*? (KJV)
Mt:11:19 (Luke:7:34): The Son of man came eating and drinking, and they say, Behold a man gluttonous, and a winebibber, a friend of *publicans and sinners*. But wisdom is justified of her children. (KJV)
Lk:15:1: Then drew near unto him all the *publicans and sinners* for to hear him. (KJV).

As one can see from this table, the *tax collectors* or *publicans* in the text were associated with *sinners*. This shows that they had no moral worth in 1st century Judaism. Their purity rating was below par. They had no worth in their society. Although, the fishermen of the day measured higher than these tax collectors, yet they belonged to the lowly. They had questionable purity rating. Both groups (the fishermen and tax collectors) belonged to the outcasts of their society. The elite of the day was not proud to associate with them.

However, Jesus did not choose from among those with first degree purity rating. He chose from among the dejected and rejected of society, from among ritually contaminated groups. He chose people who were derided by society, like Levi who was a <τέλωνης> tax collector (Lk 5,27), with low purity rating. This is also what the church should do in order to be exact and correct.

Next, Jesus had no seminary. His pedagogical method was more like that of the ancient peripatetic philosophers. In this sense, he had only a "mobile school" comparable to the Greek peripatetic schools. In which case, his disciples did not undergo formal theological education needed today in order to be a priest, minister or pastor in the churches. So if we want to do exactly what Jesus did, we have to close down all our seminaries and imitate this peripatetic style and simplicity of Jesus. This means that we have to abolish formal theological education and close down theological institutions since Jesus did not need them to form his disciples. Anything short of this becomes an interpretation of

Jesus, which we are called upon to do on the issue of the ordination of women in the church today.

Besides, Jesus chose only Jews. In the same way, the church should choose only Jews, or people of Palestinian descent. In this regard, the Jews of the Old Testament used to trace genealogy in other to establish whether one is from the priestly tribe. They wanted to be faithful to commands of Yahweh that only the sons of Aaron and Levi could be priests and Levites in Israel. So if we want to be correct in carrying out the commands of the Lord, let us begin to scrutinize descent so that only people from the Middle East can be priests or pastors in Christianity.

Further, these men were all circumcised. This is why they were called *Jewish Christians*. Therefore, circumcision should equally be a criterion for being a Christian minister. Also the place of choosing them was Palestine. In like manner, we should also be in that place to choose as Jesus did.

According to the Palestinian tradition, Jesus chose only "twelve" men. Therefore, the number of those to be chosen *must* and *should* be *only* twelve to correspond to the mind and intention of the master. Once this number is exceeded, it is no longer doing what Jesus did.

It is also on record that Jesus appointed *married men* as apostles and disciples. The first generation of Christian pastors and missionaries were not celibates. Obviously, Peter[228] and the other apostles (1Cor 9.5) were married, meaning that the foundation of Christian faith was laid on *a married institution* and not on a celibate one. If we want to do what Jesus did, let Catholicism abolish the celibate priesthood which is contrary to what the master did. If he chose *married people* to be apostles and today we choose celibates, does it mean that the master was wrong in what he did? Are we trying to correct him? In addition, by not admitting married people to the priesthood or the leadership of the church, we contradict the church of 1Timothy which prescribed marriage for church leaders.[229]

God created a celibate man in the Yahwist account of creation in Gen 2. He later abandoned this experiment, when he decided that *it was not good for the man to be alone* (Gen 2,18). On account of this, he decided to create for him an עֵזֶר (*ēzer*), a conjugal partner, a companion, a helpmate. To walk away from this is to deviate from the original mandate *to increase and multiply and fill the earth* (Gen 1,28). As we read from the New Testament texts Jesus respected this by choosing *married people* to be his apostles and disciples. Therefore, if we want to do what Jesus did, let us abolish with dispatch the celibate priesthood. We must do this in order to conform completely to his will. This is a divine act that no other one can nullify, even with the best of intentions. The fact still remains that a higher norm can never be superseded by a lower one. There is no need interpreting this away. But if we can, let us also interpret away the notion of men as the only apostles of the Lord to pave the way for the ordination of women.

Further, in order to do what Jesus did, let us pull down all the Christian cathedrals around the world and the magnificent and extravagant churches we have built so that we may worship in Jewish temples and synagogues, as Jesus and his followers did. Alternatively, let us revert to the "house churches" which was the ideal of *ekklêsia* in the New Testament. Also if Jesus appointed disciples and apostles, why do we glory in appointing priests and bishops, which Jesus did not *clearly* do? Does this constitute doing *exactly* what Jesus did? Or is it an interpretation of what he did? One sees that even when we decide not to interpret, this decision is already an interpretation in its own way. It is incumbent on us today to interpret in the light of present exigencies of the 21st century.

The second papal argument above talks about the "constant practice of the Church, which has imitated Christ in choosing only men". The question now is this: The constant practice of which church? Is it the "church of men" or the "church of God"? This is precisely one of the reasons why we have consistently maintained, in this work, that God is not a gender profiler. The evidence adduced in this work shows this to be true. The Pauline charismatic church tradition also shows that discrimination against women is unchristian and should not be continued in the name of God.

Indeed, it is not good to present God as a Supreme Being who patronizes the male gender and identifies with it in a very special way. Unfortunately, this statement by the Roman Pontiff presents God to be this type of Being. This creates the impression of gender-based charisms in the church. Of course, this is the impression already created in the *Ordinatio Sacerdotalis*[230] and *Mulieris Dignitatem*,[231] both Papal documents by another Roman Pontiff, John Paul II. Based on this manufactured gender profiling-function of the Holy Spirit, women are flatly denied ministry roles in the church, especially the priestly ministry. The arguments presented in this work go against all the reasons given here by the Pontiff. The exclusion of women from the ministerial priesthood or similar high offices in the church is not and cannot in any way be the plan of God. On the contrary, not ordaining them or recognizing them in leadership positions is what constitutes a *breach of the plan God.*

The final element of the Pontiff's argument is that "the living teaching authority has consistently held that the exclusion of women from the priesthood is in accordance with God's plan for his Church". This is where biblical interpretation comes in. Unfortunately, it is the only true member of the argument. *The problem of the ordination of women is man-made.* Everything depends on the will of man here. *The decision not to ordain women is the act of a patriarchal church, where male-domination is extolled as coming from God.* Vatican officials say "no" to the priestly ordination of women but Anglicanism endorses it. This becomes the case of "a tale of two cities". One sees that *it is not a question of the mind of God, but a matter of which "newspaper you are reading".*

Is it not the same Holy Spirit supposed to be operating in the Catholic Church that is also active in the Anglican Church? Often times we pretend as if there were different "Holy Spirits" for the different churches of God. It is utterly naive to think that one has the monopoly of the Spirit of God. Or that it rests with one more than with the others. It is also a vain act to think that the Holy Spirit favors one's own church. Fortunately, this Holy Spirit has no favorite. *He is not the member of any church or denomination.* So he does not belong to any particular church.

In view of this, the Anglican Church and those upholding the equality of man and woman through ordination and ministry roles cannot in any way be said to be against the plan of God. Instead, they are the ones upholding it. The weight of biblical evidence is in support of this position. Besides, the Holy Spirit apportions his gifts *as he wills.* Anglicanism has come to terms with this truth. Hence, it is highly commended in this work and recommended as a model for all the churches of God.

It is also in view of the awareness of the freedom of the Holy Spirit that the Roman Catholic Church in Czechoslovakia[232] under Bishop Felix M. Davidek in the early 1970s ordained married men and women priests to meet the needs of the underground church. The reason for this action was that single males, at the time in the then communist Czechoslovakia, were suspicious to the communist authorities, who clamped down on the church with impunity.

Indeed, the train has departed and there is no stopping it. Even within the Catholic tradition, it is only the ultra-traditionalist clique within the Roman Curia in Rome that stamps its opinion with the

Catholic seal, since it is in its possession. Regrettably, the word *change* is not in the dictionary of this group. Its motto is, *as it was in the beginning, so shall it be now and so shall it ever be*. This hard-line attitude shuts the door on the Holy Spirit, now made inoperative by a bureaucratic apparatus, tightly controlled and squeezed by tradition. This does not represent the position of the universal Catholic Church, where there is a yawning to let the Sprit renew the face of the church. As I have hinted, the problem is that you have an unrestrained all-powerful Catholic oligarchy that is sitting on *absolute power* in the church. Sometimes, it does not know what to do with it. Hence, it is used arbitrarily in a Machiavellian way.

5) The Role of other Churches

The ugly condition in which the woman finds herself in the Roman Catholic Church is not only akin to this tradition. What happens here also obtains in many other Christian churches, especially the conservative wing of Protestantism. The Anglican experiment is not yet a universal experience. There are still many churches that refuse to recognize women as senior pastors and preachers in the church. This means that Christianity is generally guilty of this gender profiling against women. Hence, urgent actions are needed in this 21st century to fight this Satan that has continued to possess Christianity. Both the secular and religious authorities have to be challenged. But unless women speak out, as forcefully and loudly as they can, they will not be adequately heard. *Not to say something could be misunderstood to mean saying something in support of an alienating and estranging status quo*. It could even mean giving tacit support to one's own death sentence. This means that the woman has to take her own destiny into her own hands since most of the men are very reluctant and quite unwilling to help her out of the present impasse.

It will be in vain to look onto the ruling "seniors"[233] of Christianity, who are so privileged to occupy the top echelon of leadership in the church, to provide a way out. Most of these men, by virtue of their advanced age, feel threatened by the possibility of young, dynamic and energetic women wresting the reins of power from them. Many of these "seniors" are weak and frail. As a result, they cannot really compete with the young. The mere thought of women competing with them is in itself awful. Since some of these men are already a spent force[234] the only way out is to hold onto the relic of an antiquated tradition. In order to preserve male authority and domination they try to legislate women out "through Christ our Lord", with most of the religiously sedated women unfortunately responding, "Amen".

6) Final Remarks

Indeed, the subordination of women in Christianity is simply the result of male chauvinism. It is not from God. The desire to rule, or what the German philosopher Nietzsche called "the will to power", is the cause of the discrimination against women in Christianity. The 21st century is the time to rectify this anomaly. It is time to play the game according to the norms of a charismatic Christian church. It is not for us to determine who should get which gift, though human guidance is not to be discountenanced. Charisms are gratuitously given, so is ministry. They are a *gratis* from above. Let us not turn the grace of God upside down in order to pursue our own human agenda. It is time to allow women to become leaders *in all the churches* and *at all levels*. This fits into the ideals of the gospels, the Pauline and other apostolic churches.

If we support the good principles of "equal opportunity" for all, does it make sense that many Christian churches still resist this same principle; when it comes to the question of leadership in the church? Wives of pastors and bishops should not be discriminated in work places and civil society on the basis of sex. But it is all right to discriminate against them in the church on the same grounds. This is the irony underlining the present status quo. The 21st century Christians should address this problem very urgently. The anomalies of past history against women have to be rectified. This is the basic position of the women liberation movement. Anything less than this demand is *unacceptable*. The ideals of the charismatic church enables us to set the clock right. This has to be done, and the time to do it is now.

One more thing remains to be done in this work before the last chapter. I am aware that the priesthood has already been mentioned in chapter three above in connection with the prophetic ministry of women. Since the two church traditions just examined both emphasize ordination as a special ministry of the church, it is my intention to do a more intense scrutiny here.

The reason for doing this is simple. While Roman Catholicism tightens the nooks against women participation in the priesthood of the church, Anglicanism loosens it. The traditional explanation given for the Catholic position is that Jesus instituted the priesthood by himself and admitted only men to it, while excluding women. As we saw in the last chapter, the Anglican Church now disagrees completely.

In the light of this lack of consensus, it is now my intention to show, exegetically, the tension that existed between Jesus and the priesthood of his day. This discussion will question further the idea that Jesus established a Christian priesthood. If he did not personally establish one, then, one sees that male bigotry has simply excluded women from it, using obscure divine language. Let us now turn to the next chapter for a thorough examination of these issues raised.

Chapter 8
Jesus and the Priesthood of his Day

The way the last two chapters emphasized the priesthood and the ordination of women has led to this discussion. It is intended to strengthen whatever position has already been taken about the early development of the Christian priesthood.

As the reader may recall, in chapter three above, I meticulously pointed out the tension that existed between Jesus and the priests of his day. One reason given was the rigorous demands of the purity laws of the Old Testament and the meticulous dietary regulations of the Judaism of the period. Since he was working in the prophetic tradition, these prevented Jesus from associating with this priesthood in a positive way.

As a priest in Israel, he would have had to observe these norms in order to be able to perform cultic duties worthily. The ultimate consequence for Jesus would have been to be separated from the people. But Jesus did not want this, since his messianic ministry involved intermingling with people, both blemished and unblemished. Hence, his own attitude towards this priesthood made it extremely difficult for him to make use of the priestly models of his day to define his ministry and that of his disciples.

In view of this, Luke 10,25-37 has been chosen here to show the "cat and mouse" relationship between Jesus and the priests of his day. The exegesis of this text will show how lukewarm Jesus was towards this priesthood.

As we shall soon see, based on this unhealthy relationship, it is inconceivable that Jesus would have turned around to establish the same "discarded priesthood" for his chosen disciples, or even build on its models. As this text will soon show, Jesus did not show any discernible enthusiasm for the priests of the day, nor had they any for him either. And there is no sign that he imitated the priestly model in any of his actions. In fact, our analysis of this chosen text will reveal the mind of Jesus towards this priesthood. Besides, as Witherington correctly pointed out, "early Christianity had no temples, no priests, and no sacrifices".[235]

This story (Lk 10,25-37) is one of the most interesting narratives of Luke, which clearly depicts the relationship between Jesus and the priests of his day. As we shall see, it is in every respect a repudiation of the *priestly concept of ministry* at the time. In the period in question, the priestly or Levitical ministry was temple-bound, heavily cultic and intensely ritualistic. The temple or the sanctuary was taken to be the place where God could be served. This was also seen to be his abode. Everything was done to prepare one towards this. The priest, who was the custodian of this sacred place, was evaluated by the degree of his conformity to temple guidelines and the prevailing purity laws. For him ministry began in the temple and ended in the temple the supposed place of divine presence.

This is also reminiscent of the priest or pastor today who thinks that ministry begins in the church and ends in the church. Hence, the story, which we are about to analyze, challenges this type of misconception. With it Jesus emphasizes that ministry is not confined to the priesthood or to the pastors of the church. Even a non-cleric can be a good "minister", without official anointing. Secondly, Jesus moves the concept of ministry away from rituals and cultic celebrations. Now an essential element of real Christian ministry is compassion, mercy and love, all of which women possess. These are indispensable. As one can see, it fits into the notion of διακονία (service) which has continuously underlined this work.

While Jesus did not outrightly condemn the temple liturgy or priestly ministry of the time, he equally did not propose them as models for New Testament ministry. This is the conclusion that one will see at the end of the analysis. Here, we shall see what seems to be the "secularization" of ministry, seen from the point of view of the orthodox Judaism of the time. The neighbor becomes the real temple where God is to be encountered and served. God is no longer exclusively confined to the cult or liturgy. This means that real ministry does not need to be cultic, something that underlined the priesthood of the Old Testament. It can now take place in secular and mundane places, without the temple, or sanctuary or the sacred places of Israel. This is what clearly accommodates the ministry of women.

Some people call this the story of the "Good Samaritan". While there is nothing wrong with this, yet from the main lesson of the story, I think that it is better called the story of the "Loving Samaritan".[236] This is maintained because the main point of the story was not to point out the good nature of the Samaritan but his loving and caring aspect. In the end, it is this aspect that the storyteller requires his reader to go and imitate. Let us begin the analysis involved with a reading of the text.

1) Text

[25] And, behold, a certain lawyer [νομικός] stood up, and tempted him, saying, Master, what shall I do to inherit eternal life [τί ποιήσας ζωὴν αἰώνιον κληρονομήσω]? [26] He said unto him, What is written in the law? how readest thou? [27] And he answering said, Thou shalt love the Lord thy God with all thy heart, and with all thy soul, and with all thy strength, and with all thy mind; and thy neighbour as thyself. [28] And he said unto him, Thou hast answered right: this do, and thou shalt live. [29] But he, willing to justify himself, said unto Jesus, And who is my neighbour [καὶ τίς ἐστίν μου πλησίον]? [30] And Jesus answering said, A certain man went down from Jerusalem to Jericho, and fell among thieves [λῃσταις], which stripped him of his raiment, and wounded him, and departed, leaving him half dead. [31] And by chance there came down a certain priest [ἱερεύς] that way: and when he saw him, he passed by on the other side. [32] And likewise a Levite [Λευίτης], when he was at the place, came and looked on him, and passed by on the other side. [33] But a certain Samaritan [Σαμαρίτης], as he journeyed, came where he was: and when he saw him, he had compassion [ἐσπλαγχνίσθη] on him, [34] And went to him, and bound up his wounds, pouring in oil and wine, and set him on his own beast, and brought him to an inn [πανδοχειον], and took care of him [ἐπεμελήθη]. [35] And on the morrow when he departed, he took out two pence, and gave them to the host [πανδοχει], and said unto him, Take care of him [Ἐπιμελήθητι αὐτου]; and whatsoever thou spendest more, when I come again, I will repay thee. [36] Which now of these three, thinkest thou, was neighbour unto him that fell among the thieves? [37] And he said, He that shewed mercy on him. Then said Jesus unto him, Go, and do thou likewise [Πορεύου καὶ σὺ ποίει ὁμοίως] (KJV).

As we have seen, the story begins with the lawyer, called νομικός (*nomikós*) in the text. He asked an important question: τί ποιήσας (what shall I do?), which is what ministry is all about. Indeed, Christian ministry is about doing the work of God. It is about action and activities in the *Corpus Christi* (body of Christ). At the beginning of the story, the questioner did not know what to do. In the end, he was authoritatively told what to do – "Go and do likewise" (Πορεύου καὶ σὺ ποίει ὁμοίως). This story is presented in a sort of antithetical parallelism. The table below highlights this point.

Νομικός – Lawyer	Σαμαρίτης – Samaritan
Ἰερεύς – Priest	Πανδοχεύς-Inn-keeper
Λευίτης – Levite	Πανδοχειον – Inn
Νόμος – law	Λησταις – robbers
Ναος – Temple	Ἀνθρωπός τις – a certain man

Here, we see the cherished things of Judaism being contrasted with profane things, something that should have been annoying for the Jew of the New Testament times. As we can see, in the story, the temple had no more role to play. It was only mentioned in passing, showing its irrelevance for the Christian. On another note, the personalities associated with this temple were paired with the Samaritan, who was considered to be outside of the covenant society. In the end, this Samaritan was in, while the cultic officials of Judaism were out. Here, the reader sees how Jesus apparently turned traditional values upside down. Accordingly, the Samaritan became relevant, while both the priest and the Levite became irrelevant in the story.

Here, we see a situation where the stone rejected by the builders became the chief cornerstone. In other words, the Samaritan, rejected by the Jews of the time, becomes the model and hero in the story. One sees that Jesus is now defining Christian ministry no longer in terms of temple principles, cultic models or rituals. As the text shows, the old rituals must now give way to the commandment of love, which is much-trumpeted in John's gospel. For the purposes of the analysis to follow the story is broadly divided into two main parts: Lk 10,25-29 and Lk 10,30-37.

2) Lk 10,25-29

This first part serves as the introduction to the whole story. Here, there is a dialogue going on between the νομικός (lawyer) and Jesus. The starting point of the story is this eschatological question put to Jesus by the lawyer: τί ποιήσας ζωὴν αἰώνιον κληρονομήσω-what shall I do to inherit eternal life? This sets the tone of the story and provides us also with the context of the second part, which brings in the principal characters, the priest (ἰερεύς), the Levite [Λευίτης] and the Samaritan [Σαμαρίτης]. The interesting thing about this part is that even the νομικός (lawyer) of the story, supposed to be an expert in the laws of the Old Testament, now no longer seems to be sure how to get on board the "salvation ship". Here, despite his great knowledge of the law, he was still not quite sure of what definitively constituted eternal life.[237] In order to be sure, he had to ask Jesus, whose supreme authority is now recognized in the story.

As we can see, the lawyer's question hinges on *eschatology*. It presupposes that Jesus is now the expert or specialist on eschatological matters. In view of this, the authority of this member of the Jewish hierarchy is now submitted to the one of Jesus, who is now called διδάσκαλος (*didáskalos*) teacher, the equivalent of a rabbi. With this Jesus is now recognized as the "rabbi of rabbis", the "teacher of teachers". There is a soteriological question that Jesus the teacher has the answer. The lawyer unwillingly succumbs to know this. As the great teacher that Jesus is, he now answers the lawyer's question with another one intended to make him answer his own question. Hence, Jesus asked him: ʾΕν τῳ νόμῳ τί γέγραπται-*in the law what is written?*

The answer, which this lawyer gave, is somewhat puzzling. One would have expected him to go into the details of the purity and cultic laws of the Old Testament which were so much emphasized at the time. But this did not happen. Instead, he simply played the Jesus-game by answering: "You shall love the Lord your God with all your heart, and with all your soul, and with all your strength, and with all your mind: and your neighbour as yourself." This is a striking quotation from Deut 6,5[238] and Lev 19,18.[239] It is somewhat perplexing that this is the only text that this lawyer remembers, when there is a thousand and one of them in the law books of the Old Testament.

However, one does not have to forget the fact that the whole story is mainly *didactic*. It is intended to convey a Jesus-teaching. In view of this, the narrator makes this lawyer to supply the answer that Jesus wanted now to propose as being the most important element of the law. In other words, neither the priesthood, nor the cultic laws, nor the dietary laws, nor the purity laws serves any further purpose. The impotency of these things is now radically underlined. They are ineffectual. Here, ethics becomes the operative norm, no longer elaborate rituals and cultic observances. Hence, the Lucan Jesus confirmed the lawyer's answer by saying: ʾΟρθως ʾαπεκρίθης· Τουτο ποίει καὶ ζήση-you have answered correctly; *do this, and you will live.* This is an imperative indicating what necessarily has to be done in order to live. This is now what constitutes salvation or eternal life.

In which case, the most important thing now to do is no longer to devote endless attention to the question of purity or cultic regulations, which preoccupied the priests of the day, but to love God and to love the neighbor. But one more important thing remains to be clarified. It is the concept of the neighbor. Hence, the lawyer asked: Καὶ τίς ἐστίν μου πλησίον-but who is my neighbour? This question at the core of the whole narrative. It leads to the second part of the narrative centering on the loving Samaritan. Here, we shall see that the story makes the πλησίον (neighbor) to be incompatible with the priests of the day. The separation between priest and people is highlighted in the story. This is what we shall now see.

3) Lk 10,30-37

This is the second part of the narrative. It contains the main teaching of Jesus on real ministry in the Christian community. Here, Jesus is both narrating a story and at the same time teaching. He is the "narrator-teacher". Hence, this story is technically called a *didactic narrative*. This is one of the teaching methodologies adopted by Jesus. Other instances of this same pedagogical method are found in Luke 15,11-32 (the narrative of the prodigal son) and Matt 20,1-16 (the workers in the vineyard). In these instances, the "narrator-teacher" creates life situations and uses it to bring out the main points of his teaching. In a sense, the story used to achieve this, becomes a type of teaching aid, intended to help make the teacher's thought clearer. In the analysis to follow, the role of the various characters in the story will be highlighted.

a) The Neighbor and the Needy

This segment of the story begins with the Greek phrase – ἄνθρωπος τις (*ànthrôpos tis*), which means *a certain man*. This is the way the wounded man in the story is presented. This usage is very interesting. Jesus could have used a terminology, which delineated the gender of the person involved. But he did not do this. Ordinarily, the Greek ἄνθρωπος (*ánthrôpos*), which is translated in English as *man*, is a generic word, without gender specification. It is a non-exclusive gender word. The German language has a precise word for translating this *ánthrôpos*, which is *Mensch*, meaning a "neither, nor". Here, neither the man nor the woman is implied but mankind as a whole. Like the Greek *ánthrôpos*, this *Mensch* does not specifically refer to either man or woman. It is an all-inclusive term, which includes both genders. To bring this out in English, the Greek phrase *ánthrôpos tis* is better translated as "a certain person" because the text was not interested in talking about the sex of the person in need. In other words, the wounded or needy person in the story could have been either a man or a woman.

The fact that the narrator avoided using either a definite or an indefinite article, but used an indefinite pronoun (*tis*) *a certain* person, means that no one particular gender is intended by the narrative. The life situation of the wounded person in the story means that such a one could have been a man (*anêr*) or a woman (*gynê*). These gender-bound morphological terms for man and woman were clearly and carefully avoided in the story. This hides the gender of the one in need in the story and makes this person to be *anyone in need*.

Indeed, the use of this indefinite pronoun to qualify the person involved means that the *neighbor* in need is not always determined in advance. It could be anybody, anywhere, in whatever situation, who is in need of help. This concept tears down racial boundaries and wipes out racial and religious lines. The neighbor becomes a person without frontiers. Hence, nothing prevents such a one from being helped. Not even the segregating purity laws can do this. Here, religious walls are pulled down and the world becomes a constituency or global village.

As the story progresses, this "certain person" in the story is described and presented as a person traveling ἀπὸ Ιερουσαλὴμ εις Ιεριχὼ (*apó Ierousalêm eis Ierichô*)-from Jerusalem towards Jericho. This fact makes him a *stranger* and reinforces what has already been said above. In which case, the Samaritan was helping someone he did not personally know. In other words, *he was helping a stranger*.

This means that the neighbor is not necessarily someone known to one in advance. The only reason that brought him to the wounded traveler or stranger was that he (the Samaritan) had love. This was what helped him to identify this wounded stranger as a fellow human being in need of help. Consequently, he helped him. This action squarely fits into the answer, which the lawyer gave above, about loving God and the neighbor with one's whole heart. In other words, *the true love of neighbor is not necessarily in cult or by means of elaborate rituals or the observance of burdensome dietary laws.*

The fact that this stranger was described as "half dead" shows his extreme helplessness and how desperate he was in need of his fellow human beings. If he was "half dead", he was possibly in an unconscious state and definitely needed urgent care. This is the condition of the man lying between Jerusalem and Jericho. What; then; is the attitude of the various groups of passers-by mentioned in the story?

b) The Robbers

Before we begin to answer this important question, let us look at the men who brought misfortune to the traveler in the story. Luke tells us that this "certain person" fell among robbers, who stopped him and beat him, and departed, leaving him half-dead. These robbers, in Greek, are called λησταις (*lêstais*). They were cruel and dangerous. This is shown by the fact that, they not only stopped the man, they beat him, and left him half-dead. Eusebius corroborated this act of treachery. Hence, in his *Ecclesiastical History*, describing the events that took place in Jerusalem under the reign of the emperor Nero, he writes as follows concerning these robbers:

> And the same 4 author again relates that about the same time there sprang up in Jerusalem a certain kind of robbers,[3]" who by day," as he says, "and in the middle of the city slew those who met them." For, especially at the feasts, 5 they mingled with the multitude, and with short swords, which they concealed under their garments, they stabbed the most distinguished men. And when they fell, the murderers themselves were among those who expressed their indignation. And thus on account of the confidence which was reposed in them by all, 6 they remained undiscovered. The first that was slain by them was Jonathan the high priest; and after him many were killed every day, until the fear became worse than the evil itself, each one, as in battle, hourly expecting death.[240]

One sees that these robbers were ruthless villains. At the time, they were highly dreaded and feared by the people because of their cruelty. If they could dare assassinate the high priest Jonathan, no one then was safe. One can see how irreligious they were.

These actions described by Eusebius also put the two robbers on the cross in their correct perspectives and present to us the identity of those crucified together with Jesus. We also learn about the identity of the robber who got his salvation on the cross, before even the apostles.[241] There is no gainsaying that these *lêstais* (robbers) were dangerous criminals. This can be further substantiated in the following Lucan account: "Then Jesus said to the chief priests and the captains of the temple and elders, who had come out against him, '*Have you come out as against a robber, with swords and clubs*'" (Lk 22,52)? Here, the mention of *swords and clubs*, in relation to arresting a robber, means that these robbers in the time of Jesus were indeed violent criminals. In order to overpower them, dangerous weapons were needed to achieve this. So we see that the traveler on his road from Jerusalem to Jericho had a very rough time with these *lêstais* (robbers).

Possibly, the fear of these murderous and bloodthirsty robbers may have dissuaded the priest and Levite in the story from going to help the wounded man in the story. Possibly, on account of this potentially life-threatening situation, they decided to play it prudently, and go away quietly. They were probably afraid of being also attacked by these robbers, who may still have been in hiding waiting for their next victim to attack and plunder.

However, the text now makes it clear that there is a price to pay for loving the neighbor. It can be *costly* and *risky*. As the text highlights, the Samaritan did not count this cost of loving his neighbor. He *gambled* with his own life to save life. *He risked in order to serve his neighbor.* This is typical of John 10,15 and 15,13.[242] Here, he has shown himself to be an ideal disciple, without even been officially enrolled as one.

At this juncture, we are almost at the main point of the whole story. Jesus begins the next sub section of the story with a contrast between the priest/Levite and the Samaritan. This he did with "Now. . . So. . . But." This *but* used in relation to the Samaritan is "contrastive," separating the action of the priest/Levite with that of the Samaritan. With the use of this *but*, Jesus signaled that two levels of actions are involved, one desirable the other undesirable. The various actions of the priest, the Levite and the robbers are undesirable. On the contrary, what the Samaritan did is desirable. The unfortunate thing here is that both the priest and the Levite are classified with the robbers in the story. *This is in no way an endorsement of the priesthood of the day.* Nor is it commendatory.

c) The Priest and the Levite

Jesus continues to prepare the way for the narrative climax. He is gradually going towards the crescendo of the story. In these two verses (Luke 10. 31-32), he makes it clear that the endpoint of the story goes beyond the priesthood of the day. He presents its occupants in bad light.

As one sees, Luke 10, 31-32 is aimed at the priests and Levites, who were supposed to be very exemplary in their society. However, Jesus scores them very low. One sees a dense critic against the persons associated with the Old Testament cultic institution. In a sense, by means of this story, Jesus hit the priests of his day very hard. They felt that they were nearer to God because of their association with the temple. However, instead of identifying with them, Jesus punched into the very heart of Old Testament Judaism. How is the action of the priest and the Levite to be explained?

The vocation of Israel was based on the understanding that the people should be pure and holy. In fact, the God of the Sinai-theophany based his covenant with Israel on this holiness. Hence, in Exo 19.6, he said to the Israelites that they shall be to him מַמְלֶכֶת כֹּהֲנִים (*mamleket kōhănîm*) a kingdom of priests and קוֹי קָדוֹשׁ (*qôy qādôš*) a holy *nation*. Not only that the nation is to be קָדוֹשׁ (*qādôš*) holy, the individual is also expected to be holy as Leviticus underlines: "You shall be holy to me; for I the LORD am holy, and have separated you from the peoples, that you should be mine" (Lev 20,26). Separation from the other nations becomes one of the main characteristics of the old covenant. Hence, this line of separation becomes the line of confrontation. Line crossing becomes contamination.

But how is this whole idea of holiness to be realized? It was through a rigorous observance of the law, seen also as the revelation of God. Within this cultural and religious contexts, the excellent example and embodiment of an ideal Jew and a free Israelite was supposed to be the priests and the Levites, who belonged to a super class in the Jewish society of their day. They occupied the topmost echelon of the Jewish hierarchy. The guiding principle for each of these priests is seen in Lev 21,6. There, we read:

> They [the priests] shall be holy to their God, and not profane the name of their God; for they offer the offerings by fire to the LORD, the bread of their God; therefore they shall be holy. 7 for the priest is holy to his God. 8 You shall consecrate him, for he offers the bread of your God; he shall be holy to you; for I the LORD, who sanctify you, am holy.

On account of this radical and emphatic demand to be holy, strict purity guidelines were put in place to help the priest to be clean and holy. These were characterized with a number of prohibitions. In the light of this, he was not supposed to marry either a harlot or a divorced woman (Lev 21,7). His hair was neither to hang loose nor was he allowed to rend his garments (Lev 21,10). Even the edges of his beards were not supposed to be shaved off, nor was he supposed to make tonsures upon his head or make any cuttings in his flesh (Lev 21,5). The most relevant prohibition to our own context is the following:

> The priest who is chief among his brethren, upon whose head the anointing oil is poured, and who has been consecrated to wear the garments. . . shall not go in to any dead body, nor defile himself, even for his father or for his mother; neither shall he go out of the sanctuary, nor profane the sanctuary of his God (Lev 21,10-12).

One sees here that the priest was even forbidden from having any contact with the dead. To do otherwise, was to contract impurity. In view of this persistent situation of impurity, the law says: "And the LORD said to Moses, 'Say to Aaron, None of your descendants throughout their generations who has a blemish may approach to offer the bread of his God'" (Lev 22,1).[243] This puts the priest and the Levite in the Lucan story in their proper religious contexts and perspectives.

It is not to be forgotten that Luke tells us in 10,30 that the robbers, who stopped and beat the man, left him *half-dead.* This means that this wounded man in the story was probably impure. In a sense, then, he was potentially an impurity-carrying agent. On account of this, he was capable of rendering both the priest and the Levite in the story unclean. He remained a potential source of ritual contamination and pollution for these "holy people". In other to escape being "contaminated", they passed by and could not help the wounded. [244]

So, in the story, the fear of impurity contributed in deterring the priest and the Levite from coming near a supposedly dead man. If they had come near him, it could have made them unworthy of entering the temple. This would have rendered them incapable of offering any sacrifice there or even in participating in the ritual meals until they were purified. This is maintained because of this legal provision of Leviticus, which says:

> Whoever touches anything that is unclean through contact with the dead or a man who has had an emission of semen[245]. . . the person who touches any such shall be unclean until the evening and shall not eat of the holy things unless he has bathed his body in water (Lev 22,4b-6).

Here, one sees that impurity was a great ritual obstacle. It had a disabling effect on ritual figures. One sees why Jesus could not have opted for this as a paradigm for Christian ministry. In any case, on account of this legal provision, both the priest and the Levite were seemingly impeded from going to help the wounded man in the story.

In this story, we see a critical reappraisal of the Old Testament laws vis-à-vis the New Testament concept of love as enunciated by Jesus himself. With this he brought love and not law to the center of Christianity.[246] The constant conflict between Jesus and the *de iure* (by law) religious authorities of his day centered also on questions of correct legal observation and interpretation of these laws. Now and then Jesus gave his own legal opinion, almost always in conflict with the understanding of the religious authorities of his day.

Apart from the re-interpretation and reappraisal of the purity laws taking place in Luke 10, another example of this practice is seen in the Sabbath day conflicts. In relation to this, Matthew tells the following story in connection with the man with the withered hand.

[9] And when he was departed thence, he went into their synagogue: [10] And, behold, there was a man which had his hand withered. And

they asked him, saying, Is it lawful to heal on the sabbath days? that they might accuse him. [11] And he said unto them, What man shall there be among you, that shall have one sheep, and if it fall into a pit on the sabbath day, will he not lay hold on it, and lift it out? [12] How much then is a man better than a sheep? Wherefore it is lawful to do well on the sabbath days. [13] Then saith he to the man, Stretch forth thine hand. And he stretched it forth; and it was restored whole, like as the other. [14] Then the Pharisees went out, and held a council against him, how they might destroy him. [15] But when Jesus knew it, he withdrew himself from thence: and great multitudes followed him, and he healed them all (KJV: Matt 12,9-15).

One sees here, as in the case of the story of the "loving Samaritan", that two things are equally involved here:
a) Meticulous faithfulness to the letters of the law which forbade work on a Sabbath as a requirement for keeping the Sabbath holy.[247]
b) The question of "doing good" or acts of love vis-à-vis legal observance.

In other words, the question at stake is formulated as "either, or": Love or Law?[248] In Luke 10, the answer is in favor of love and this was what helped to propose the Samaritan as a model. Matthew adds the element of "doing good" which helps to underline this Lucan understanding. This becomes normative for Christians. It is now what defines the Christian, who now has a vocation *to do good* and not to be preoccupied with elaborate legal observances. If Jesus turns his back on the priesthood, this becomes quite understandable in the light of this new understanding on his own part. So whenever this "doing good" or love runs into conflict with the law, this act of "doing good" takes precedence. Accordingly, Mark summarized this principle as follows: "The sabbath was made for man, not man for the sabbath" (Mk 2,27). In view of this, the universal brotherhood and sisterhood of man and woman is uncompromisingly stressed.

If Jesus had problems with these legal observances and the priests of the day were in the vanguard of these laws, it becomes increasingly difficult to see how he could have opted for this paradigm, either during or after his earthly ministry. *Ab initio* (from the beginning), he had a problem with the priestly institution. He did not associate with it in a positive way. Almost every action of his, in respect of the priests of his day, was a critique. He was not even seen visiting or eating with any of them. The relationship between them was anything but friendly or cordial. This story of the loving Samaritan underscores this point.

d) The Loving Samaritan

The first thing to be noted here is that Luke dedicates three verses (10,33-35) to this character, whom he called, *Samarítês tis* (Σαμαρίτης τις) – a certain Samaritan. This character plays a pivotal role in the narrative. He is the center of gravity. The whole story revolves around him. As the Greek reader can see, grammatically, the phrase-*Samarítês tis* (Σαμαρίτης τις-has neither a definite, nor an indefinite article. Instead, the grammatical construction follows the same indefinite pronominal construction of the wounded in the story called *anthrôpos_tis* (a certain person).

In view of this parallel, the one who played the heroic role in the story is simply "a certain Samaritan". As we can see, this narrative character is both unnamed and unknown. This means that the Samaritan in the story could have been a man or woman, even though the female morphology, which is Σαμαριτις (*Samaritis*),[249] was not used. All the same, the story is told in such a way that both male and female are accommodated. In other words, both genders are recognized due to the grammatical use of this indefinite pronoun. Hence, the Samaritan in the story could be anybody playing the role assigned to this person.

e) The Samaritans in Josephus and the Old Testament

Although Samaria appears in the Old Testament in about hundred instances, the word Samaritan was almost not used. As the evidence shows, it is probably attested only in 2Kgs 17,29. The relevant text reads:

> [29] Howbeit every nation made gods of their own, and put them in the houses of the high places which the Samaritans had made, every nation in their cities wherein they dwelt. [30] And the men of Babylon made Succothbenoth, and the men of Cuth made Nergal, and the men of Hamath made Ashima, [31] And the Avites made Nibhaz and Tartak, and the Sepharvites burnt their children in fire to Adrammelech and Anammelech, the gods of Sepharvaim. [32] So they feared the Lord, and made unto themselves of the lowest of them priests of the high places, which sacrificed for them in the houses of the high places. [33] They feared the Lord, and served their own gods, after the manner of the nations whom they carried away from thence (KJV: 2Kgs 17,29-33).

As can be seen from this text, the Jews of the time associated the Samaritans with idolatry and the worship of false gods. In other words, these Jews did not believe that they were worshipping the true God, like themselves. As we know, the Samaritans occupied Samaria, the northern part of the biblical Israel. Even though they were living in an Israelite territory, yet the Jews maintained that these people were non-Jews. The reason for this was that they were said to be the descendants of those brought from Babylon to populate Samaria after many of the Jews were deported from the land.

This line of thought is found in Josephus who points out that these Samaritans were called the Cutheans. According to him, they are called this way because they were brought out of the country called Cuthah, which is a country of Persia.[250] In other words, they were deported from this Cuthah to the land of Samaria to fill the vacuum created by the deportation of Jews. This position was reiterated elsewhere by Josephus, as follows:

> Now as to Shalmanezer, he removed the Israelites out of their country, and placed therein the nation of the Cutheans, who had formerly belonged to the inner parts of Persia and Media, but were then called *Samaritans*, by taking the name of the country to which they were removed.[251]

However, these Samaritans did not accept this Jewish interpretation of their history. Accordingly, they maintained that they were the descendants of the Israelite remnants left behind after the fall of Samaria. This explains why they espoused the laws of Moses, as enshrined in their own version of the Pentateuch called the *Samaritan Pentateuch*. How can these two different positions be reconciled?

Evidence from history shows that both positions contain some elements of truths. Obviously, not every Jew was deported from Samaria after the fall of the Northern Kingdom of Israel. Some were left behind, while foreigners were also deported to Samaria from other lands. The Jewish remnants now living with foreigners intermingled and intermarried with them contrary to the advice of Tobit to his son Tobias in these words: "Beware, my son, of all immorality. First of all take a wife from among the descendants of your fathers and do not marry a foreign woman, who is not of your father's tribe; for we are the sons of the prophets" (Tobit 4,12). Besides, Josephus accused these Samaritans of playing double standards. According to him, they had to do this in order to protect their own interests. On this, he says:

> And when they see the Jews in prosperity, they pretend that they are changed, and allied to them, and call them kinsmen, as though they were derived from Joseph, and had by that means an original alliance with them; but when they see them falling into a low condition, they say they are no way related to them, and that the Jews have no right

to expect any kindness or marks of kindred from them, but they declare that they are sojourners, that come from other countries.[252] Further, as far as Josephus is concerned, these Samaritans are simply "enemies to the tribes of Judah and Benjamin."[253] The greatest flash point occurred during one of the Jewish festivals, when the Samaritans were accused of desecrating the Jewish temple with corpses. Josephus narrates this incidence in these words:

> As Coponius, who we told you was sent along with Cyrenius, was exercising his office of procurator, and governing Judea, the following accidents happened. As the Jews were celebrating the feast of unleavened bread, which we call the Passover, it was customary for the priests to open the temple-gates just after midnight. When, therefore, those gates were first opened, some of the Samaritans came privately into Jerusalem, and threw about dead men's bodies, in the cloisters; on which account the Jews afterward excluded them out of the temple, which they had not used to do at such festivals; and on other accounts also they watched the temple more carefully than they had formerly done.[254]

One sees that Jews and Samaritans were no bedfellows. From the first moments of their history, they had animosity towards each other. For Jews, these Samaritans were never taken to be one of them. Hence, there was constant tension and friction between the two peoples, even in the time of Christ.

f) Tension between Jews and Samaritans

The aversion and friction, which existed between Jews and Samaritans, are typical of a north-south type divide. One of the contentious issues was the attitude towards Yahweh, the God of Israel. The Jews of the time accused the Samaritans of worshipping the gods of the foreign settlers in Samaria.[255] In other words, they were charged with idolatrous behavior. These foreigners are said to have brought their own gods along with them, which now causes the problem seen in 2kgs 17,29ff above. Hence, there is now a syncretism in place. In relation to these foreign gods, Josephus said: "each of them, according to their nations, which were in number five, brought their own gods into Samaria, and by worshipping them, as was the custom of their own countries".[256] As Josephus said, on account of this idolatrous act, these Samaritans paid a terrible price. Hence, Josephus said:

> They provoked Almighty God to be angry and displeased at them, for a plague seized upon them, by which they were destroyed; and when they found no cure for their miseries, they learned by the ora-

cle that they ought to worship Almighty God, as the method for their deliverance.[257]

How, then, did these Samaritans come to know about the God of Israel and the law of Moses? Josephus responds by saying that the reaction of these Samaritans to these ravaging plagues was that they sent word to Babylon for some of the captured Israelite priests to be sent to them. He summarized what happened in these words:

> So they sent ambassadors to the king of Assyria, and desired him to send them some of those priests of the Israelites whom he had taken captive. And when he thereupon sent them, and the people were by them taught the laws, and the holy worship of God, they worshipped him in a respectful manner, and the plague ceased immediately; and indeed they continue to make use of the very same customs to this very time, and are called in the Hebrew tongue Cutlans, but in the Greek tongue Samaritans".[258]

In this regard, the presence of other gods is deemed to compromise the cult of Yahwism, which in itself is an affront to the radical monotheism of Israel expressed in the *shema* in these words: אֱלֹהֵינוּ יְהוָה אֶחָד יְהוָה יִשְׂרָאֵל שְׁמַע (šəma' yiśrā'ēl *yǝhwāh ĕlōhênû yǝhwāh ehād*)-*Hear Oh Israel: The Lord our God is one Lord* (Deut 6,4). The radical emphasis here is on יְהוָה אֶחָד (*yǝhwāh ehād*) – *one Lord*. This is the heart of the cult of Yahwism. It underlines its radical *monotheism* and belief in one Lord and one God.

In the time of the monarchy, the kings of Israel were judged on this note. This was their litmus test. They passed or failed on this point. In view of this, king Ahab was judged so harshly based on this principle (1kgs 16,30). If the Samaritans are viewed negatively, it is because they did not also pass this test of radical Yahwism.

Besides, while the Jews worshipped in Jerusalem, the Samaritans worshipped at Gerizim. Accordingly, there were two separate temples, the Jewish temple in Jerusalem and the Samaritan temple at Gerizim. In addition, they had their own bible called the *Samaritan Pentateuch* different from the Masoretic text, since they believed that this is only what is scripture.[259] We have also indication of this in John 4,20. To bring these differences to a head, the anger of the Samaritans boiled when the high priest John Hyrcanos destroyed their temple around 128 BC.[260]

g) The Samaritans in the New Testament

Statistical evidence shows that the Samaritans did not feature in Mark's gospel. Matthew mentioned them only once in chapter 10 in a way that recreates the tension between Jews and Samaritans. The relevant text says:

> These twelve Jesus sent out, charging them, 'Go nowhere among the Gentiles, and enter no town of the Samaritans, but go rather to the lost sheep of the house of Israel' (Matt 10,5-6).[261]

Here, we see that the Jewish Christian sources classify these Samaritans together with Gentiles. *It was thought that salvation was not for these Samaritans.* Hence, the twelve were not supposed to go to evangelize them since it was considered pointless doing that. However, as we shall soon see, Luke takes a different approach. Following his universalistic approach, he shows that salvation is *also* for them.

The tension between the Samaritans and Jews in the New Testament period is further highlighted by these words from the Samaritan woman at the well of Jacob in John's gospel. In response to Jesus' request for water to drink, the woman said: "How is it that thou, being a Jew, askest drink of me, which am a woman of Samaria? for the Jews have no dealings with the Samaritans" (KJV: John 4,9).

I think that this text adequately highlights the problem quite well. Elsewhere, in John, the Jews revealed their thoughts also towards these Samaritans, when they said to Jesus in John 8,48: *The Jews answered and said to him, have we not correctly said that you are a Samaritan and have the devil* –᾿Απεκρίθησαν οἱ Ιουδαιοι καὶ εἰπαν αὐτω, Οὐ καλως λέγομεν ἡμεις ὅτι Σαμαρίτης εἰ σὺ καὶ δαιμόνιον ἔχεις? Here, one sees that the opponents of Jesus labeled him a Samaritan, showing that he was not recognized as one of them. This was intended to degrade and demean him. In other words, the Jews were being derogatory.

Further, we can see that the word *Samaritan* is associated with δαιμόνιον (*daimónion*) the demon. Josephus confirmed this mentality, when he said that these Samaritans are "evil and enviously disposed to the Jews".[262] The reader sees that the enmity between Jews and Samaritans continued in the time of Jesus and even beyond.

The Samaritans featured prominently in Luke, sometimes in high profile situations. In this gospel, they are mentioned in three instances. The first is in 9.51-56, where these Samaritans refused Jesus passage through their territory. This confirms the tension already pointed out above in both Matthew and John. The second is in 10.30-37-the case of the "loving Samaritan", which is presently under analysis. The third is in Lk 17,11-19, the cleansing of the ten lepers, where the only one that returned to thank Jesus was a Samaritan. The first of these texts reads:

When the days drew near for him to be received up, he set his face to go to Jerusalem. 52 And he sent messengers ahead of him, who went and entered a village of the Samaritans, to make ready for him; 53 but the people would not receive him, because his face was set toward Jerusalem. 54 And when his disciples James and John saw it, they said, "Lord, do you want us to bid fire come down from heaven and consume them?" 55 But he turned and rebuked them. 56 And they went on to another village (Luke 9,51-56).

This shows that, even Luke the "friend" of the Samaritans, was aware also that they had problems with Jews. Their refusal of Jesus passage was not because of his person but because of his nationality. Here, there is the case of both racial and religious profiling. The problem between Jews and Samaritans at the time also extended to strangers wishing to pass through Samaritan territories to Jewish ones. Hence, they could not permit Jesus to pass through their village *en route* to Jerusalem.

The anger of the Jewish disciples of Jesus also highlights the enmity between them as Jews and these Samaritans. Hence, they wanted their master to permit them in turn to call down destruction upon these Samaritans *via* fire from heaven. However, Jesus rebuked them because of this. He was not to be seen to be equally nationalistic like his disciples. He could not take sides in the racial dispute going on. He transcended this situation, even though his disciples thought that he was one of the nationalists of their own time.

Apart from the various texts above, which cast the Samaritans in a somewhat bad light, the New Testament exalted them in three other high profile instances. As the pieces of evidence show, the texts in question lifted them up more than the expectation of any orthodox first-century Jew of the period. The first of these is the text of the Loving Samaritan under analysis. The second is the cleansing of ten lepers.[263] And the third is in John.[264]

This extended study of the Samaritans is intended to put them in their correct context in the story of the loving Samaritan. These were people treated as *outcasts* and *renegades*. They were considered to be the enemies of God's people. They were anomalous persons. As we have seen above, they were not even friendly to Jesus, though he was kind to them. Yet this is the person now chosen, instead of someone from among the chosen people.[265] This is the person now proposed as a model.

What Jesus did was quite revolutionary, something no other orthodox Jew of the day would have done under any circumstance. Here, the "pariah" is praised, while the cultic officials of the Judaism of the day were *repudiated*. Their action was not endorsed. Hence, Jesus goes forward now to offer new ideas about purity and holiness.

In this story, we see that Jesus is constantly distancing himself from the priesthood and priestly paradigms. Apparently, these did no satisfy him. As far as he is concerned, they measured below par. The harsh and intense nature of the critique involved seems to close all the doors and windows on this priesthood. There is nothing in the story to suggest that Jesus had the intention of refining and adapting it to his ministry or even of eventually recommending it to his followers. What one sees here is a Jesus, who is turning his back on the models of the priesthood. He bluntly refused to define himself in sacerdotal terms. Instead, he prefers to define himself in terms of his own ideas. The messiah could not be held captive by the norms of purity and elaborate legal observances. This was cumbersome for him.

h) Jesus and the Concept of Purity

The time has now come to answer the initial question: Who is my neighbor? The answer is contained in Lk 10,36-37. Here, Jesus refers the question put earlier by the lawyer back to him to answer it by himself. It is now up to him to answer the question: who is my neighbor? The text made no mistake in reminding this lawyer that the two personages he is about to refuse to recognize as being a neighbor to the wounded are a priest and a Levite, highly respected cultic personalities in Israel. These were supposed to have taught their fellow Jews what being a neighbor is all about. But in this story, *they failed the litmus test.* Hence, once Jesus asked this lawyer: "Which of these three, do you think, proved neighbor to the man who fell among the robbers," the lawyer simply said, "The one who showed mercy on him." As we can see, he cleverly avoided saying, the Samaritan.

However, what is important here is that the lawyer forgot all the ritual laws about purity and used mercy as the measuring rod or defining norm. Here, it is not the priest and Levite, who were obsessed with ritual purity and cultic observances, but the Samaritan ignorant of these ritual laws, who is now recognized and endorsed as the model to be imitated.

Once more, implied in this story is a critique of the occupants of the priesthood of the day. In this regard, it is interesting that the two representatives of the priestly class (the priest and the Levite) were mentioned, thereby sparing none of them. In other words, *the Jewish priesthood, as a whole, is on trial in Luke 10.* Here, we see a subtle attack on the Jewish priesthood of the day. It seemed to be so preoccupied with externals like ritual purity, cultic observations and meticulous observance of the dietary laws that the more important matter of caring for the neighbor was relegated to the background.[266]

As we can see, Jesus wanted to show that to love is more important than these observances, something which recalls that famous Old Testament saying in 1Sam 15,22.[267] As far as Jesus is concerned, if a law becomes an obstacle towards being a neighbor, then, it no longer serves its purpose. Also, the mere fact of occupying the priestly office is no longer a guaranteed criterion for holiness or high purity rating.[268]

Indeed, the command, which Jesus gave to the lawyer, implies a *redefinition* of the concept of purity and a new understanding of the notion of holiness. These too have a bearing on ministry in the New Testament. It is no longer ritualistic or about a set of laws. It is now about doing, and about being a neighbor to others. It is no longer about ritual ceremonies. Ministry is no longer about liturgical rites and rubrics. New Testament ministry transcends these. In a sense, no priesthood is needed any more to carry this out. This is what accommodates the ministry of women in the church today. The task of being a neighbor to others belongs to all Christians.

When Jesus said to the lawyer: "go and do likewise", he means that the lawyer should not imitate the priest and the Levite who were so obsessed with ritual purity. These people are no longer proposed as ideals and models to be imitated. Consequently, the priesthood they represent is also discarded.

On the contrary, the person, whose action is now proposed as an ideal to be imitated, is the supposedly sinful and renegade Samaritan. This is something that no first-century Jew would have found easy to accept. The lesson that one learns from this unit (as well as in the New Testament as a whole) is that Christianity is a practical way of life and not simply a system of religious rituals or cultic observances. This new understanding does not augur well for a Christian priesthood.

i) Final Thoughts

This story is representative of the way Jesus approached the priests and the priesthood of his day. It is not surprising that the priests championed the course of his arrest and eventual crucifixion. Hence, he was condemned to death by the same priesthood that it challenged. In which case, one can rightly speculate that the priests of the day had some scores to settle with him. The time for this presented itself during the arrest. But, then, why did the relationship between Jesus and these priests deteriorate to the point of violence against him? A number of factors contributed to this. As we shall soon see, both sides contributed to this tragic saga.

On the side of Jesus, he had constant contacts with persons legally declared impure in his native Palestine. To worsen matters, there is no evidence that Jesus underwent ritual purification or decontamination. This was part of what angered the priests of the day, who were so obsessed with ritual cleanness. It is also the reason why the religious authorities of the day, who felt that Jesus engaged in acts considered anomalous in the Judaism of the period, confronted him in Mk 7. In this regard, as the pieces of evidence show, he came in contact with dead people, be it in the case of Lazarus (John 11,1-53), or in the case of the widow's son at Naim (Luke 7,11-17), or in the case of the centurion's daughter (Mk 5,35-43). This violates the letters of Lev 21,11 and Haggai 2,13.

Next, in contrast to Lev 21,17-23, he had contacts with the lame (Matt 11,5; 15,30-31; 21,14), people with different infirmities ((Lk 5,15; 8,2)) and with blind people (John 9). He touched lepers (Mk 1,40-45) in contravention of the legal provision of Num 5,2. He had contact with menstruants in the traditional impure state, as seen in the case of the woman with the issue of blood (Mk 5,25-34), something that Lev 15,19-30 forbade. Equally annoying for his contemporaries was the fact that he drove away those selling in the temple (John 2,13-22), and even taught in this same temple without the necessary permission. This angered the Jewish authorities, who questioned his authority to do this (Matt 21,23).

Further, his program of exorcism led the Jews to accuse him of demon possession (Matt 9,34; 12,24). This shows that he was regarded as an impure person by the religious authorities of his day for which they had no remorse to put him to a violent death. In addition, he openly broke the Sabbath day laws. In this regard, he allowed his disciples to pluck ears of corn on a Sabbath (Matt 12,1-8), while he himself healed on a Sabbath (Matt 12,9-14). He had association with such impure persons like sinners and tax collectors (Matt 9,11). He had no good words for the religious authorities of his day. As far as he was concerned, they were hypocrites and whitewashed graves (Matt 23,27). Their father is the devil.[269] These things put together led to his arrest and summary crucifixion. In which case, Jesus was crucified as one who was disobedient to the laws of his land. In other words, he was executed for committing "religious treason". Even if he wanted, he could not have qualified for the priesthood of the day.

However, in Mark 7, Jesus rejects this type of evaluation. As we can see, he distinguishes between *human traditions* and the *revelation of God.*[270] This type of distinction enabled him to prove that he was not breaking any law of God. He points out that the point of controversy is nothing but human traditions, which he variously called "the tradition of men" (Mk 9,8) and "your tradition" (Mk 7,9).

Of course, Jesus is right in making this important distinction since the issues involved in the dispute centers on the prevailing purity laws, which prescribed some ritual washing or purification under various circumstances. Some of these laws had to do mainly with *bodily hygiene*, even though they were given religious value. This, notwithstanding, to break any of these laws made one unclean. Accordingly, Jesus accused his opponents of neglecting the commandment of God and holding fast to the tradition of men (Mk 7,8).[271]

On the side of the priests, they showed open displeasure with the acts of Jesus (Matt 21,15). It is interesting that they were the ones who questioned his authority to teach in the temple (Matt 21,23). Even at the end of one of his parables these priests were the ones who interpreted it to be directed against them (Matt 21,45). Accordingly, they wanted to get hold of him but were restrained, at this stage, for fear of the people (Matt 21,46; also Matt 26,5). This is an indication that Jesus had favor with the common people.

These priests were the ones who finally took the decision to kill Jesus in the palace of the high priest Caiaphas (Matt 26,3-4). Not only this, they were also the ones who connived with Judas to deliver him up to them. In this regard, they cut a deal with Judas to give him thirty pieces of silver with which he delivered Jesus to them (Matt 26,14-15). After this act of betrayal, the priests sent the great multitude that came with swords and arrows in the company of Judas Iscariot to arrest Jesus (Matt 26,47). It did not end here. Also those who sought false witness against Jesus were also these priests (Matt 26,59). The final decision to deal with Jesus by putting him to death was also taken by the priests (Matt 27,1). They were also the ones who put him on trial (Matt 27,12). In other words, it was the priesthood that put him to a violent death, even though Roman soldiers were used to carry this out.

These priests were also the ones who persuaded the multitude to demand the release of the murderer Barabbas instead of the release of the innocent Jesus (Matt 27,20). They were also among the party mocking Jesus (Matt 27,47). They also went to Pilate to demand that the tomb of Jesus be well safeguarded to avoid his disciples stealing his body (Matt 27,62-65). In connection with this, it was also these same priests that manufactured the *theft theory* in relation to the resurrection of Jesus (Matt 28,11-13).

When all these things are fitted together we see why Jesus kept an arm's length with the priesthood of his day. Based on this he could not have instituted any priestly office. Of course, the New Testament Christians did not in any way pretend that they had one. Hence, no one among them was ever called a priest. This means that the argument that it came from Jesus, which is used as a reason for not ordaining women priests, is quite preposterous. Circumstantial evidence is insufficient here in trying to establish a Christian priesthood. Consequently, *Jesus could not have forbidden women from practicing what he did not establish.* If we cannot prove with absolute certainty that he established a priesthood for Christians how can we really argue that he excluded women from such a priesthood? If we have clear evidence in favor of prophets, we do not have that in relation to a Christian priesthood.

In the light of this study, the reader sees that everything depends entirely on the will of the male clergy controlling the religious destiny of women. One sees that the real argument is not christological. It is not good to impute gender-obsession to the innocent Jesus. He stands above the present gender struggle. His will is that men and women should be collaborators doing the work of the kingdom and not detractors. We are all workers in the vineyard of the Lord. Hence, name-calling should stop.

There is no need promoting tension between gender and ministry in the name of Jesus. The gifts of God cannot be distributed based on gender. The "no male, no female" slogan in Galatia (Gal 3,28) should guide us in our distribution of ministry roles in the church today. So no one should be excluded on biological grounds.

Besides, Jesus left the paradigm of the pastor-shepherd for his church (cf. John 10). This accommodates but men and women. *Therefore, if and when we want to ordain women, we can.* With this in mind, we shall now go to the last chapter of this work, dealing with general matters affecting the womenfolk and the struggle for emancipation.

Chapter 9
Gender and Emancipation

Our study of the role of women in the ministry of the church has led to this final reflection. In the course of our study, we have seen how two church traditions tried to interpret and implement the demands of the apostle Paul and the New Testament.

However, we wish to note here that the struggle for emancipation is not only connected with religion. It affects the secular world as well. Indeed, it is a well-known fact that women have suffered not only in religious history or in the ancient world but also in the secular world. They have been the "oppressed of every creature". Recent examples from contemporary history will suffice here.

1) Enfranchising the Disenfranchised

As the facts of political history show, life was not easy for women, even in the advanced countries of the world, the so-called champions of freedom and democracy. For long, freedom and democracy were only the "prerogatives" of men in these places. The oppression and exploitation of women reached such a point that women decided to take their own destiny into their hands. This is something that the Christian women are called upon to do today in relation to their rightful place in the church. They have to seize the initiatives and change the tide of church history and tradition in their favor. The "waiting game" has not achieved much and should be declared over. It is in vain hoping that men would be enthusiastic enough to take the initiative to tear down the walls of subordination and discrimination.

After all, this is their effective instrument of control and dominance in both the church of God and the secular world.

This realization was what led women in the 20th century British society to challenge the subordinating status quo, which made them second class creatures, leaving them *without voting rights*. At the time, on account of this female disenfranchisement the "right to vote" became of cardinal importance to women. It was important for them to take up this matter by themselves since the status quo favored the men, who were unwilling partners to effect any change that would give equal franchise to both men and women. It would have been naive for women to continue to wait for these men to take the initiative to change the male status quo since they had nothing to lose by allowing things to be the way they were. To do anything to the contrary would have meant shooting themselves in the leg. The women read the handwriting on the wall and understood it very well. So they decided to take their own destiny into their own hands and began to agitate to be enfranchised. This began a struggle with a successful outcome.

As was to be expected, this bold and courageous initiative was met with hostility on the part of men. Notwithstanding, it did not deter women. And luckily, male opposition was short-lived. Consequently, the first franchise of women became a reality in 1918. However, the franchise-bar was raised well beyond that of men. Hence, the voting age for women at the time was 30 years and above. In other words, inequality continued to exist.

All the same, this hard won victory, no matter how limited, shows that women in the various churches today cannot be resting on their oars. They have to intensify their struggle because God is on their side, even when church history and tradition have not been on their side.

It has to be pointed out here also that the long disenfranchisement of women was not only in Britain. Women equally suffered this fate in the *United States of America*, the "bastion of freedom and democracy". Unfortunately, the "right to vote" for women was also an issue here. Once more, women were on the offensive. They had to demand to be enfranchised like their male counterparts. This led to the proposal of the "right to vote" amendment to the US Constitution as far back as 1878. One would have thought that progress would have been made on this front as soon as the proposal was made. This was not the case. It had to wait for over forty years before the men controlling the destiny of women could give it a hearing. After a long period of dilly-dallying and procrastinating, the proposal was finally ratified in 1920 as the *19th Amendment*[272] of the US constitution. So it became law.[273]

As one can see, it took over forty years for a consensus on the matter to be reached. The reason for this long delay was that the men, who were controlling the destiny of women, did not want this amendment to succeed. Just like in the case of Britain, opposition to it was equally very stiff here.

One sees that these "defenders" of freedom, forgot to defend the freedom and right of women to vote. Hence, the franchise right was denied women. Even the founding fathers of America could not remember this in 1781 when the first constitution of the United States was ratified. It needed so much struggle on the part of women and the 19th Amendment to make women suffrage a reality.[274]

These two examples show that women have to fight for their rights. Men have not always proven to be reliable and dependable partners in the fight for women rights. Only when too much pressure is brought to bear on them can they reluctantly effect the necessary changes. This is what we have learnt in the fight for women suffrage in both Britain and the United States of America.

Therefore, Christian women are called upon in this book to intensify their struggle in order to get their rightful places in the ἐκκλησία του θεου (ekklêsia tou theou) church of God. If they are waiting for their male pastors, bishops, priests and church leaders to effect this, they may have to wait ad infinitum.

The examples seen above have shown that men are never in a hurry to cede power to women, especially when the status quo favors them. This means that more women activists are needed in the church in order to gain more ministry roles for women. The struggle has to intensify. It is important for women to challenge their unjust situations in the churches with the same vigor that they challenged their disenfranchisement in the world.

2) The Status of Women Today[275]

The condition of women today is improving compared with what it used to be in the past. In this regard, it is quite interesting that the preamble to the United Nations' Charter of 1945 made explicit reference to equal rights for women. This may have encouraged many nations of the world to rethink policies that promote and encourage the subordination of women to men. As a result, throughout much of the contemporary world women are gradually emerging from centuries of subordination and confinement to the household. However, this progress has been uneven. In addition, it has sometimes suffered reversals.

Even till today, despite all the hullabaloos about human rights, equal opportunity and freedom for all, the American society (for instance) is still a male-dominated one. Though serious efforts have been made, and are still being made, yet *gender profiling* persists. Some men are not so enthusiastic about the principles of equality with women. Hence, the long and arduous fight for The *Equal Rights Amendment* (ERA) to the US Constitution suffered a setback on June 30, 1982, though it was earlier approved by the US. *House of Representatives* in 1971 and the *Senate* in 1972.[276] The reason for this debacle was because it fell three states short of the needed thirty-eight needed for the measure to pass.[277] This is understandable since men are always the majority in all the state legislatures in the US.

However, there is a bit of hypocrisy here. Following the mockery on marriage that began in San Francisco in February 2004 allowing the so-called same sex marriage, some people in America support this cultural joke on the ground that it is protected by the "equal protection clause" of the US constitution. However, they also forget that the *Equal Rights Amendment* was defeated in 1982. Women's rights should not be protected, but gay rights should be protected.

On the political scene, the highest political achievement that women have made in a place like the US is their attempt to run for the vice presidential race, *though without success*. However, on the judicial front, a limited achievement has been recorded. In 1981, the first woman was appointed to the US Supreme Court. Currently two women are sitting in this court. As for Britain, it had to wait till 1974 before getting its first female Prime Minister.[278]

On the religious front, we have Teresa of Avila, Saint Catherine of Siena, Edith Stein, and the great Mother Teresa of Calcutta, winner of the 1979 Nobel Peace Prize. She dedicated her life to the service of the poor of Calcutta in India. One can see that not many women have attained great religious heights, though numerous men abound. This means that religion has not really been promoting adequately the welfare of women. It seems to have a stifling effect on them.

Here, it is sad to note that while the secular world has taken steps universally to ensure equal voting rights for women and men, the institutionalized Christian churches are quite reluctant implementing this. Women are forbidden from voting or choosing ecclesiastical functionaries. The Roman Catholic Church is most guilty in this respect due to the intransigence of Rome. Women cannot join in the selection process of their priests, not to talk of voting to elect a bishop or a Pope. This is entirely a male action, those to whom the Holy Spirit of Roman Catholicism has endorsed and recognized to vote for office bearers and be voted. Isn't the secular world ahead of us in ensuring and enshrining women's rights, though we put on a "holier than thou" attitude?

3) Looking Towards the Future

There is still much room for improvement. A lot is left to be done. Both the political state and the religious world should do more, beyond mere posturing. It should be more action and less talking. For instance, the female world is anxiously waiting to see when the US will elect her first woman president. It would be such a nice thing to see a Mrs. President in the *White House* as commander-in-chief of the armed forces of the United States of America. We are still to see the German State elect its first woman chancellor. Or when Japan will elect a woman Prime Minister. Or when a woman president will preside in the Kremlin in Russia. Or when China will elect a woman president.

On the religious level, despite the roadblocks being mounted on the way for the women liberation movement I am still optimistic about the future. With the initiative of the Anglican Church to ordain women, a *point of no return* has already been reached. It is now *forward ever, backward never*. No matter how tough, no matter how difficult, no matter how odious this task may be victory will be achieved in the end.

In this place, I recall one of the war songs that the Biafran side in the Nigeria-Biafra civil war (1967-1970)[279] used to express its optimism in the outcome of the war. The words of the song are:

> *We are Biafrans*
> *Fighting for our nation*
> *In the name of Jesus*
> *We shall conquer.*

In the same way, women are like those on a war footing. This is what every liberation struggle looks like. However, these women are advised not to lose their temper to the point of abandoning their principle of "non violence". Belligerence will not be able to win this struggle. Besides, sympathy to this noble course may be lost. But firmness of purpose and strong resolve will be very important weapons. Like the Biafrans, mentioned above, the "war" song of this women liberation struggle should now be:

> *We are women*
> *Fighting for our freedom*
> *In the name of Jesus*
> *We shall conquer.*

Indeed, women will triumph in the end. More patience is only what is needed. It is in this hope and optimism that the closing message of the Fathers of the *Second Ecumenical Council of the Vatican* to women on the 8th of December 1965, deserves to be recalled here:

> The hour is coming, in fact has come, when the vocation of women is being acknowledged in its fullness, the hour in which women acquire in the world an influence, an effect and a power never hitherto achieved. That is why, at this moment when the human race is undergoing so deep a transformation, women imbued with a spirit of the Gospel can do so much to aid humanity in not falling.[280]

The prophesied "hour" in the text has to be now. It has to be in this 21st century. This third millennium of Christianity is full of expectations in relation to women. In view of this, the world is anxiously waiting to see when the Roman Catholics will elect their first woman Pope to sit in the Vatican to be addressed as "Her Holiness, Pope Victoria 1". This applies also to the other mainstream churches resistant to change. In this regard, the world also wants to see a woman archbishop of Canterbury, to be addressed as "Her Excellency, the archbishop of Canterbury". The same holds for the patriarchates of the Greek and Russian orthodox churches. Why can't a woman be a Patriarch, an archbishop or a Pope? Beyond the human veil that blurs our vision, is it a theological impossibility? By no means!

It is only the "theology" of our own making, and not the theology of Jesus Christ and Paul, that has created this ugly problem for women. Since nobody speaks from no-where it is not surprising that we have been taken captive by the patriarchal world of Christianity. The influence has been tremendous and incalculable.[281] In this regard, I repeat here what I have said in my earlier publication on *Biblical Exegesis and Inculturation in Africa in the Third Millennium*:

> This is an unfortunate accident of history made possible through the might of imperial Rome and some of the emperors like Constantine the great and Charles the Great. Instead of Jerusalem and Antioch, original centers of Jewish Christianity, Rome swallowed up everything. The consequence, for Church history, is that Jerusalem is only remembered as the cradle of Christianity. But Roman culture, law, and Roman outlook on life came to be adopted as the Christian way of life, thus replacing Jerusalem. European version of Christianity became universalized to the extent that everything Roman is now Christian.[282]

This is the ugly predicament in which we find ourselves today. It is important not to forget it. Otherwise, we will be deceived with the theology of our own making and the ecclesiology of our own fabrication. The time has come for us to go back to the sources of faith, without allowing our church traditions to blur our vision. Otherwise, we may be developing a "theological cataract" without being aware that this is the case. This may mean gradually losing our "theological sight" without even realizing that this is taking place.

It is quite unacceptable that we are still handcuffed and leg-chained by the traditions of our own making, when the world that helped to mislead us now democratizes and makes sincere and genuine efforts to break the shackles of the past. This is one reason why women are suffering today. Therefore, this 21st century is the time to break the fetters because God is on the side of this struggle called *women liberation*. Equality cannot only be a paper work or something delivered only from the church pulpit. It has to be practical and concrete.

Indeed, the woman has to be equal with the man since both of them are *joint heirs of grace* (1Peter 3,7). There has to be true emancipation for the woman and equal ministry access for all, irrespective of gender. The woman has to be released from her "detention", from the "house arrest" where men have kept her a prisoner for centuries. She has to break loose her chains. She has to burst her fetters. She has to liberate herself from bondage. A new act of deliverance is urgently needed for her, just like Moses delivered the oppressed Hebrews from inhumanity. Some men are willing to join in this "crusade" but women must lead the way for there to be total success.

However, this new act of "setting the woman free" is not intended to lead her to *total* independence from the man. By no means! This work is simply about the inter-dependence of the sexes. It is about mutual coexistence based on unbiased principles of equality, equity and fairness. Therefore, a relationship of reciprocal respect has to exist. So the *equality of the sexes has to be the hallmark of this new relationship in this 21st century*. This is what makes the Pauline version of Christianity relevant to the liberation of women today. This movement becomes then a *freedom movement*. As this work shows, Paul has enunciated its principles very clearly. In effect this becomes a "handbook of women liberation".

Rightly, this book is about *gender and ministry* in the early church and the church today. In this age, when democratization is considered a political jewel and freedom taken to be its heart, this topic becomes all the more interesting. If democracy enshrines the principles of equality between man and woman, today what is the contribution of Christianity and Christians towards this? Does the 21st century Christianity proclaim the same equality between man and woman in all things? What effort has been made to restore the woman to the level of equality with man in the Christian churches? Does equality not include leadership positions in these churches? This fluid situation links women liberation with Pauline Christianity.

I still remember that English song of old: *It's not an easy road* Indeed, all those involved in this struggle to give women their due places in the world and in the church should bear this in mind. It has never been easy and will not be easy. So it will continue not to be an easy road. But the struggle *must* continue without looking behind. There should be no resting on the oars until final victory is won. Indeed, fellow theologians and exegetes, fellow liberation fighters for the total emancipation of women, anger is in our hearts, but no rancor.

This is why we have resorted to theologizing instead of vandalizing. Our principles must be guided by the late Dr. Martin Luther King, Jr., who preached non-violence to achieve civil rights issues in the American society. In view of this, our principle must be: *No sword, but peace* – *šālôm*. The road may be too rough, *but the tough will keep going* because *when the going gets tough, the tough keeps going*. Women issues must be constantly kept on national and ecclesiastical agendas. Therefore, there should be no relenting. We have to continue to build on the progress made so far. This leads us now to the final conclusion of this exegetical work on *Gender and Ministry in Early Christianity and the Church Today*.

Summary and Conclusion

The time has come to conclude this work on *gender and ministry*. The approach to be adopted here is a simple one. In the first place, a chapter by chapter summary of the work will be made. This will be a recapitulation of the main ideas of each chapter. The aim is to help the reader to sum up what has been read in the main parts of the book. This means that this section of the work is not intended to be a substitute for the actual reading of the work. After the summary part of this section, the final conclusions will be stated. Let us now begin with the summary aspect.

Summary of Work

As the reader my recall, this investigation began with the *first chapter* dealing with the Pauline usage of the Greek term *synergós*, for fellow worker, which he used to describe some of those who worked with him. In the course of our study, we saw that there were those whom Paul repeatedly called his *coworkers* or *fellow workers*. These were his close companions or associates in spreading the good news. In a sense, they were the *evangelists* of Pauline Christianity. The most interesting thing found in our study is that these *fellow workers* included both women and men. Names were mentioned in this respect. Here, equality was emphasized and the demon of discrimination was exorcised.

As we further demonstrated in this chapter the women fellow workers of Paul were highly placed women in the church. There is evidence that they were leaders in the house churches. One example given was Prisca, who owned a house church together with her husband Aquila. This practice was also shown to be a feature of the apostolic church in Acts, where women too presided over the house churches. One name mentioned here was Mary, the mother of John Mark. The overall presentation showed that these women participated in the leadership of the house churches of the day.

This led us to the *second chapter* dealing with the question of women apostles in early Pauline Christianity. The principal text analyzed was Rom 16,7. The argument here was highly technical based on morphology and the evidence of textual criticism. Two varying names were mentioned in our text as an apostle-*Iounian* (Junia/Junias) and *Ioulian* (Julia). Which one should we take? First of all, we presented a morphological argument, maintaining that the name *Iounian*, as an accusative case, could be translated as Junia (an *attested* feminine name) or Junias (an *unattested* masculine name). Here, we opted for the former, which is *Junia*.

Then, we turned to textual criticism. Here, the case for *Iounian* (Junia) and *Ioulian* (Julia) was made since both are contained in different manuscripts of Rom 16,7. As the manuscript evidence shows we saw that there is an overwhelming manuscript support in favor of the name *Iounian* (Junia). On the other hand, the support for *Ioulian* (Julia) was very scanty, thereby creating insufficient witnesses in favor of this name. *However*, we refused to conclude the discussion based on the principle of "majority carries the vote". In view of this, based on chronological evidence about the various manuscripts, the document p[46] (dating around AD 200) containing Julia (*Ioulian)* was preferred. The simple reason for doing this was that the next closest document to this p[46] was dated 4th century AD. As a result, we concluded that the name in the text is Julia (*Ioulian*). However, it was changed at a later date to a name looking like a masculine one (*Iounian*) by someone obsessed with patriarchal logic. Whatever the case maybe, whether one takes Junia or Julia, the person mentioned in Rom 16,7 is a *woman*. This leaves us with the strongest possibility of *a woman apostle* in Pauline Christianity, thereby producing more evidence of equality between man and woman in the Pauline churches.

The *third chapter* dealt with the question of women and the prophetic ministry in the early church. We noted that this ministry was never a one-gender affair, unlike the priesthood which was exclusively reserved for men. Hence, notable women like Miriam and Deborah were prophetesses in the Old Testament. And Anna was also a prophetess in the New Testament. As we also saw, both Paul and the apostolic church in Acts permitted the ministry of prophetesses without any reservation

In the course of this chapter we made a striking discovery from the text of *Didache* where the author advised the community involved, saying, "give these first fruits to the prophets. For they are your high priests". In view of this link between prophecy and priesthood in the 2nd century, we argued that a distinctive Christian priesthood had not yet developed at this time. This fitted into our assertion that the priesthood is the product of church history and tradition.

However, the main argument here was that if women were already prophets and the *Didache* says that prophets are your priests, then women too were priests based on the idea of the priesthood of the time. And if *Didache* excluded them, this would be an obvious deviation from the apostolic practice, as shown by Paul in 1Cor 11,5. So we concluded that the exclusion of women from ordination or leadership ministry in the church is man-made and not from God.

Finally, in this chapter, the prophetic ministry of Jesus was considered. Our insistence here was that the Jesus of Nazareth *was not a priest*. As we showed, the main reason for this is that his contemporaries knew him as a prophet, including his disciples. Of course, he saw himself also as a prophet. All his activities were prophetic and his messianic agenda was also a prophetic one.

On the contrary, he was never seen performing any cultic or priestly action. He had even a *questionable* relationship with the temple of the day. This favors the ministry of women in the church, since Jesus did not propose an exclusive male paradigm as a standard for ministry in the church. He used something that is elastic enough to accommodate both men and women. Hence, the prophetic ministry favors the ministry of women in the church today.

This led us to the *fourth chapter* where the controversial text of 1Cor 14,33b-35 was critically analyzed. Here, we went on the defensive due to the dilemma that this text posed for our study of Paul and the ministry of women in the church today. As we saw, the text unambiguously imposed a ministry ban on women. In view of this, a question arose as to whether this is *authentically* a Pauline text or not. This question arose because of discrepancies in the manuscript transmission. In order to answer this question our analysis here was detailed and thorough. Examining different manuscripts we saw that there was no consensus as to what to do with this particular text, as early as the history of textual transmission of the New Testament. Accordingly, different scribes behaved differently in relation to the text in question. While some placed it at the margin, others left it were it is now, and others moved it to the end of 1Cor 14. This was the first key needed to unlock the problem posed by the authorship of the text.

Further analysis was made in order to come to a firm conclusion. In this place, 1Cor 14,33b-35 was compared with the text of 1Tim 2,11-15. The similarities were striking, suggesting an affinity between the two. Then the internal evidence was considered. The text was found to be "out of alignment" when it is examined in the context of the charismatic discussion going on in 1Cor 14.

In view of all the pieces of evidence, we concluded that *the text is not Pauline*. It belongs to the pastorals or a similar tradition of the New Testament household codes. We, then, cautioned against using it in the name of Paul to whip women or to deny them leaderships rights. Finally, we pointed out that this text frivolously promotes gender profiling. In view of this, its use should be discouraged since biblical texts have been used in past history in ways that brought despair, sadness and tearful sorrows to humanity.

Then, the *fifth chapter* was considered dealing with the gospels and the ministry of women. Here, we tried to show, against the position of Roman Catholicism on the ministry of women in the church today, that the gospels support ministry roles for women. In this regard, we noted that women were in fact the real followers of Christ in the gospel traditions. They were the ones who followed him till death. They proved to be the disciples of the cross. On the other hand, the gospel accounts tell us that all the men fled during the passion events. Only the women followed him at this crucial moment. They walked the *via crucis* (way of the cross) with their Lord and master, who even advised them to weep for him no more, but for their children.

Next, we also noted that women were the first commissioned evangelists, in post-resurrection Christianity, sent with a *mandate* to announce to "the eleven" and the other disciples the good news of the resurrection. If the risen Lord made them the "preachers of preachers"- the "evangelists of evangelists", how could this constitute an argument against their ministry in ordained capacity, or their roles as pastors and church leaders, we asked. Finally, we cautioned against making the priesthood *the sacrament of unequal opportunity*

At this point, a measured attention was given to the *sixth chapter* dealing with Roman Catholicism and the ministry of women today. Here, we saw that the practice of this denomination, on the question of the ordination of women and ritual leadership roles for them, represents the repudiated tradition of 1Cor 14,33b-35. In view of this, we pointed out that to deny women priestly ordination is to ostracize them. As was indicated, *this is wrong*. It is a standard case of gender profiling in the Christian church by an all-powerful male clergy. Instead of ordination, subordination is offered to women. Here, we showed that evidence from both Paul and the apostolic church is incompatible with this practice. Hence, we pointed out that leadership was also a gift of the Spirit and women as prophets participated in it. Their role in the "house churches" helped to underline this point.

In the course of this study, we strongly maintained that the arguments on which the Roman Catholic decision is based are shaky and faulty. In view of this, we cautioned against decreeing people into silence, or using church might to achieve this. As we indicated, if this approach succeeded in the past, it will not succeed in this 21st century. Times have changed. Only dialogue can be of use now, but not dialogue for its sake. The age of monologue called teaching by *ex cathedra* is over. Past dogmas are now resting in libraries and archives of history. Many no longer pay attention to most of them. It does not pay to teaching for its sake.

In this regard, we noted that "infallible" authorities have shown themselves to be *fallible* in the past, even when they tried to explain it away in order to maintain the logic of their professed infallibility. In this place, the brutal inquisition and the so-called "holy crusades" were among the things recalled from the history books to underline this point. Hence, we warned against repeating past mistakes of church history in new forms.

The *seventh chapter* was a follow-up discussion to the Catholic understanding of ordination. This dealt with the issue of the Anglican ordination of women. This bold and courageous step was highly commended in this work. The other churches are called upon to imitate it. The weight of biblical evidence is on the part of the Anglican Church on this point. Women cannot be seen to demean the priestly ministry or senior ministry positions in the church. Instead, they make it more meaningful.

The attitude of Catholicism and Anglicanism led us to consider in details the perspectives of Jesus on the priesthood of his day in *chapter eight*. Our point of departure was the text of Luke 10, dealing with the loving Samaritan. The involvement of the priestly establishment in the story made it an attractive one for the study. Here, the concept of the purity was examined in relation to the priesthood of the day. One striking thing was that the strict nature of the purity and dietary laws would have inhibited Jesus from achieving the things he did. Second, the idea of a priestly consecration would have dedicated Jesus exclusively to the cult. Consequently, this would have separated him from the people. But this would have run against the ministry of Jesus in the New Testament. Further, the tension between Jesus and the priests was examined. The final conclusion reached here is that Jesus could not have established this hostile priesthood for his disciples. Also, his models of ministry, like the pastor-shepherd, are anything but priestly. This leaves us with one result: That the priesthood is a post-Jesus development. In which case, one cannot Jesus as a basis for not ordaining women priests.

Finally, the *last chapter* was considered. This deals with the struggle for emancipation in the secular world. Here, we saw that women were subordinated also at the political level. However, the women took their destiny in their own hands and won the right to vote for themselves both in Britain and America. We urged the Christian women to emulate the good example of the women who led the *Protest Movement* of the 19th century and beyond.

General Conclusions

At the beginning of this work, we set out to find out the relationship between gender and ministry in the New Testament and the church today. In the course of our study, we saw that Pauline Christianity did not tolerate gender discrimination. The apostolic church also maintained this principle since women were leaders in its house churches. If the church was first of all a "house church" and women were leaders in this church, why should they be excluded from leadership roles in the church today? As we saw in our study, Roman Catholicism ignored this question, while the Anglican Communion took it seriously and opened up all the ministry doors to women in its church. Here, they followed the non-discriminatory practice of the early church, as seen in Paul, the gospels and the apostolic church.

It is true that whenever the issue of the ordination of women is raised, it is also about the ability of women to be Christian leaders, to be power brokers in the church. However, as we saw during our study, this was not a problem in Pauline Christianity which guaranteed equality for all Christians, irrespective of gender or race. In view of this, the present situation in which women are prevented from playing certain ministry roles in some of the churches creates and leaves firmly in place two unequal classes, the ruler (men) and the ruled (women). This is what has provoked the protests led by the women liberation movement. The 21st century Christians must address this legitimate grudge. There is no need calling names or issuing intimidating church documents to gag or to muzzle in order to prevent the truth from being heard. *The time has come to confront the past and rectify accumulated centuries of anomalies against the women.*

Indeed, the present alienating status quo needs a radical rethinking in this third millennium of Christianity. This sense of urgency is necessitated by the fact that a church that supports human rights should not be insulated from these same human rights. Their violations in the name of God are neither theologically excusable nor are they to be acts worth pardoning or condoning in this third millennium of the Christian religion. *Pauline Christianity and the practice of most of the early Christians motivate us today to struggle for equal rights and equal opportunity in the church today.* It obliges us to fight for the liberation of women and all peoples in the world. Above all, it teaches us that the movement to liberate women is a *freedom movement.* In other words, those who fight for this equality are "freedom fighters", though male bigotry sometimes terms them "renegades". Indeed, these people are the "Salvation Army" of women. In this way, the women liberation movement becomes also a *movement for the emancipation of women.* To be against this is to be against the freedom, which Christ has won for all us.

Further, in the course of our inquiry, we saw that the allocation of ecclesiastical roles on the exclusive basis of gender was not a feature of Pauline Christianity. Paul's insistence on the charismatic nature of his Christianity reinforces this position. In this community, both men and women had equal opportunity to be prophets, deacons and apostles. Above all, they served also as the *fellow workers of Paul.* There was no obvious sexual discrimination. Indeed, we saw a real quest to create a truly egalitarian Christian society. Hence, Paul becomes the author of equity and fairness in Christianity. He stands for justice for all, irrespective of gender.

As we prepare to conclude this work, it is important to underline one more thing which I consider crucial. The struggle for the liberation of women should not in any way create "gender strife" between the sexes. It is not about gender warfare, though there is a *gender struggle* going on. Otherwise, it would have been pointless writing this book. Also it is not a battle of women versus men, as if they were two opposing armies facing each other in the war front. *This book is against every form of injustice, be it against the woman or against the man.* Both belong to the οἰκείος της πίστεως (*oikeíos tês písteôs*) *household of faith* (cf. Gal 6,10). Mutual respect should always be kept in mind. *It is also immoral to replace one form of discrimination with another.*

The stand taken in this book is that the relationship between man and woman should be that of *equals*. But this equality should be based on mutual tolerance between the sexes. Therefore, a universal brotherhood or sisterhood is advocated in this work. Christianity belongs to all Christians. It is our duty to build it up. The battle of the sexes in Christianity will not advance the Christian faith in a world that is increasingly becoming irreligious and over-secularized. It is important not to become lawless Christians, taking the laws into our hands. Respect for the religious authorities of Christianity is also called for in this work. However, if respect is demanded, it should also be given. This should be a two-way traffic.

Indeed, the struggle continues for we are no longer in an age when the opinion of one man becomes universalized and imposed as the *will of God*. No amount of decrees or doctrinal intimidation can deter the 21st century man or woman from the path of truth. In the past, only the clergy monopolized theological education. This is no longer the case today because the study of theology has ceased to be a clerical prerogative. Even some non-clerics are today more theologically informed than many pastors.

Since no one has the monopoly of the Spirit of God, no one also has the monopoly of truth. It is mere arrogance to think that one possesses this. *Every act of injustice against women is immoral and must be rectified, no matter who is doing it, and no matter in whose name it is being carried out.* It is all in vain trying to use the name of God or his Holy Scripture to cover up our discriminatory practices against women in our present day church. *We may have succeeded for a long time but we will not succeed forever.* Now is the time to put an end to it. Christianity is neither a "one-man show" nor a gender affair. In other words, different people have different assignments, regardless of gender. Hence, Paul says, "for just as the body is one and has many members, and all the members of the body, though many, are one body, so it is with Christ" (1Cor 12,12). All hands must now be on deck to realize this important objective.

Even the quarreling Corinthians seem to be better than we are today because their dispute was not gender-based. The gender question was never raised in this church. It never preoccupied Corinthian Christians to ask their master Paul whether some of the charisms should be reserved only for the male members of their church community or not. Since the equality of the sexes was recognized and upheld, this question was irrelevant. The same advice, which Paul gave to the competing Corinthians, he gives us today in 1Cor 14,1: "Be eager in pursuit of love." This should be the motto of 21st century Christianity. There should be a "hot pursuit" of love. If we do this, it will help to heal the wounds caused by centuries of divisions among Christians. Besides, it will humble us to say to women: *nostra culpa* (it is our fault). *We owe them this unqualified apology.* This is part of what true *agapê* is all about. Finally, we should resolve not to discriminate against them any more in any shape or form and under whatever pretext, be it secular or religious.

In the light of the acts of Paul we are called upon in this third millennium to rethink our gender-profiling attitude towards women in the church and in our world today. If early Pauline Christianity preached and practiced equality in the church under the slogan-*no male, no female*-this means that it is not impossible to do the same in this 21st century. Now is the time to begin this. Therefore, this work is a call to all Christians to help fight inequality wherever it exists. It is a call to all the Christian churches to eschew pride and open their topmost hierarchy to women. To do this is not capitulation but heroic and historic. In this regard, the example of the Anglican Church should be imitated by all.

With this final remarks this work on *Gender and Ministry in early Christianity and the Church today* is now concluded. However, the struggle continues till equality is achieved between man woman both in the church and in our world. Our ultimate goal is the full and unhindered participation of women in the ministry of the churches. May they no longer be discriminated against or profiled any more in the churches or by any government in the world, in the mighty Name of Jesus the Lord we pray, Amen!

Endnotes

[1] This work presupposes the seven-letter theory of Paul in which seven out of the thirteen letters ascribed to him are accepted to be indisputably Pauline, while the remaining six are taken to be secondary Pauline literature. With this in mind, in this table, we have used asterisk (*) to indicate deutero-Pauline occurrences.

[2] W. H., Ollrog, *Paulus und seine Mitarbeiter*, Neunkirchen-Vluyn, 1979; E. E. Ellis, "Paul and his Co-Workers," NTS 17, 1970-71, 437-452; B. Witherington, *Women in the Earliest Churches*, 104-117 (this is specifically on Paul's coworkers); Bertram, "συνεργός," TDNT VII, 871-876.

[3] These are Ephesians, Colossians, Titus, 1Timothy and 1Peter.

[4] Bertram, "συνεργός," Theological Dictionary of the New Testament VII, 871. Henceforth, cited as TDNT in the work.

[5] Bertram, "συνεργός", TDNT VII, 874.

[6] Perhaps, this Prisca is also the woman missionary known to Luke as Priscillia (Acts 18,2).

[7] As Acts 18,2 tells us that this Aquila was the husband of Prisca. He was a Jew from Pontus. Later he converted to Christianity and played great missionary roles together with the wife Prisca.

[8] P. Lampe, "Prisca", in: *The Anchor Bible*, Volume 5, 467.

[9] P. Lampe, "Prisca", in: *The Anchor Bible*, Volume 5, 467.

[10] P. Lampe, "Prisca", in: *The Anchor Bible*, Volume 5, 467.

[11] The idea of building big churches and cathedrals began to take place in the 4th century Byzantine Empire under the emperor Constantine the Great.

[12] P. Lampe, "Prisca", in: *The Anchor Bible*, Volume 5, 468.

[13] P. Lampe, "Prisca", in: *The Anchor Bible*, Volume 5, 468.

[14] The text in question says: "After this he [Paul] left Athens and went to Corinth. 2 And he found a Jew named Aquila, a native of Pontus, lately come from Italy with his wife Priscilla, because Claudius had commanded all the

Jews to leave Rome. And he went to see them; 3 and because he was of the same trade he stayed with them, and they worked, for by trade they were tent-makers " (Acts 18,1-3).

[15] The text reads: "Greet Prisca and Aquila, and the household of Onesipho-rus" (2Tim 4,19).

[16] B. Byrne, *Paul and the Christian Woman*, Homebush 1988, 73.

[17] Hauch, "κοπιάω", TDNT III, 828.

[18] Hauch, "κοπιάω", TDNT III, 829.

[19] See: V. Abrahamsen, "Women at Philippi: The Pagan and Christian Evidence," *Journal of Feminist Studies in Religion* 3 (Fall 1987) 17-30.

[20] Greek texts used in this work are from *The Greek New Testament*, edited by, K. Aland, M. Black, C. M. Martini, B. M. Metzger and A. Wikgren, third edition (corrected).

[21] William F. Arndt & F. Wilbur Gingrich, *A Greek-English Lexicon of the New Testament and other early Christian Literature*, Chicago: The University of Chicago Press, second edition, 1979, p.77. Henceforth, cited only as "Arndt & Gingrich, *Lexicon*" in this work.

[22] The text reads: "Only, conduct yourselves in a way worthy of the gospel of Christ, so that, whether I come and see you or am absent, I may hear news of you, that you are standing firm in one spirit, with one mind struggling together [*synathlountes*] for the faith of the gospel" (NAB: Phil 1,27).

[23] Henry George Liddell & Robert Scott, *A Greek-English Lexicon*, revised and augmented by Henry Stuart Jones, Oxford: The Clarendon Press, repr. 1977, p.34. Henceforth, cited only as "Liddell & Scott, *Lexicon*" in this work.

[24] We can see that the English words *athlete* and *athletic* are derived from this group of words.

[25] Liddell-Scott, *Lexicon*, 34.

[26] See, for instance, "The Martyrdom of Saint Polycarp", 18,3.

[27] Liddell & Scott, *Lexicon*, 34.

[28] Letter of Ignatius to Polycarp 3,1-2. E-Text from "Welcome to the Catholic Church" on CD Rom by Harmony Media Inc., Oregon.

[29] Liddell & Scott, *Lexicon*, 34.

[30] Stauffer, "ἀθλέω-συναθλέω", TDNT I, 167.

[31] Stauffer, "ἀθλέω-συναθλέω", TDNT I, 167.

[32] Ignatius, "Letter to Polycarp", 1,3. E-Text from „Welcome to the Catholic Church.

[33] Ignatius, "Letter to Polycarp", 2,3. E-Text from „Welcome to the Catholic Church.

[34] Stauffer, "ἀθλέω-συναθλέω", TDNT I, 167.

[35] Arndt & Gingrich, *Lexicon*, 783.

[36] See: Amadi-Azuogu, C.A., *Biblical Exegesis and Inculturation*, 317-321; Scott, Hafemann, *Suffering and Ministry in the Spirit: Paul's Defense of His Ministry in II Corinthians 2:14-3,3*, Eerdmans, 1990.

[37] This text reads: "So also our beloved brother Paul wrote to you according to the wisdom given him, speaking of this as he does in all his letters. There are

some things in them hard to understand which the ignorant and unstable twist to their own destruction, as they do the other scriptures" (2Pet 3,15b-16).

[38] I wish to point out here, as well, that there are many honest pastors and ministers of the gospel who are really ministering to Christ's people. The fact that there are misguided, disgruntled and misdirected pastors and preachers does not mean that every pastor or minister is bad. Far be it! Indeed, there are *model pastors and preachers*, worth-imitating. So my critique is not just a blanket one. I respect these and other conscientious pastors and ministers of the gospel, who are laboring, like Paul and his ministers did. I recognize, in as much as there are *fake pastors* with *bogus ministry*, that there are also *true ones*.

[39] This is what fires up the so-called "prosperity gospel", which I call the "lotto gospel". Hence, we have the "name it and claim it" movement. Here, faith is reduced to mere quest for the material. God's blessing is defined only in terms of the material. Hence, spirituality becomes materialism and theology is anthropologized.

[40] In the true sense of the Greek word *ekklesia* for church, these are not really churches. They are *Christian fellowships* – a gathering of a group of Christians to fellowship with one another in the name of Christ. The real church is an institution, with defined structures. *It is not privately owned*, as it is the case with the "churches" in question, functioning more like a *private enterprise*. In many of the cases, the death or disengagement of the pastor means the end of the "church". Unlike the situation in a real church, there is no continuity. These churches have the life span comparable to that of a mushroom. Hence, they are called the "mushroom churches". On the other hand, in a real church, no one person is indispensable. Here, continuity is an essential hallmark. Besides, no person's death spells doom for the church in question. With or without the pastor of such a church, life continues in the church community.

[41] This is one of the differences between Jewish Christianity and Hellenistic Christianity. On the one hand, Jewish Christianity linked apostleship to the Palestinian twelve, who were all males. On the other hand, Hellenistic Christianity recognized it as a charismatic gift not reserved for any particular person or group in the community. This Hellenistic Christian approach opened the possibility of being apostle to everybody, irrespective of gender.

[42] The following is recommended for further reading. R. E. Brown, "The Twelve and the Apostolate", in: *The New Jerome Biblical Commentary*, edited by R. E. Brown, J. A. Fitzmyer and R. E. Murphy, New Jersey, 1990, 1377-1381; F. H. Agnew, "On the origin of the term *apostolos*", CBQ 38, 1976, 49-53; F. H. Agnew, "The origin of the NT apostle-concept", JBL 105, 1986,75-96; R. D. Culver, "Apostles and the apostolate in the New Testament", Bsac 134, 1977, 131-143; F. Hahn, "Der Apostolat in Urchristentum", KD 20, 1974, 56-77; E. Käsemann, "Die Legitimität des Apostels", *Zeitschrift für die Neutestamentliche Wissenschaft* 41, 1942,33-71; K. Kertelge, "Das Apos-

telamt des Paulus", BZ 14, 1970, 161-181; W. Schmithals, *The office of apostle in the early church*, Nashville, 1969.

[43] To translate *apóstolos* as "apostle" (or in Latin as *apostolus*) is like rendering the Greek *parakletos* as "Paraclete", which says almost nothing of the word translated. In both cases, what we have is closer to a transliteration.

[44] Rengstorf, "ἀπόστολος", TDNT I, 407.

[45] Rengstorf, "ἀπόστολος", TDNT I, 413.

[46] Josephus, *Jewish Antiquities*, 17, 300.

[47] This Greek phrase, *hapax legomenon*, is a technical term, which literally means "reading once". In biblical studies, it is used to refer to instances where a word or something occurred *only once*.

[48] The Hebrew transliterations in this book are based on Thomas Lambdin's *Introduction to Biblical Hebrew*, London: Darton, Longman and Todd, 1971, repr. 1980.

[49] The reader may not know that there are many manuscripts of the *Greek New Testament* of the Bible. Among these are the *four major ones* called the *uncials*. The *Codex Vaticanus* is one of them. It contains the entire New Testament, unlike some of the other manuscripts, which do not. It is housed in the Vatican library in Rome. This is one of the most important manuscripts in the study of the New Testament. It is taken to be a highly authoritative manuscript, *being the earliest of all the manuscripts*. It dates 4th century B.C.

[50] The *Codex Alexandrinus* is also one of the four major manuscripts of the New Testament. Like the other uncials or major manuscripts, it contains the whole of the New Testament. It dates 5th century and is housed in London.

[51] Cf. Rengstorf, TDNT I, 413.

[52] F. Brown, S. R. Driver & C. A. Briggs, *Hebrew and English Lexicon of the Old Testament*, Oxford: translated by E. Robinson, Clarendom Press, repr. 1977, p. 1018. **Henceforth, cited as BDB.**

[53] Rengstorf, "ἀπόστολος", TDNT I, 416.

[54] Rengstorf, "ἀπόστολος", TDNT I, 417.

[55] Rengstorf, "ἀπόστολος", TDNT I, 418.

[56] Rengstorf, "ἀπόστολος", TDNT I, 422.

[57] Rengstorf, "ἀπόστολος", TDNT I, 422.

[58] See: J. A. Fitzmyer, "The Letter To The Romans", in: *The New Jerome Biblical Commentary*, edited by R. E. Brown, J. A. Fitzmyer and R. E. Murphy, New Jersey, 1990, 868.

[59] I am aware of the fact that the *Revised Standard Version* of the Bible translated this same word as *messengers*. Though this is also legitimate, yet I do not find any reason to follow it since it simply covers the problem. The RSV's translation (messenger) explains the role of these apostles in 2Cor 8,23.

[60] Didache xi, in: *The Early Christian Fathers: A Selection Of The Fathers From St. Clement Of Rome To St. Athanasius*, trasl. by H. Bettenson, London 1969, 51.

[61] Craig, S Keener, *Paul, Women & Wives*, 242.

[62] This follows also the pattern in Rom 16.3:᾽Ασπάσασθε Πρίσκαν καὶ᾽Α-κύλαν.

[63] The interested reader wishing to know more about this textual problem can see: J. A. Fitzmyer, "The Letter to the Romans", in: *The New Jerome Biblical Commentary*, edited by R. E. Brown, J. A. Fitzmyer and R. E. Murphy, New Jersey, 1990, 831 §9-10.

[64] It occurred only once.

[65] The text reads: "And I tell you, you are Peter, and on this rock I will build my church, and the powers of death shall not prevail against it. 19 I will give you the keys of the kingdom of heaven, and whatever you bound on earth and shall be bound in heaven, and whatever you loose in heaven shall be loosed in heaven."

[66] These translations of the New Testament have Junias: ASV, DBY, ICB, NASB NASU RSV YLT and JB.

[67] These translations have Junia: BBE, KJV, NKJV, NRSV and WEX.

[68] J. A. Fitzmyer, "The Letter To The Romans", in: *The New Jerome Biblical Commentary*, edited by R. E. Brown, J. A. Fitzmyer and R. E. Murphy, New Jersey, 1990, 868.

[69] Keener, Craig S., *Paul, Wives and Wives*, p.241.

[70] James D. G. Dunn, *Romans 9-16*, Word Biblical Commentary, volume 38B, Texas, 1988, 894.

[71] James D. G. Dunn, *Romans 9-16*, 894.

[72] Craig, S Keener, "Women in Ministry", in Beck, James R. and Blomberg, Craig L. (eds.), *Two Views on Women in Ministry*, p.35.

[73] Keener, Craig S., *Paul, Wives and Wives*, p.242; R. R. Schulz, "Romans 16,7: Junia or Junias?" *Expository Times* 108-110; V. Fabrega, "War Junia(s), der hervorrangede Apostel (Rom 16,7) eine Frau?" *Jahrbuch für Antike und Christentum* 27-28 (1984-85) 47-64; Spencer, Aida Besancon, *Beyond the Curse: Women Called to Ministry*, p. 101.

[74] Keener, Craig S., *Paul, Wives and Wives*, p.242.

[75] James D. G. Dunn, *Romans 9-16*, 894.

[76] James D. G. Dunn, *Romans 9-16*, 894.

[77] James D. G. Dunn, *Romans 9-16*, 894.

[78] Brooten, Bernadette. "Junia . . . Outstanding among the Apostles (Rom 16.7)." In *Women Priests: A Catholic Commentary on the Vatican Declaration* (ed. Leonard Swidler and Arlene Swidler; New York: Paulist, 1977) 141-144.

[79] David E. Aune, *Revelation 1-5*, Word Biblical Commentary, volume 52, Texas, 1977, 203.

[80] Chrysostom, Homily on Romans 16, in Philip Schaff, ed, *A Select Library of the Nicene and Post-Nicene Fathers of the Christian Church*, vol. II. Grand Rapids: Wm. B. Eerdmans Pub. Co., 1956, p. 555.

[81] John Chrysostom, *On The Epistle To The Romans*, Homily XXXI. Rom 16,7.

[82] R. E. Brown, "The Twelve and the Apostolate", in: *The New Jerome Biblical Commentary*, edited by R. E. Brown, J. A. Fitzmyer and R. E. Murphy, New Jersey, 1990, 1381.

[83] R. E. Brown, "The Twelve and the Apostolate", in: *The New Jerome Biblical Commentary*, edited by R. E. Brown, J. A. Fitzmyer and R. E. Murphy, New Jersey, 1990, 1381.

[84] J. A. Fitzmyer, "The Letter To The Romans", 868.

[85] James D. G. Dunn, *Romans 9-16*, 894.

[86] Craig S. Keener, *Paul, Women & Wives*, p.242.

[87] The text reads: "And when Jesus was come into Peter's house, he saw his wife's mother laid, and sick of a fever" (KJV: Matt 8,14).

[88] The relevant text says: "A bishop then must be blameless, the husband of one wife, vigilant, sober, of good behaviour, given to hospitality, apt to teach" (KJV:1Tim 3,2).

[89] Bernadette Brooten, *Junia. . .Outstanding among the Apostles*, 141.

[90] Bernadette Brooten, "*Junia. . . Outstanding among the Apostles*" 142.

[91] This information is based on *The Greek New Testament*, edited by, K. Aland, M. Black, C. M. Martini, B. M. Metzger and A. Wikgren, third edition (corrected).

[92] The attention of the reader is also drawn to the fact that there is also another manuscript designated as D (05), which is properly called the codex Bezae. This document contains only the gospels and Acts. It is not the manuscript in question here.

[93] There is also G (011) in London and Cambridge (also IX century) . It contains only the gospels.

[94] These uncials are the codex Sinaiticus (א) in London, the codex Alexandrianus (A) in London, the codex Vaticanus (B) in Rome and the codex Ephraemi (C) in Paris.

[95] This information is based on *The Greek New Testament*, edited by, K. Aland, M. Black, C. M. Martini, B. M. Metzger and A. Wikgren, third edition (corrected).

[96] For a similar position, see: B. Byrne, *Paul And The Christian Woman*, 72.

[97] It has to be noted here that the English word *prophet* is the anglicized form of the Greek *prophêtes*.

[98] Friedrich, "προφετεύω", TDNT VI, 829.

[99] Krämer, "προφήτης", TDNT VI, 783.

[100] Friedrich, "προφετεύω", TDNT VI, 829.

[101] Friedrich, "προφετεύω", TDNT VI, 829.

[102] Friedrich, "προφετεύω", TDNT VI, 851.

[103] Liddell & Scott, *Lexicon*, 1539.

[104] Krämer, "προφήτης", TDNT VI, 783.

[105] Krämer, "προφήτης", TDNT VI, 783.

[106] Rengstorf, "ἀπόστολος", TDNT I, 409.

[107] Friedrich, "προφετεύω", TDNT VI, 829.

[108] Friedrich, "προφετεύω", TDNT VI, 829.

[109] Krämer, "προφήτης", TDNT VI, 791.

[110] *Letters of Jerome, Letters LII-LV*, Letter to Furia, LIV, 17. Also, Augustine, *City of God*, chapter 15.

[111] At some point in the history of the Old Testament, it seems that the prophets were even above the priests. This helps to explain why they could openly criticize the priests. An example of this can be seen in the encounter between Amos and the priest Amazia (Amos 7,14).

[112] *Letters of Jerome, Letters LII-LV*, Letter to Furia, LIV, 16. E-Text from: The Early Church Fathers Series in WinHelp Format *A 37-volume electronic collection of writings from the first 800 years of the Church* programmed in WinHelp by: Maged Nabih Kamel, http://www.geocities.com/Athens/7084. Converted to HTML Help format by Graham Ranson. © 1996 Dr. Maged N Kamel Boulos. This special edition is freeware and the *plain* text of *The writings of Early Church Fathers* is in the *public domain*. Elsewhere, in this work, this source will only be cited as "The Early Church Fathers in WinHelp Format". See: http: //www.Zeitun-eg.org.

[113] Eusebius, *Ecclesiastical History*, Book III, XXXI. E-Text from "The Early Church Fathers in WinHelp Format".

[114] Eusebius, *Ecclesiastical History*, Book V, XVIII,3. E-Text from "The Early Church Fathers in WinHelp Format".

[115] Among other instances, see *Apostolic Constitutions*, Book V, chapter VII; Augustine, *City of God*, Bk I, chapter LII.

[116] Abraham J. Heschel, *The Prophets*, New York and Evanston: Harper and Row, Publishers, 1962, p. 10.

[117] Abraham J. Heschel, *The Prophets*, 10.

[118] The relevant text says: "Now Pashur the son of Immer the priest, who was also chief governor in the house of the Lord, heard that Jeremiah prophesied these things. Then Pashur smote Jeremiah the prophet, and put him in the stocks that were in the high gate of Benjamin, which was by the house of the Lord" (KJV: Jer 20,1-2).

[119] One known example of this is the following text: "Then said they, Come and let us devise devices against Jeremiah; for the law shall not perish from the priest, nor counsel from the wise, nor the word from the prophet. Come, and let us smite him with the tongue, and let us not give heed to any of his words" (KJV: Jer 18,18).

[120] These subordination texts simply subjugate the woman to the man. Hence, in these texts, the woman is commanded to be submissive to the man (see: Eph 5,21-24 and Col 3,18). The Ephesian community even demanded this submissiveness to be in all things, when it emphatically said: Eph:5:24: "Therefore as the church is subject unto Christ, so let the wives be to their own husbands in every thing" (KJV: Eph 5,24).

[121] Didache, 13,1-7. E-Text from "Welcome to the Catholic Church" on CD Rom by Harmony Media Inc., Oregon.

[122] On this see the discussion of the *house churches* above in chapter one. There we showed that even women presided over the Eucharist, contrary to the thinking of later Roman Catholicism.

[123] Didache, 15,1. E-Text from "Welcome to the Catholic Church"

[124] This word *androcracy* is a compound word coined from two Greek words, *anêr* (*andros*) = man and *kratein* = to rule. This combination gives us a "rule by men".

[125] Chapter 8 tries to put these pieces together. There, the argument against a Christian priesthood will become more pointed and sharper.

[126] These are some of the texts: Exo 23,19; 34,26: Lev 2,12.14; 23,17.20: Neh 10, 32-39.

[127] The text says: "And the high places of Isaac shall be desolate, and the sanctuaries of Israel shall be laid waste; and I will rise against the house of Jeroboam with the sword" (KJV: Am 7,9).

[128] This text reads: To what purpose is the multitude of your sacrifices unto me? saith the Lord: I am full of the burnt offerings of rams, and the fat of fed beasts; and *I delight not in the blood of bullocks, or of lambs, or of he goats.* [12] When ye come to appear before me, who hath required this at your hand, to tread my courts? [13] Bring no more vain oblations; incense is an abomination unto me; the new moons and sabbaths, the calling of assemblies, I cannot away with; it is iniquity, even the solemn meeting. [14] Your new moons and your appointed feasts my soul hateth: they are a trouble unto me; I am weary to bear them. [15] And when ye spread forth your hands, I will hide mine eyes from you: yea, when ye make many prayers, I will not hear: your hands are full of blood. [16] Wash you, make you clean; put away the evil of your doings from before mine eyes; cease to do evil; [17] Learn to do well; seek judgment, relieve the oppressed, judge the fatherless, plead for the widow" (KJV: Isaiah 1,11-17). See also Isaiah 58.

[129] Didache, 15,1-2. E-Text from "Welcome to the Catholic Church"

[130] *Eisegesis* is a type of subjective hermeneutics where the interpreter approaches the sacred text with preconditions and preconceived ideas. Sometimes, the interpreter superimposes his or her own ideas to enable the text to say what the one has in mind or would want it to say.

[131] On the other hand, *exegesis* is objective hermeneutics where the interpreter approaches the sacred text with a "wanting to know" attitude. The individual submits oneself to one's findings. Here, there are no pre-conditions and no preconceived ideas. Even if there is, it is not allowed to determine the outcome of the investigation. The individual resigns oneself to one's exegetical findings or conclusions.

[132] If Hebrews declared Jesus a priest, nothing suggests that a similar thing was said of the disciples of Jesus.

[133] The *institution narratives* refer to those texts in which Jesus instituted the Eucharist *via* the Last Supper.

[134] This draws our attention to the charism of *kybernêsis* (1Cor 12,28) by which people became leaders in the charismatic community. Obviously proph-

ets and prophetesses enjoyed this particular charism too. However, things began to change with the institutionalization and politicization of Christianity beginning with the post New Testament Christianity and the emperor Constantine.

[135] In this regard, we have already seen that the Old Testament recognized Miriam and the others as prophetesses, while the New Testament recognized Anna, the four daughters of Philip and the unnamed prophetesses of the Pauline community (cf. 1Cor 11,5).

[136] Something similar takes place also in the narrative of the "Loving Samaritan" in Luke 10,29-37. Here, neither the priest, nor the Levite was praised in the story. The person chosen, as model for the neighbor, was the Samaritan who was even considered to be outside the covenant society by the orthodox Jewish mentality of the time. As we can see, this is by no means a priestly narrative. Instead, *it is an anti-priestly story.* Chapter 8 will devote more time to this.

[137] This is a strong indication that the Old Testament world believed in the doctrine of *reincarnation,* a belief, which is also very strong among the contemporary Igbos of Eastern Nigeria in Africa.

[138] See: Amadi-Azuogu, C. A., *Biblical Exegesis and Inculturation,* 75-77.

[139] The relevant text reads: "[1]The Spirit of the Lord GOD is upon me, because the LORD has anointed me to bring good tidings to the afflicted; he has sent me to bind up the brokenhearted, to proclaim liberty to the captives, and the opening of the prison to those who are bound; [2] to proclaim the year of the LORD's favor, and the day of vengeance of our God; to comfort all who mourn;" (Isaiah 61,1-2).

[140] Here, Paul continues with this puzzle and makes the body of the Christian the temple of the Holy Spirit (1Cor 3,16-17 and 6,19).

[141] These authors, among others, support this view: Meeks, Wayne A., "The Image of the Androgyne: Some Uses of a Symbol in Earliest Christianity," *History of Religions* 13 (1974) 203-204; Meeks, Wayne A., *The First Urban Christians: The Social World of the Apostle Paul,* New Haven: Yale University, 1983, 125; H. Conzelmann, *1 Corinthians A Commentary on the First Epistle to the Corinthians,* Transl. by James W. Leitch, Hermeneia Commentaries, Philadelphia: Fortress, 1975, 246; Scroggs, R., "Paul and the eschatological woman, *Journal of the American Academy of Religion* 40 (1972) 284.

[142] Craig S. Keener, *Paul, Wives and Wives: Marriage and Women's Ministry in the Letters of Paul,* Peabody, Massachusetts: Hendrickson Publishers, 1992, fifth printing, 2001, p. 75.

[143] My emphasis on theological education does not in any way diminish the role and importance of the Holy Spirit in the church. Even with all the theological know how in the world, without the Holy Spirit, our preaching and theologizing will be empty. In this regard, I have seen a *seven-year-old* minister preaching the gospel of salvation. Even without formal theological education this child was able to be effective in the ministry. But this exception does not make the theological seminaries, faculties and schools irrelevant. This has

to be emphasized because without formal education the bible could not have been translated in the first place.

[144] In my recent discussions with Prof. Craig Keener he also told me that he is now moving towards this interpolation theory. May be his subsequent publications will reflect this change.

[145] D. G. Horrell, *The Social Ethos of the Corinthian Correspondence: Interests and Ideology from 1Corinthians to 1Clement*, Edinburgh, 1996, 184.

[146] Cf.: W. O., Walker, "The Burden of Proof in Identifying Interpolations in the Pauline Letters," NTS 33, 1987, 610-618. J., Murphy-O'Connor, "Interpolations in 1 Corinthians" CBQ 48, 1986, 81-94.

[147] For some information, see; B. Witherington III, *Women in the Earliest Churches*, New York, 1988, 90-104 (This is on 1Cor 14,33b-36); W. O. Walker, "The Burden of Proof in Identifying Interpolations in the Pauline Letters," NTS 33, 1987, 610-618; B. Byrne, *Paul and the Christian Woman*, 59-65.

[148] See; B. M. Metzger, *Textual Commentary*, 565.

[149] D. G. Horrell, *The Social Ethos of the Corinthian Correspondence: Interests and Ideology from 1Corinthians to 1Clement*, Edinburgh, 1996, 186.

[150] D. G. Horrell, *The Social Ethos of the Corinthian Correspondence*, 194.

[151] I recognize that 1Cor 11,2-16 has its own problems. But this is not the place to go into the discussion involved.

[152] For views maintaining this pseudo-Pauline authorship, see also: B. Byrne, *Paul and the Christian woman*, 62-65.

[153] See, for instance, Elizabeth Shüssler Fiorenza, *In Memory Of Her*, 230-233.

[154] D. G. Horrell, *The Social Ethos of the Corinthian Correspondence*, 1996, 185.

[155] See, Trible, Phyllis, *Texts of Terror: Literary-Feminist Readings of Biblical Narratives*, Philadelphia: Fortress, 1984.

[156] I am aware that there are some scholars who accept these household codes as authentically Pauline. Craig S. Keener is one of them. This position is seen in his book, *Paul, Women & Wives*, Peabody, Massachusetts: Hendrickson Publishers, 1992, fifth printing, 2001. While I recognize that this work is impressive, nevertheless, it seems to me also that Keener was mixing up evidence by assuming that all the thirteen letters in the Pauline tradition belong to him. It would have been better if he argued out this point before proceeding with his assumption. It may be necessary for him to clarify this point in another work. Otherwise, I do not accept that the household codes, which show a post-Pauline situation, are from Paul himself. This is the position in this book.

[157] J. Murphy-O'Connor, "The First Letter To The Corinthians", in: *The New Jerome Biblical Commentary*, edited by R. E. Brown, J. A. Fitzmyer and R. E. Murphy, New Jersey, 1990, 811.

[158] E. E. Ellis, "The sentenced wives of Corinth (1Cor. 14.34-35)", in: New Testament Textual Criticism: Its significance for Exegesis," essays in honor of Bruce Metzger, E. J. Epp and G. D. Fee (eds.), Oxford, 1981, 213-220.

[159] This is said because the subordination of women in the Ephesian community, for instance, is in the home, where the wife is to be submissive to the husband in all things (Eph 5,21-24).

[160] Tertullian, "De Virginibus Velandis 9," in: H. Bettenson, *The Early Christian Fathers*, 151.

[161] Arndt & Gingrich, *Lexicon*, 749.

[162] The next chapter will be dedicated to this particular topic.

[163] Arndt & Gingrich, *Lexicon*, 303.

[164] These are the first five books of the Old Testament beginning with Genesis. It is also called the Septuagint, with the siglum >LXX<.

[165] A group of these fundamentalists was seriously cautioned by Titus. He addressed the group in this way: "For there are many insubordinate men, empty talkers and deceivers, especially the circumcision party; they must be silenced, since they are upsetting whole families by teaching for base gain what they have no right to teach. One of themselves, a prophet of their own, said, "Cretans are always liars, evil beasts, lazy gluttons." This testimony is true. Therefore rebuke them sharply, that they may be sound in the faith, instead of giving heed to Jewish myths or to commands of men who reject the truth. To the pure all things are pure, but to the corrupt and unbelieving nothing is pure; their very minds and consciences are corrupted. They profess to know God, but they deny him by their deeds; they are detestable, disobedient, unfit for any good deed (Titus 1,10-16).

[166] Arndt & Gingrich, *Lexicon*, 25.

[167] In biblical scholarship, the term *pseudepigrapha*, which literally means *false writing*, is different from *apocrypha*, which means *hidden*. While *apocrypha* is more of a Protestant term used to refer to books outside the Hebrew Canon, which the Roman Catholics include in their own bible and term the same books in question *deutero-canonical*, *pseudepigrapha* is used to refer to all other books outside the canon of the bible. Examples of *pseudepigrapha* are the ascension of Elijah, the book of Jubilees, the Testament of the Twelve Patriarchs for the Old Testament and the gospel of Mary, the Acts of Peter, for the New Testament. Examples of apocrypha from a Protestant perspective are Maccabees, Tobit, Wisdom, etc. For the Roman Catholic biblical tradition, these are not *aprocrypha*, they are the *deutero-canonical* books, recognized also as sacred scripture. These books pertain only to the Old Testament. Both Protestants and Roman Catholics accept all the books of the New Testament as scripture.

[168] What of the texts of the *household codes* dealing with the obedience of slaves to their masters, are these too inspired?

[169] Oepke, "γυνή," TDNT I, 782.

[170] Cf. Kraemer, R.S. *Gender and Christianity*. New York: Oxford, 1998; Meeks, W.A., "The Image of the Androgyne: Some Uses of a Symbol in Earliest Christianity," *History of Religions* 13 (1974), 165-208.

[171] Cf. Kroeger, Catherine Clark, and James R. Beck, (eds.), *Women, Abuse,*

and the Bible: How Scripture Can Be Used to Hurt or Heal, Grand Rapids: Baker Books, 1996.

[172] The *inquisition* is one of the blunders of church history. This was essentially the use of ecclesiastical courts to deal with the so-called heresies. Such courts had the jurisdiction to seek out and prosecute the so-called heretics of the time. The man widely associated with this is Pope Gregory IX, known as the Pope of the inquisition. He was the one who instituted the papal inquisition in 1231. As part of the punishment for the convicted heretics he gave instructions that they should be seized and burnt alive, even by the secular authorities of the day. The most unfortunate thing about this whole process is that scripture was invoked. In view of this, Luke 14,23 was used to support this practice as being endorsed by God. In other words, at the time, this barbaric act was simply seen as the plan of God.

[173] Here, the attention of the reader is drawn to the controversy in Mk 7 between Jesus and the Pharisees on the question of the "tradition of the elders". For commentary on this, see: C. A., Amadi-Azuogu, *Biblical Exegesis and Inculturation*, 74-81.

[174] Josephus, *Antiquities*, XV.xi.5. This text from Josephus reads: "Now this inner enclosure had on the southern and northern quarters three gates. . . but the temple further inward in that gate was not allowed to the women. . . ."(translated by William Whiston).

[175] This term "infancy narratives" is used to refer to the stories relating to the infancy of Jesus in Matthew and Luke. These include, the annunciation, the birth of the messiah, the purification of Mary, the killing of the holy innocents, the flight into Egypt, the return from Egypt, etc.

[176] This term *Heilsgeschichte* is a German word, sometimes, used in theological journals to refer to salvation history. The word itself is a compound word, *Heil* (salvation)+ *Geschichte* (history). This is how it comes to mean *salvation history*, when combined.

[177] See the following instances which showed a struggle among the disciples for hierarchical importance: Mk 9,34; Lk 9,46 & 22,24; Matt 18,1.

[178] On this see the text of the request of the two sons of Zebedee in Mk 10,35-40 and the reaction of anger shown by the other disciples in Mk 10,41 that these two brothers were trying to outmaneuver them.

[179] The old adage holds well here: *A friend in need, is a friend indeed*. The male disciples failed this important litmus test, while women emerged victorious. Even unto death, they were still searching for the grave where their acknowledged Lord and master was laid.

[180] The relevant text of Acts, reads: "When they therefore were come together, they asked of him, saying, Lord, wilt thou at this time restore again the kingdom to Israel?" (KJV: Acts 1,6)

[181] Luke 22,24-27 underlines this point. The text reads: "A dispute also arose among them, which of them was to be regarded as the greatest. [25] And he said to them, "The kings of the Gentiles exercise lordship over them; and those in authority over them are called benefactors. [26] But not so with you; rather let

the greatest among you become as the youngest, and the leader as one who serves. [27] For which is the greater, one who sits at table, or one who serves? Is it not the one who sits at table? But I am among you as one who serves."

[182] This text of Luke 24,19-21: "And they said to him, "Concerning Jesus of Nazareth, who was a prophet mighty in deed and word before God and all the people, [20] and how our chief priests and rulers delivered him up to be condemned to death, and crucified him. [21] But we had hoped that he was the one to redeem Israel. Yes, and besides all this, it is now the third day since this happened."

[183] John 12,1-8 has a variation of this narrative, though the "*kiss* section" is omitted here. However, the anointing portion is present. See, also, John 11,2.

[184] In this place, we ask, is it better for us today to make a faithless male disciple a bishop or a faithful female disciple? Should the criterion be gender or authentic faith in the man Jesus? Unfortunately, gender is the measuring rod, regardless of the unfaithfulness of the male minister. In this regard, it is the male folks who are bringing disrepute to the Catholic Church in America due to the scandalous homosexual acts of some o its clergy. So it is the men who have brought disrepute to this Church and not the women. Yet, this Church steadfastly refuses to ordain women. The dishonored male is still preferred to the women whose honor is still intact.

[185] The following text critical information is taken from *The Greek New Testament*, the edition used in this work. So see the critical apparatus to Matt 10,3 on Θαδδαιος.

[186] In this place, it is curious that the KJV used Lebbedeus, not attested in any serious manuscript of Matthew. I do not know how it arrived at this. Besides, as can be seen in the table above, it is questionable, attested in one obscure manuscript.

[187] Curiously, the KJV translated this as *brother of James*. Maybe, it is using another manuscript. Otherwise, this "genitive of belonging" is used describe "son of" in similar contexts. Its correct translation in the context is Judas son of James, as we have it above. Also, see, Zerwick-Grosvenor, *Grammatical Analysis of the Greek New Testament*, see note on Luke 6,16.

[188] The text of Mk 13,3 reads, "And as he sat upon the mount of Olives over against the temple, Peter and James and John and Andrew asked him privately" (KJV). Similarly, see, also, John 12,22.

[189] The relevant text reads, "One of his disciples, Andrew, Simon Peter's brother, saith unto him, There is a lad here, which hath five barley loaves, and two small fishes: but what are they among so many?" (KJV: John 6,8-9)

[190] This word *evangelist* is the anglicized version of the Greek *euaggelistês* (εὐαγγελιστής). It has two senses, one primary, and the other secondary. The primary one is a *proclaimer* of glad tidings. In other words, he or she is the preacher of the good news. After the resurrection, women were the first to be commissioned to do this. The secondary one is the "author" of a gospel. For more, see "εὐαγγελιστής", TDNT II, 736-737.

[191] With the suicide of Judas, the tradition this time knows only of the *Eleven*

and not the *Twelve*.

[192] The detailed discussion surrounding this particular position will be made in the next chapter of this work.

[193] It is not enough giving them bits and bits of "carrots" just to calm them down. Is it not insulting to women to reduce them only to the level of altar girls, choristers, washing altar linens, cooking and serving in rectories? This is simply a degradation of womanhood.

[194] Beyer, "διακονέω", TDNT II, 82.

[195] The case of his Excellency, Joseph Cardinal Ratzinger baffled me too. As a doctoral student at the University of Bonn, Germany, I happened to come in contact with some of his published works. His area of specialization is systematic theology. Reading his published works as a German professor and some of the things coming out from his office in Rome as Cardinal Ratzinger creates more confusion in me. The two sets of information do not add up. They are at odds. This leads me to conclude that it is all about power and influence. Other wise, how could one simply throw overboard what he taught over the years as a professor in order to be a leader in the church?

[196] "Area 51" is a closed United States' military zone, which is situated in the state of Nevada. It is an "off limit area". In the context of our discussion, the ordination of women becomes this off limit "Area 51".

[197] C. A. Amadi-Azuogu, *Biblical Exegesis and Inculturation*, p.51.

[198] Part of this disappointment was also because the laws governing priestly celibacy was not only retained, but also made stricter.

[199] *The New Code of canon law: in English translation*, Prepared by: The Canon Law Society Of Great Britain and Ireland, London 1983, 183.

[200] Third instruction on the correct implementation of the constitution on the sacred liturgy of 5th September 1970.

[201] *Microsoft Encarta College Dictionary*, New York: St. Martin's Press, 2001, p.1028.

[202] Cf. W. Carter, "Getting Martha out of the Kitchen: Luke 10:38-42. Again," CBQ 58.2 (1996) 264-280.

[203] These seven sacraments are baptism, confirmation, reconciliation, holy orders, anointing of the sick, holy Eucharist, and matrimony.

[204] This can happen, when a catholic priest is laicized, marries in the Catholic Church and perhaps receives the sacrament of the sick, at some point in time. This sequence can make it possible for such a male to receive all the seven sacraments, something which can *never* happen in the case of the woman because she is forbidden from receiving the sacrament of holy orders.

[205] "BISHOP: Cleric Ends Isolation, Renounces Wife", in: *Los Angeles Times*, Saturday, August 25, 2001, p. A5.

[206] The various investigations of the sex abuse scandal in the Catholic in America have accented this very fact. Various reports have shown that there was cover-up at the highest level. The church did not want the world to know that this problem is endemic. But the truth has been blown to the open. This is no longer the top secret it used to be.

[207] I do not intend to imply that there are no priests sincerely trying to live this life. But the exception does not make the norm. This tiny minority does not show that celibacy is working. To the contrary, it shows that it is failing and fading.

[208] Here, we are equally in a situation, *where men also take these vows but women keep them for them.* In other words, if the priesthood were to be based on fidelity to the vow of celibacy, women would be and should have been the first ones to be considered for sacred ordination. Unfortunately, however, here it is not about virtue but about legalism, which has guaranteed ordination for men only.

[209] The *lieutenant governor* is the US equivalent of what in some countries is called the deputy governor.

[210] Elizabeth, H. Verdesi, *In But Still Out: Women in the Church.* Philadelphia: Westminster, 1976.

[211] This is the document of John Paul II, *On Reserving Priestly Ordination to Men Alone* (in Latin: "Ordinatio Sacerdotalis") of May 22, 1994.

[212] This is said because it was never debated in any world forum of the Catholic Church. Nor was there a council convoked to discuss it, nor a world synod of bishops to openly debate the matter. The Pope does not have the monopoly of the Holy Spirit. Hence, something similar to the Lambeth Conference of 1988 should have taken place. Instead, the Pope treated the whole problem as his personal matter. If the Pope spoke in the name of Catholicism on the question of the inquisition and spoke wrongly, why do we have to believe that he has not spoken wrongly, once more, on this matter affecting women? The Anglican approach has to be adopted to handle this problem. Until this is done the agitation won't go away.

[213] It was this very document that provoked this present author into participating in the discussion. I guess that there are others too participating on this or similar ground.

[214] This is said because the question of who is a priest and who is not, is not about salvation but about the internal administration of the church. So soteriology is not the main point here.

[215] Congregation for the Doctrine of the Faith and Morals, "Declaration Inter Insigniores on the Question of the Admission of Women to the Ministerial Priesthood", (October 15, 1976), in: *AAS (1977) 100.*

[216] This compound word *androcracy* is a coinage of this author. It has been derived from two Greek words: *anêr-andros* = man as a male creature, and *kratos* – which means might or power, and so rule. So it means "rule by men". Hence, based on the popular definition of democracy, "*androcacy*" is hereby defined as *the government of the people, for the people, by men.* Male domination is radically emphasized here.

[217] These Crusades were military campaigns undertaken by the Christian crusaders to take back the Holy Land from the Muslim occupants of the time. They took place between the 11th and the 14th century AD. Two Popes are outstanding in connection with these wars. The first is Pope Urban II, who in

fact launched the first Crusade (1096-99). The second is Pope Innocent III, who is connected with the Fourth Crusade (1202-04). One sees that the church played a prominent role in the execution of these so-called "holy wars".
[218] On this see the discussion above on "prophets and priests" in the Didache. Chapter 8 will also be dedicated to this topic exclusively.
[219] In: *Insegnamenti di Paolo VI*, XIV (1976) 1017. (The document is translated as: "The Teachings of Paul VI").
[220] These conflicting responses by the Roman Catholic and Anglican Churches towards the ministry of women in the church today leads one to ask this important question. How can we explain this apparent contradiction in Christendom since both mainstream churches have access to the same divine source, the bible? Is the biblical revelation self-contradictory? This is where we see the relationship between biblical hermeneutics and the ministry of women in the church today. In other words, the ministry of women is not divorced from biblical interpretation. What we have seen is two different hermeneutic approaches. Of course, it tells us that the way you interpret the sacred texts automatically affects your attitude towards *gender and ministry* in the church. A fundamentalist interpretation leads to a fundamentalist application. This is where one sees the unbroken link between ministry and hermeneutics. As long as we have to use the bible, we will always be interpreting it. In view of this, we have this "tale of two cities".
[221] The *Lambeth Conference* is meeting of all the national churches within the Anglican tradition to discuss matters affecting the Communion. It is more of an episcopal conference since it is basically a conference of bishops. Usually, it is called every ten years. The first one was held in 1867. This conference was named after the *Lambeth palace*, formerly the Lambeth house, in London, which is the official residence of the archbishop of Canterbury. From 1867–1968 the Lambeth Conference took place here. However, since 1978, it now takes place in Canterbury, England. This conference is an important forum for discussion matters of importance to the Anglican Communion. It has no central or authoritative government. The bishops meet and deliberate as equals, with the archbishop of Canterbury as host and chairman (See, "Lambeth Conference" and "Lambeth" in Encyclopedia Britannica, Inc., 1994-2002, on CD-ROM).
[222] For my detailed commentary on this "tradition of the elders", see my earlier work on *Biblical Exegesis and Inculturation*, p.74-81 and 298-299.
[223] Cf. Katie Sherrod, "*First female bishops find warm welcome at Lambeth Conference,*" Anglican Communion News Service, Note 1705, 1998-AUG-3.
[224] See, "Lambeth Conference" in Encyclopedia Britannica, Inc., 1994-2002, on CD-ROM.
[225] Letter of Donald Coggan, Archbishop of Canterbury, to Pope Paul VI, 9 July 1975. As published by www.womenpriests.org!
[226] Paul VI, "Response to the Letter of His Grace the Most Reverend Dr. F. D. Coggan, Archbishop of Canterbury, Concerning the Ordination of Women to the Priesthood", (November 30, 1975), in: *Acta Apostolica Sedis* 68 (1976)

599.
[227] For instance, the whole question of "conception by a spirit" is unprecedented in Palestinian Judaism but clearly attested in Hellenistic Judaism, as well as Hellenistic Christianity. Hence, the Lucan virginal conception, which involves a spirit, becomes a contribution of Hellenistic Christianity. This will now be elaborated upon by means of a digression. In his work, "Jungfrauensohn und Krippenkind", published in *Botschaft und Geschichte*, Martin Dibelius points out that the Palestinian Judaism understands the Holy Spirit as an organ of inspiration, but not as a creative power of life (M. Dibelius, "Jungfrauensohn und Krippenkind: Untersuchung zur Geburtsgeschichte Jesu im Lukas-Evangelium", in: *Botschaft und Geschichte*, Band I, Tübingen 1953, 30. Original text: "Das palästinensische Judentum faßt den heiligen Geist als Organ der Inspiration, aber im allgemeinen nicht als schöpferische Lebensmacht"). In other words, the Holy Spirit is not connected with human generation in Palestinian tradition. How, then, can the role of the Holy Spirit in the generation of Jesus be explained? In response, Dibelius went ahead to show that this whole idea of generation by a spirit is typically Hellenistic. Hence, he pointed out that Hellenistic mentality knows of situations in which a god approaches a mortal woman and generates in her the embryo of life, without sexual intercourse with the woman (M. Dibelius, "Jungfrauensohn und Krippenkind", in: *Botschaft und Geschichte*, 33). This takes place only through the generative powers of the god involved, which is asexual, without sexual intercourse. This shows how Hellenistic ideas filtered into the New Testament and helped to shape it (C.A. Amadi-Azuogu, *Paul and the Law in the Arguments of Galatians*, 263-264). If this contribution by Hellenistic Christianity is accepted, the contribution of Hellenistic Christianity towards ministry in the church should also be respected and accepted.
[228] The text to this effect reads, "And when Jesus was come into Peter's house, he saw his wife's mother laid, and sick of a fever. And he touched her hand, and the fever left her: and she arose, and ministered unto them" (KJV: Matt 8,14-15).
[229] The text of 1Timothy in question reads, "A bishop then must be blameless, the husband of one wife, vigilant, sober, of good behaviour, given to hospitality, apt to teach; Not given to wine, no striker, not greedy of filthy lucre; but patient, not a brawler, not covetous; One that ruleth well his own house, having his children in subjection with all gravity; (For if a man know not how to rule his own house, how shall he take care of the church of God?)" (KJV: 1Tim 3,2-5).
[230] *Ordinatio Sacerdotalis* by John Paul II (*On Reserving Priestly Ordination to Men Alone*), May 22, 1994.
[231] *Mulieris Dignitatem*, August 15, 1988 ("On the Dignity and Vocation of Women") by Pope John Paul II.
[232] The Czechoslovakia Republic is now an anachronism of history because it no longer consists. Now, it exists as two countries, Czech Republic and Slovakia, both in Eastern Europe.

[233] This word "senior" is used here in the sense of the elderly and the aged, like a senior citizen. In many countries, they include people who are 60 years and above.

[234] Here, think about the Catholic Pontiff, John Paul II, who holds firmly onto power, even though he has slurred speech.

[235] B. Witherington III, *Conflict and Community in Corinth,* 231.

[236] The German caption is also acceptable: *Der barmherzige Samariter.* This brings out the emphasis in the story. The issue at stake is not the goodness of the Samaritan, which could point to sinlessness, but his loving action towards the neighbor. Despite the fact of sin, this Samaritan did something that Jesus now recognizes, endorses and proposes as a model to be imitated. This single act of love covers for this Samaritan a multitude of sins (cf. 1Pet 4,7). This is the way Jesus presented to us his own moral and spiritual perspectives.

[237] One evaluating this lawyer should be able to point out some amount of humility on his own part in asking what to do in order to gain life everlasting. This lawyer, in Greek *nomikos,* belonged also to the Jewish religious hierarchy. He was a highly placed religious official. Despite this, he still did not know what precisely was needed to gain eternal life. But do we have this type of humility today, especially among the church hierarchy? Do we not think that for one to become a bishop, for instance, is automatically to know everything and all that it entails to gain eternal life? Do we have the courage of this lawyer to say that we don't know or is it not that the bishop knows everything and has the last word?

[238] The text reads: Deut 6,5: "And thou shalt love the Lord thy God with all thine heart, and with all thy soul, and with all thy might" (KJV).

[239] Lev 19,18: "Thou shalt not avenge, nor bear any grudge against the children of thy people, but thou shalt love thy neighbour as thyself: I am the Lord" (KJV).

[240] Eusebius, *Ecclesiastical History,* Book II, Chapter 20,4-6. E-Text from "The Early Church Fathers in WinHelp Format".

[241] The unfortunate thing is that some later Christian traditions refuse to recognize this hard fact that the thief was the first reported person to be saved from the saving events of the cross. Instead, these traditions prefer to orchestrate the feast of St. Stephen on Dec the 26, as if that event took place before the event of the cross. In fact, whereas the Bible tells us specifically that the thief received his salvation on the cross, on the very day of the crucifixion, the same Bible was silent in the case of Stephen.

[242] These two texts read: "As the Father knoweth me, even so know I the Father: and I lay down my life for the sheep" (KJV: John 10,15). "Greater love hath no man than this, that a man lay down his life for his friends" (KJV: John 15,13).

[243]. For more details about this list of prohibitions, see Lev 22.

[244] In this story, we see that religious laws intended to keep the priest and the levite holy became obstacles towards doing actually what God would have wanted them to do in this instance. These laws of "holiness" became obstacles

towards loving the neighbor. Is this not possible today? Are there no situations in which laws and rules made to protect the holiness of church officials become obstacles to fulfilling the will of God? The story of the loving Samaritan would have required the priest and the Levite to ignore the laws they were observing and help the wounded. But they were very legally minded and were ruled by the letters of the law. If, however, they had set aside the laws and helped the wounded man, they would have been praised for showing love. There are conditions in which one will have to set aside rules and do what the situation demands, especially if it is deemed to be in accordance with the will of God the supreme law giver. This is the case for the Greek *epieikeia*. The priest and the Levite in the story did not know this. Hence, they could not be proposed as models. Laws cannot be sheepishly and uncritically implemented.

[245] On account of this problem, since nocturnal emissions are also included here, the high priest had to stay awake on the eve of the *Yôm kippûr* – "Day of Atonement" so as not to contaminate himself with the seminal fluid. This *Yôm kippûr* was normally celebrated once a year. This was the only day in the year in which the high priest entered the "Holy of Holies." See Lev 16 for the ritual prescription of this ceremony.

[246] From this it becomes clear that there are situations in which laws are superseded, even if they are made by a religious authority. Jesus tries to correct some of the Old Testament idea of God. We do not have a law-minded God interested only in punishing every breach of the law no matter the circumstance. The God, whom Jesus came to reveal, is not one who knows only legal prescriptions in the law code. The God that is made manifest in Jesus Christ is not an unintelligent God, who cannot see reasons beyond the written law. He is not taken captive by it.

[247] See the Decalogue of Exo 20,8-11 and its alternative version in Deut 5,12-15).

[248] Of interest is the fact that the Johannine Jesus was very insistent and consistent in maintaining that "*God is love.*" But he never said: God is law!" Even within the Pauline tradition, love receives an unmitigated and undiluted emphasis. It is not only the fulfillment of the law (Gal 5,14; Rom 13,8-10), it is the greatest (1Cor 13,13). We see that there is a New Testament consensus that makes New Testament ethics and morality love-oriented.

[249] This feminine form-Σαμαριτις (*Samaritis*)-was used in John 4,9 in respect of the Samaritan woman who met Jesus at the Jacob's well.

[250] Josephus, *Jewish Antiquities*, Book 9:14,3.

[251] Josephus, *Jewish Antiquities*, Book 10:9,7. Text from: *The Works of Flavius Josephus* translated by William Whiston. E-Text from: http://www.ccel.org/j/josephus/JOSEPHUS.HTM.

[252] Josephus, *Jewish Antiquities*, Book 9:14,3, translated by William Whiston.

[253] Josephus, *Jewish Antiquities*, Book 11:4,3, translated by William Whiston.

[254] Josephus, *Jewish Antiquities*, Book 18:2,2, translated by William Whiston.

[255] J. Jeremias, "Σαμαρίτης", TDNT VII, 89.

[256] Josephus, *Jewish Antiquities*, Book 9:14,3, translated by William Whiston.

[257] Josephus, *Jewish Antiquities*, Book 9:14,3, translated by William Whiston.

[258] Josephus, *Jewish Antiquities*, Book 9:14,3, translated by William Whiston.

[259] J. Jeremias, "Σαμαρίτης", TDNT VII, 91.

[260] J. Jeremias, "Σαμαρίτης", TDNT VII, 89.

[261] This text is an indication of the early Jewish Christian opposition to the Hellenistic Christian mission. A saying like this purported to have come from Jesus would have been used to support such an opposition. This cautions us against using texts to interpret women down in the church.

[262] Josephus, *Jewish Antiquities*, Book 11:4,9, translated by William Whiston.

[263] This text reads: "On the way to Jerusalem he was passing along between Samaria and Galilee. [12] And as he entered a village, he was met by ten lepers, who stood at a distance [13] and lifted up their voices and said, "Jesus, Master, have mercy on us." (Picture) [14] When he saw them he said to them, "Go and show yourselves to the priests." And as they went they were cleansed. [15] Then one of them, when he saw that he was healed, turned back, praising God with a loud voice; [16] and he fell on his face at Jesus' feet, giving him thanks. Now he was a Samaritan. [17] Then said Jesus, "Were not ten cleansed? Where are the nine? [18] Was no one found to return and give praise to God except this foreigner?" [19] And he said to him, "Rise and go your way; your faith has made you well" (Luke 17,11-19).

[264] The text says:[39]And many of the Samaritans of that city believed on him for the saying of the woman, which testified, He told me all that ever I did. [40] So when the Samaritans were come unto him, they besought him that he would tarry with them: and he abode there two days. [41] And many more believed because of his own word; [42] And said unto the woman, Now we believe, not because of thy saying: for we have heard him ourselves, and know that this is indeed the Christ, the Saviour of the world. [43]: Now after two days he departed thence, and went into Galilee. [44] For Jesus himself testified, that a prophet hath no honour in his own country (KJV: 4,39-44).

[265] This story also challenges the concept of election.

[266] Jesus makes the same critique in Matthew. The text says: "Woe unto you, scribes and Pharisees, hypocrites! for ye pay tithe of mint and anise and cummin, and have omitted the weightier matters of the law, judgment, mercy, and faith: these ought ye to have done, and not to leave the other undone (KJV: Mt:23,23).

[267] The text reads: "And Samuel said, Hath the Lord as great delight in burnt offerings and sacrifices, as in obeying the voice of the Lord? Behold, to obey is better than sacrifice, and to hearken than the fat of rams" (KJV: 1Sm 15,22).

[268]. This is equally a lesson for the church today, especially where the so-called hierarchical structure is overemphasized, as if this were the essence of Christianity. If Jesus were to be here today, this critique that he made against the priests of his day he would probably redirect to those who occupy the priestly office. He would not be happy with anyone creating ecumenical obstacles, which make it difficult for Christians to love one another. He may not even agree with our strict theological interpretation and application of some of the sacraments in which we

forget that the main reason for them is love, and not to bind people (in the case of marriage and divorce) with heavy burden. Possibly, we are not even better than the priests and Pharisees of the time of Jesus. Let it be known to us that holiness does not come from the top to the grass roots. God can also propose the common people as the model to be imitated. If Jesus were to come back today, he may not say: Go and do like the priests and pastors of the church. If he had little to do with the Jewish priesthood of his day (also supposed to come from God) what guarantee do we have that if he were to come back to us today that he would change this attitude?

[269] The text to this effect says: "Ye are of your father the devil, and the lusts of your father ye will do. He was a murderer from the beginning, and abode not in the truth, because there is no truth in him. When he speaketh a lie, he speaketh of his own: for he is a liar, and the father of it" (KJV Jn:8,44).

[270] These two sets of things (the *commandment of God* and the *tradition of men*) are not supposed to be opposed to one another. In fact, when there is the correct harmony and the right understanding and application, the tradition (*paradosis*) can become very valuable in understanding the revelation of God. In other words, tradition (*paradosis*) is not opposed to the commandment of God (*hê entolê tou theou*) as such. But a poor harmony could lead to a *misunderstanding* of this same revelation. The way the traditional materials involved are used and the type of weight and importance one gives to them could create problems. In other words, whenever *tradition* is made to stand above the word of God or when *authority* stands above the word of God, there is bound to be friction.

[271] Whatever our analysis may be, *the text of Mk 7 is in no way to be taken to be an argument that the Marcan Jesus was against human traditions.* Instead, it is the attitude towards these *traditions* that is called into question. In Mk 7, as one sees, there is a misplaced emphasis which, in effect, leads to a misplaced priority. These traditions seem to have received more attention than what Jesus calls the "commandment of God." The proper balance, which should have existed between the two, seemed to be lacking. A one-sidedness existed and Jesus refused to endorse this. Here, Jesus rightly distinguished between two things: *the tradition of men* and *the commandment of God.* This still holds for us today. We may be quarreling over *paradosis* (tradition) to the extent that the main thing the commandment of God (*hê entolê tou theou*) suffers or becomes even neglected. In view of this, human law may become more emphasized than the divine law itself.

[272] The text of this amendment reads: "The right of citizens of the United States to vote shall not be denied or abridged by the United States or by any State on account of sex. Congress shall have power to enforce this article by appropriate legislation."

[273] The following literature is useful for further reading: DuBois, Ellen C., Feminism and Suffrage: The Emergence of an Independent Women's Movement in America, 1848-1869 (1978); Flexner, Eleanor, Century of Struggle:

The Woman's Rights Movement in the United States, rev. ed. (1975); Fulford, Roger, Votes for Women (1970); Kraditor, Aileen S., The Idea of the Woman Suffrage Movement, 1890-1920 (1965); Morgan, David, Suffragists and Democrats: The Politics of Woman Suffrage in America (1971); Pankhurst, S., The Suffragette Movement (1931; repr. 1971); Scott, Anne F. and Andrew M., One Half the People: The Fights for Woman's Suffrage (1975); Severn, William, Free But Not Equal (1967); Stanton, Elizabeth Cady, et al., eds., The History of Woman Suffrage, 6 vols. (1881; repr. 1971).

[274] I have selected Britain and US as examples. The pattern shows a widespread default on women's suffrage. For instance, it was just in 1971 that Switzerland finally gave women the vote. This shows that it has not been easy for women, no matter where.

[275] Evans, R. J., The Feminists (1977); Hymowitz, C., and Weissman, M., A History of American Women (1978); Iglitzin, L., and Ross, R., eds., Women in the World (1976); Newland, K., The Sisterhood of Man: The Impact of Women's Changing Roles on Social and Economic Life around the World (1979); Pomeroy, S., Goddesses, Whores, Wives, and Slaves: Women in Classical Antiquity (1976); Rosenberg, Rosalind, Divided Lives: American Women in the Twentieth Century (1992); United Nations, The World's Women, 1970-1990: Trends and Statistics (1991).

[276] This may also be the situation with the United States' proposed constitutional amendment on the sanctity of marriage as an institution between a man and a woman.

[277] See: Mansbridge, Jane, Why We Lost the ERA (1986); Mathews, Donald G., and DeHart, Jane S., ERA and the Politics of Gender (1990); Wolgast, E. H., Equality and the Rights of Women (1980).

[278] Although women generally have acquired the vote, still they do not exercise political power in proportion to their numbers. It is still a minority rule. Notwithstanding, I am also aware of the fact, on the political level, that a few women have attained the highest political office. In this regard, Indira Gandhi was twice Prime Minister of India (1966 to 1977) and (1980 to 1984). Corazon Aquino became the president of the Philippines in 1986 through a popular revolt following her nearly robed election victory. Golda Meir was Prime Minister of Israel from 1969 to 1974. Margaret Thatcher, Britain's first female Prime Minister, ruled from 1987-1990. Violeta Barrios de Chamorro was elected president of Nicaragua in 1990. Benazir Bhutto became Prime Minister of Pakistan in 1988. Elizabeth II, Queen of the United Kingdom of Great Britain and Northern Ireland, was crowned on June 2, 1953. Ever since then, she has been both head of the royal family and a ceremonial head of state. Sirimavo Bandaranaike was a two-term Prime Minister of Sri Lanka (1960-65 and 1970-77).

[279] The Nigeria-Biafra war was a war of genocide carried out against the Igbo nation in the East of Nigeria by the rest of the races of Nigeria represented by the Hausa-Fulani tribe in the North and the Yoruba tribe in the West. It lasted for 30 months. It was unleashed as a result of the pogrom in the North and

West against the Igbo race. As a result of this, the Igbo nation declared its unilateral independence from the rest of Nigeria on May 30th 1967 as the "Republic of Biafra". Following this, war broke out on July 16th 1967 and ended on Jan 12th 1970 due to the combined forces of the OAU, with logistics from Great Britain and its allies.

[280] See: *Acta Apostolica Sedis* (AAS) 58 (1966) 13-14.

[281] In this regard, the feudal system and the politics of Europe helped to shape European Christianity. This blend was exported around the world as Christianity. There is no gainsaying that the idea of church hierarchy was shaped mainly by Middle Ages' Europe. Some liturgical dressings today are vestiges from the European past.

[282] C. A. Amadi-Azuogu, *Biblical Exegesis And Inculturation In Africa*, 3, footnote #4.

Bibliography

Abrahamsen, Valerie Ann, *Women and Worship at Philippi,* Astarte Shell Press, Portland, Maine, 1995.

Abrahamsen, Valerie Ann, "Women at Philippi: The Pagan and Christian Evidence," *Journal of Feminist Studies in Religion* 3 (1987) 17-30.

Abrahamsen, Valerie Ann, "Women in Early Christianity," *Oxford Companion to the Bible,* 814-18. Ed. Bruce M. Metzger and Michael Coogan. Oxford and New York: Oxford University Press, 1993.

Agnew, F. H., "On the origin of the term *apostolos*", *Catholic Biblical Quarterly* 38 (1976) 49-53.

Agnew, F. H., "The origin of the NT apostle-concept", *Journal of Biblical Literature* 105 (1986) 75-96.

Allen, Ronald and Beverly, *Liberated Traditionalism: Men and Women in Balance,* A Critical Concern Book. Multnomah, 1985.

Amadi-Azuogu, Adolphus, C., *Biblical Exegesis and Inculturation in Africa in the Third Millennium,* Enugu-Nigeria: SNAAP Press, 2000.

Amadi-Azuogu, Adolphus, C., *Paul and the Law in the arguments of Galatians: A Rhetorical and Exegetical Analysis of Galatians 2,14-6,2,* Bonner Biblische Beiträge Band (BBB) 104, Weinheim, Germany: Beltz Athenäum, 1996.

Arlandson, J. M. *Women, Class, and Society in Early Christianity: Models from Luke-Acts.* Peabody, MA: Hendrickson, 1997.

Ashley, B. M., *"Justice in the Church: Gender and Participation (The McGivney Lectures of the John Paul II Institute for Studies on Marriage and Family, 1992),"* Catholic University of America Press, 1996.

Bahr, C. J., "Paul and letter writing in the fifth century", *Catholic Biblical Quarterly* 28 (1966) 465-477.

Barnett, P. W., "Women in the church: with special reference to 1 Tim 2," *The Bible and women's ministry* (1990) 49-64.

Barron, B., "Putting women in their place: 1 Timothy 2 and evangelical views of women in church leadership," *JETS* 33(1990) 451-459.

Baumert, N., *Frau und Mann bei Paulus: Überwindung eines Mißverständnisses,* Würburg, 1992.

216

Beck, James R. and Blomberg, Craig L. (eds.), *Two Views on Women in Ministry*. Grand Rapids, Michigan: Zondervan Publishing House, 2001.

Behr-Sigel, Elisabeth, *The Ministry of Women in the Church*, Redondo Beach, CA: Oakwood Publications, 1991.

Belleville, Linda L., *Women Leaders and the Church: Three Crucial Questions*, Grand Rapids Michigan: Baker Books, 2000.

Bernard, J., "Quelques notes sur la femme dans la Bible," *Mélanges de Science Religieuse* 47 (1990) 67-104.

Bertram, "συνεργός", TDNT VII, 871-876.

Bettenson, H. (trasl.), *The Early Christian Fathers: A Selection Of The Fathers From St. Clement Of Rome To St. Athanasius*, London, 1969.

Beyer, "διάκονος", TDNT II, 88-93.

Bilezekian, Gilbert, *Beyond Sex Roles: What the Bible Says about a Woman's Place in Church and Family*, 2d ed. Grand Rapids, Michigan: Baker, 1985.

Bliss, Kathleen, *The Service and Status of Women in the Church*, London: SCM Press, 1952.

Bloesch, Donald G, *Is the Bible Sexist? Beyond Feminism and Patriarchalism*, Westchester, IL: Crossway Books, 1982.

Boldrey, Richard, and Joyce Boldrey, *Chauvinist or Feminist? Paul's View of Women*, Grand Rapids: Baker, 1976.

Boomsma, Clarence, *Male and Female, One in Christ: New Testament Teaching on Women in Office*, Grand Rapids: Baker, 1993.

Børreson, Kari Elisabeth, *Subordination and Equivalence: The Nature and Purpose of Women in Augustine and Thomas Aquinas*, Washington, D. C.: University Press of America, 1981.

Boston, L., "A Womanist Reflection on 1 Corinthians 7:21-24 and 1 Corinthians 14:33-35," *Journal of Women and Religion* 9-10 (1991), 81-89.

Bowman, A. L., "Women in ministry: an exegetical study of 1 Timothy 2:11-15," *Bibliotheca Sacra* 149 (1992) 193-213.

Bristow, J.T., *What Paul Really Said About Women*, San Francisco: Harper, 1991.

Brooten, B., "Junia ... Outstanding among the Apostles (Rom 16.7)." In *Women Priests: A Catholic Commentary on the Vatican Declaration* (ed. Leonard Swidler and Arlene Swidler; New York: Paulist, 1977) 141-4.

Brooten, B., *Women Leaders in the Ancient Synagogue*, Brown Judaic Studies no. 36, Chico, CA: Brown Judaic Studies, 1982

Brooten, Bernadette, "Early Christian Women and Their Cultural Context: Issues of Method in Historical Reconstruction." In *Feminist Perspectives on Biblical Scholarship* (ed. Adela Yarbro Collins; Biblical Scholarship in North America 10; Chico, California: Scholars Press, 1985) 65-91.

Brown, F., Driver S. R., & Briggs, C. A., *Hebrew and English Lexicon of the Old Testament*, Oxford: translated by E. Robinson, Clarendom Press, repr. 1977.

Brown, R. E., "The Twelve and the Apostolate", in: *The New Jerome Biblical Commentary*, edited by R. E. Brown, J. A. Fitzmyer and R. E. Murphy, New Jersey, 1990, 1377-1381.

Brunner, Peter, *The Ministry and the Ministry of Women*, St. Louis: Concordia Publishing House, 1971.

Burtchaell, James Tunstead, *From Church to Synagogue: Public Services and Offices in the Earliest Christian Communities*, New York, NY: Cambridge University Press, 1992.

Byrne, B., *Paul and the Christian Woman*, Homebush, 1988.

Byrne, Lavinia, *Women at the Altar. The Ordination of Women in the Roman Catholic Church*, Collegeville, MN: The Liturgical Press, 1994.

Byrne, Lavinia, *Women Before God*, 2nd edition, SPCK, London, 1995.

Caird, G. B., "Paul and Women's Liberty", BJRL 54 (1972) 268-281

Carter, W., "Getting Martha out of the Kitchen: Luke 10:38-42. Again," *CBQ* 58.2 (1996) 264-280.

Cartledge, Mark J., "Charismatic Prophecy: A Definition and Description", *Journal of Pentecostal Theology* 5 (1994): 79-120.

Castelli, Elizabeth A., "Gender, Theory, and *The Rise of Christianity*: A Response to Rodney Stark." *Journal of Early Christian Studies* 6 (2 1998) 227-57.

Castelli, Elizabeth A., "Heteroglossia, Hermeneutics, and History: A Review Essay of Recent Feminist Studies of Early Christianity." *Journal of Feminist Studies in Religion* 10 (2 1994) 73-98.

Castelli, Elizabeth A., "Paul on Women and Gender." In *Women and Christian Origins* (ed. Ross Shepard Kraemer and Mary Rose D'Angelo; New York: Oxford University Press, 1999) 221-35.

Cerling, C. E., "Women ministers in the New Testament church?" *JETS* 19 (1976) 209-215.

Chapman, J., "*Last Bastion: Women Priests; the Case for and Against,*" Heinemann, 1989.

Chaves, M., *Ordaining Women: Culture and Conflict in religious Organizations*, Harvard University Press, 1997.

Chittister, Joan, *Women, Ministry and Church*, New York: Paulist Press 1983.

Chow, John K., *Patronage and Power: Studies on Social Networks in Corinth*, Sheffield Academic Press, 1997.

Clark, Elizabeth, A., "Early Christian Women: Sources and Interpretation." In *That Gentle Strength: Historical Perspectives on Women in Christianity* (ed. Lynda L. Coon, Katherine J. Haldan and Elisabeth W. Sommer; Charlottesville: University of Virginia Press, 1990) 19-35.

Clark, Elizabeth, A., *Women in the Early Church*, Message of the Fathers of the Church Series, Vol.13. Wilmington, Del: Michael Glazier, 1983.

Clark, Stephen B., *Man and Woman in Christ: An Examination of the Roles of Men and Women in Light of Scripture and the Social Sciences*, Ann Arbor: Servant Books, 1980.

Cloke, Gillian, *This Female Man of God: Women and Spiritual Power in the Patristic Age, A.D. 350-450*. New York: Routledge, 1995.

Clouse, Bonnidell, and Robert G. Clouse, (eds.), *Women in Ministry: Four Views*, Downers Grove, IL: InterVarsity Press, 1989.

Cohen, S. J. D., "Menstruants & the Sacred in Judaism and Christianity," in *WHAH* 273-300

218

Cohen, S.J.D., "Women in the Synagogues of Antiquity," *Conservative Judaism* 34 (1980), 23-29.

Conner, Kevin J., *The Ministry of Women*, Melbourne, Australia: KJC Publications, 1984.

Cooper, K., "Insinuations of Womanly Influence: An Aspect of the Christianization of the Roman Aristocracy," *JRS* 82 (1992) 150-164

Corley, Kathleen E., "Feminist Myths of Christian Origins." In *Reimagining Christian Origins. A Colloquium Honoring Burton L. Mack,* (ed. Elizabeth A. Castelli and Hal Taussig; Valley Forge, Pennsylvania: Trinity Press International, 1996) 51-67.

Corrington-Streete, Gail P., "Sex, Spirit, and Control: Paul and the Corinthian Women." In *Ritual, Power, and the Body: Historical Perspectives on the Representation of Greek Women* (ed. C. Nadia Seremetakis; New York: Pella, 1993) 95-117.

Cotter, Wendy J., "Women's Authority Roles in Paul's Churches: Countercultural or Conventional?" *Novum Testamentum* 36 (1994) 350-72.

Croskery, J., "Christian Work of Women in the Early Church," *ExpT* 15 (1903-04) 111-115.

Culver, R. D., "Apostles and the apostolate in the New Testament", *Bibilotheca Sacra* 134 (1977) 131-143.

D'Angelo, M.R., "Re-Membering Jesus: Women, Prophecy, and Resistance in the Memory of the Early Churches," *Horizons* 19 (1992) 199-218.

Daniélou, J., "Le ministère des femmes dans l'Église ancienne," *La Maison-Dieu* 61 (1960) 70-96.

Daniélou, Jean, *The Ministry of Women in the Early Church*, Faith Press, Leighton Buzzard, 1974.

Doughty, D.J., "Women and Liberation in the Churches of Paul and the Pauline Tradition," *Drew Gateway* 2 (1979), 1-21.

Dunn D. G, J., *Romans 9-16*, Word Biblical Commentary, volume 38B, Texas, 1988.

Edwards, Ruth B., *The Case for Women's Ministry*, in Biblical Foundations in Theology, SPCK, 1989.

Ellis, E. E., "Paul and his Co-Workers", NTS 17 (1970-71) 437-452.

Ellis, E. E., *Pauline Theology: Ministry and Society*, Grand Rapids, Michigan, 1989.

Evans, Mary J., *Woman in the Bible: An Overview of All the Crucial Passages on Women's Roles*, Foreword by Donald Guthrie. Downers Grove, IL: InterVarsity Press, 1983.

Fabrega, V., "War Junia(s), der hervorrangede Apostel (Rom 16,7) eine Frau?" *Jahrbuch für Antike und Christentum* 27-28 (1984-85) 47-64.

Ferder, Fran, *Partnership: Women and Men in Ministry*, Notre Dame, IN: Ave Maria Press, 1989.

Field, Barbara (Ed.), *Fit for this Office (Women and ordination)*, Collins Dove, Melbourne, 1989.

Finegan, J., "The original form of the Pauline collection", HTR 49 (1956) 85-103.

Fitzmyer, J. A., "The Letter To The Romans", in: *The New Jerome Biblical Commentary*, edited by R. E. Brown, J. A. Fitzmyer and R. E. Murphy, New Jersey, 1990, 830-868.

Fitzmyer, J. A., and Snyder, E. H., "Did Paul Put Down Women in 1 Corinthians 14,34-36?" *BTB* 11 (1981), 10-12.

Foh, Susan T., *Women and the Word of God: A Response to Biblical Feminism*, Phillipsburg, NJ: Presbyterian & Reformed, 1979.

Foster, H. E., "Jewish and Graeco-Roman Influences upon Paul's Attitude Toward Women," (U. of Chicago Ph.D. dissertation, 1934).

France, R. T., *"Women in the Church's Ministry: A Test-Case for Biblical Interpretation,"* Eerdmans Publishers, 1997.

Friedrich, G., "Lohmeyers These über das paulinische Briefpräskript kritisch beleuchtet", TLZ 81 (1956) 343-346.

Fuchs, L., *We Were There: Women in the New Testament*. New York: Alba House, 1993.

Funk, A., *Status und Rollen in den Paulusbriefen*, Innsbruck, Tyrolia, 1981.

Funk, J., "Klerikale Frauen?" in *Österreichisches Archiv für Kirchenrecht* 14 (1963) 274-280.

Gamble, H., "The redaction of the Pauline letters and the formation of the Pauline corpus", JBL 94 (1975) 403-418.

Gilbert, Bilezikian, *Beyond Sex Roles: A Guide for the Study of Female Roles in the Bible*, Grand Rapids, MI: Baker Book House, 1985.

Giles, Kevin, "A Critique of the "Novel" Contemporary Interpretation of 1 Timothy 2:9-15 Given in the Book, Women in the Church", Part I', *Evangelical Quarterly* 72:2 (2000) 151-67.

Giles, Kevin, "Women in the Church: A Rejoinder to Andreas Kostenberger", *Evangelical Quarterly* 73:3 (2001) 225-245.

Giles, Kevin, 'A Critique of the "Novel" Contemporary Interpretation of 1 Timothy 2:9-15 Given in the Book, Women in the Church. Part II', *Evangelical Quarterly* 72:3 (2000) 195-215.

Giles, Kevin, *Patterns of Ministry among the First Christians*, North Blackburn, Victoria: Collins Dove, 1989.

Gordon, A. J., "The Ministry of Women," *Missionary Review of the World* 7 (1894) 910-921.

Gordon, Clark, "The Ordination of Women," in John Robbins, *Scripture Twisting in the Seminaries* (Jefferson, MD: Trinity Foundation (1985) 70-71.

Graham, R.W., "Women in the Ministry of Jesus and in the Early Church," *Lexington Theological Quarterly* 18 (1983), 1-42.

Grant, R. M., "Neither Male Nor Female," Biblical Research 37 (1992), 5-14.

Grenz S. J. & Kjesbo, D. M., *"Women in the Church: a Biblical Theology of Women in Minstry,"* Intervarsity Press, 1995.

Grenz, Stanley, and Denise Muir Kjesbo, *Women in the Church: A Biblical Theology of Women in Ministry*, Downers Grove, IL: InterVarsity Press, 1996.

Groothuis, Rebecca, *Good News for Women: A Biblical Picture of Gender Equality*, Grand Rapids: Baker, 1997.

Groothuis, Rebecca, *Women Caught in the Conflict: The Culture War between Traditionalism and Feminism*, Grand Rapids: Baker, 1994; reprint, Wipf and Stock, 1997.

Grudem, Wayne, *The Gift of Prophecy in the New Testament and Today*, Wheaton: Crossway, 1988.

Gryson, Roger, *The Ministry of Women in the Early Church*. Translated by Jean Laporte, Hall, Mary, Louise. Collegeville MN: The Liturgical Press, 1976.

Gundry, Patricia, *Neither Slave nor Free: Helping Women Answer the Call to Church Leadership*, Harper & Row, 1987.

Gundry, Patricia, *Woman Be Free!* Grand Rapids, MI: Zondervan, 1977.

Hagen, J. S. (ed.), *Gender Matters: Women's Studies for the Christian Community*, Grand Rapids: Zondervan, 1990.

Hahn, F., "Der Apostolat in Urchristentum", KD 20 (1974) 56-77.

Harvey, Susan Ashbrook, "Women in Early Byzantine Hagiography: Reversing the Story." In *"That Gentle Strength": Historical Perspectives on Women in Christianity* (ed. L. Coon, K. Haldane and E. Sommer; Charlottesville: University Press of Virginia, 1990) 36-59.

Harvey, Susan Ashbrook, "Women in Early Syrian Christianity." In *Images of Women in Antiquity* (ed. Averil Cameron and Amélie Kuhrt; Detroit: Wayne State University Press, 1985) 288-98.

Hauke, Manfred, *Women in the Priesthood? A Systemic Analysis in the Light of the Order of Creation and Redemption*, San Francisco: Ignatius Press, 1988.

Hayne, Léonie, "Thecla and the Church Fathers." *Vigiliae Christianae* 48 (1994) 209-218.

Heine, S., *Women and Early Christianity*. Minneapolis, MN: Fortress, 1988.

Hoffman, Daniel, "Tertullian on Women and Women's Ministry Roles in the Church." In *The Spirit and the Mind: Essays in Informed Pentecostalism* (ed. Donald N. Bowdle, Terry L. Cross and Emerson B. Powery; Lanham, Maryland: University Press of Ameia, 2000) 131-55.

Holmberg, Bengt, *Paul and Power: The Structure of Authority in the Primitive Church as Reflected in the Pauline Epistles*. Philadelphia: Fortress, 1980.

House, H. Wayne, *The Role of Women in Ministry Today*, Nashville: Thomas Nelson, 1990; rev. ed., Grand Rapids: Baker, 1995.

Houston, Graham, *Prophecy: A Gift for Today?* Downers Grove: IVP, 1989.

Howe, Margaret E., *Women and Church Leadership*, Grand Rapids: Zondervan, 1982.

Huber, Elaine C., *Women and the Authority of Inspiration: A Reexamination of Two Prophetic Movements from a Contemporary Feminist Perspective*. Lanham, Maryland: University Press of America, 1985.

Hugenberger, G.P., "Women in Church Office: Hermeneutics or Exegesis? A Survey of Approaches to 1 Tim 2:8-15 [emphasis on marital relationship]," *JETS* 35 (1992), 341-60.

Hull, Gretchen Gaebelein, *Equal to Serve: Women and Men in the Church and Home*, Old Tappan, NJ: Revell, 1987.

Hunt, Susan, and Peggy B. Hutcheson, *Leadership for Women in the Church*, Foreword by D. James Kennedy. Grand Rapids: Zondervan, 1991.

Hurley, J. B., "Did Paul Require Veils or the Silence of Women? A Consideration of 1 Cor. 11:2-16 and 1Cor. 14:33b-36," *Westminster Theological Journal* 35 (1973), 190-220.

Hurley, James B., *Man and Woman in Biblical Perspective*, Grand Rapids: Zondervan, 1981.

Ide, A. F., *God's Girls: Ordination of Women in the Early Christian and Gnostic Churches*, Tanglewould Press, 1986.

Irvin, D., "The Ministry of Women in the Early Church: The Archeological Evidence", *Duke Divinity School Review* 2 (1980) 76-86

Jean, Laporte, *The Role of Women in Early Christianity*, New York and Toronto: Edwin Mellen, 1982.

Jensen, Anne, *God's Self-Confident Daughters: Early Christianity and the Liberation of Women*, trans. O. C. Dean. Louisville: Westminster John Knox, 1996.

Jewett, Paul K., *The Ordination of Women*, Grand Rapids, Michigan: Eerdmans Publishing Company, 1980.

Jewett, Paul King, *Man as Male and Female*, Grand Rapids: Eerdmans, 1975.

Käsemann, E., "Die Legitimität des Apostels", *Zeitschrift für die Neutestamentliche Wissenschaft* 41 (1942) 33-71.

Kee, H.C., "The Changing Role of Women in the Early Christian World," *Theology Today* 49 (1992), 225-38.

Keener, Craig S., *Paul, Wives and Wives: Marriage and Women's Ministry in the Letters of Paul*, Peabody, Massachusetts: Hendrickson Publishers, 1992, fifth printing, 2001.

Kendall, Patricia, *Women and Priesthood: A Selected and Annotated Bibliography*. Philadelphia: Episcopal Diocese of Pennsylvania, 1973.

Kertelge, K., "Das Apostelamt des Paulus", *Biblische Zeitschrift* 14 (1970) 161-181.

Kienzle, Beverly Mayne and Pamely J. Walker, (eds.), *Women Preachers and Prophets through Two Millenia of Christianity*, Berkeley: University of California Press, 1998.

Klawiter, Frederick C., *The New Prophecy in Early Christianity: The Origin, Nature and Development of Montanism, A.D. 165-220*. Ph. D. Dissertation; Chicago, 1975.

Knight, George W., *The Role Relation of Men and Women*, Chicago: Moody Press, 1985.

Knox, J., "A note on the format of the Pauline corpus", *Havard Theological Review* 50, 311-314.

Kostenberger, A. J., Schreiner, T. R., Baldwin, H. S. (eds.), "Women in the Church: A Response to Kevin Giles", *Evangelical Quarterly* 73:3, 2001, 205-224.

Kostenberger, A. J., Schreiner, T.R., Baldwin, H.S. (eds.), *Women in the Church: A Fresh Analysis of 1 Timothy 2,9-15*, Grand Rapids, Michigan: Baker, 1995.

Kraemer, Ross Shephard, "Jewish Women and Christian Origins: Some Caveats." In *Women and Christian Origins* (ed. Ross Shepard Kraemer and Mary Rose D'Angelo; New York: Oxford University Press, 1999) 35-49.

Kraemer, Ross Shephard, *Gender and Christianity*, New York: Oxford, 1998.

Kroeger, Catherine Clark, and James, Beck R., (eds.), *Women, Abuse, and the Bible: How Scripture Can Be Used to Hurt or Heal*, Grand Rapids: Baker Books, 1996.

Kroeger, Richard Clark and Kroeger, Catherine Clark, *I Suffer Not a Woman: Rethinking I Timothy 2:11-15 in Light of Ancient Evidence*, Grand Rapids, Michigan: Baker Books, 1992.

Kydd, Ronald, *Charismatic Gifts in the Early Church*, Peabody, MA: Hendrickson, 1984.

Lampe, P., "Prisca", in: *The Anchor Bible*, Volume 5, 467-468.

Lees, Shirley, *The Role of Women - 8 Prominent Christians Debate Today's Issues*, Leicester, England: Intervarsity Press, 1984.

Leonard, E. A., "St Paul on the Status of Women", *Catholic Biblical Quarterly* 23 (1950) 311-320.

Levison, J. R., "Judith 16:14 and the Creation of Woman", *Journal of Biblical Literature* 114.3 (1995) 467

Lewis, C.S., "Priestesses in the Church?" *God in the Dock*, ed. Walter Hooper, Grand Rapids: William B. Eerdmans Publishing Company, 1970.

Lösch, "Christliche Frauen in Korinth (IKor 11,2-16)", TQ 127 (1947) 216-261.

Louis, Bouyer, *Woman in the Church*, Ignatius, 1979.

MacDonald, Margaret Y., "Rereading Paul: Early Interpreters of Paul on Women and Gender." In *Women and Christian Origins* (ed. Ross Shepard Kraemer and Mary Rose D'Angelo; New York: Oxford University Press, (1999) 236-53.

MacDonald, Margaret Y., "Reading Real Women through the Undisputed Letters of Paul", In *Women and Christian Origins*, 199-220.

MacDonald, Margaret Y., *Early Christian Women and Pagan Opinion: The Power of the Hysterical Woman*. New York: Cambridge University Press, 1996.

Margaret, Howe, E., *Women and Church Leadership*, Grand Rapids, MI: Zondervan, 1982.

Maximos, Bishop of Pittsburgh, *Women Priests?* Holy Cross Orthodox Press, Brookline, MA, 1976.

McKenna, Mary Lawrence, *Women of the Church, Role and Renewal*, New York: P. J. Kenedy & Sons, 1967.

Mealand, D. L., "Positional stylometry reassessed: Testing a seven epistle theory of Pauline authorship", NTS 35 (1989) 266-286.

Meeks, W.A., "The Image of the Androgyne: Some Uses of a Symbol in Earliest Christianity," *History of Religions* 13 (1974) 165-208.

Meeks, Wayne A., *The First Urban Christians: The Social World of the Apostle Paul*, New Haven: Yale University, 1983.

Melton, J. Gordon, *Women's Ordination: Official Statements from Religious Bodies and Ecumenical Organisations*, Detroit, Michigan: Gale Research Inc., 1991.

Merklein, H., *Studien zu Jesus und Paulus*, WUNT 43, Tübingen, 1987.

223

Meyers, Carol, Toni Craven and Ross S. Kraemer, (eds.), *Women in Scripture: A Dictionary of Named and Unnamed Women in the Hebrew Bible, the Apocryphal/Deuterocanonical Books, and the New Testament*, Grand Rapids, Michigan/Cambridge: Wm. B. Eerdmans/Houghton Mifflin, 2000.

Mickelsen, Alvera, (ed.), *Women, Authority, and the Bible*, Downers Grove, IL: InterVarsity Press, 1986.

Mitchell, E. P. (ed.), *Women: To Preach or not to Preach; 21 Outstanding Black Preachers say Yes*, Judson Press, 1991.

Mitton, C. L., *The formation of the Pauline courpus of letters*, London, 1955.

Mollenkott, Virginia Ramey, *Women, Men, and the Bible*, Nashville: Abingdon, 1977.

Moltmann, E. und J., "Menschwerdung in einer neuen Gemeinschaft von Frauen und Männern", EvTh 42 (1982) 80-92.

Moo, D. J., "1 Timothy 2:11-15: Meaning and Significance," *Trinity Journal* 1 (1980) 62-83.

Morris, Joan, The Lady Was A Bishop: *The Hidden History of Women with Clerical Ordination and the Jurisdiction of Bishops*, New York: McMillian, 1973.

Murphy O'Connor, Jerome, *"St. Paul: Promoter of the Ministry of Women"*, in 'Priests and People' August-September 1992 Vol. 6 Nos. 8,9.

Murphy-O'Connor, J., "The First Letter To The Corinthians", in: *The New Jerome Biblical Commentary*, edited by R. E. Brown, J. A. Fitzmyer and R. E. Murphy, New Jersey, 1990, 798-815.

Murphy-OConnor, J., "Interpolations in 1 Corinthians" CBQ 48 (1986) 81-94.

Nadell, P. S., *"Women Who Would Be Rabbis: A History of Women's Ordination, 1989-1985,"* Beacon Press, 1998.

Neuer, Werner, *Man and Woman in Christian Perspective*, Trans., Gordon Wenham, Westchester, IL: Crossway, 1991.

O'Connor, Sr. Francis Bernard, CSC, *"Like Bread, Their Voices Rise!"* - *Global Women Challenge the Church*, Ave Maria Press, 1993.

Oepke, "γυνή", TDNT I, 776-789.

Ollrog, W. H., *Paulus und seine Mitarbeiter*, Neunkirchen-Vluyn, 1979.

Osburn, C. D., "The Interpretation of 1 Cor. 14:34-35," *Essays on Women* (1993) 219-42.

Osiek, C., "Women in the Church," TBT 32 (1994a) 228-233.

Padgett, A., "Paul on Women in the Church: The Contradictions of Coeffure in 1 Corinthians 11,2-26", JSNT (Journal for the Study of the New Testament) 20 (1984) 69-86.

Pagels, E., "Paul on women: A response to recent discussion", JAAR 42 (1974) 538-549.

Parvey, Constance F., (ed). *Ordination of Women in Ecumenical Perspective*. World Council of Churches, Geneva, 1980.

Parvey, Constance F., "The Theology and Leadership of Women in the New Testament." In *Religion and Sexism*, pp. 117-149. Edited by Rosemary Radford Ruether. New York: Simon and Schuster, 1974.

Pelser, G. M. M., "Women and Ecclesiastical Ministries in Paul", Neotestamentica 10 (1976) 92-109.

224

Peter Brunner, *The Ministry and the Ministry of Women,* St. Louis: Concordia Publishing House, 1971.

Piper, John, and Wayne Grudem, (eds.), *Recovering Biblical Manhood and Womanhood: A Response to Evangelical Feminism,* Westchester, IL: Crossway, 1991.

Plevnik, J., *What are they saying about Paul,* New York, 1986.

Plisch, U.-K., "Die Apostelin Junia: Das exegetische Problem in Rom 16.7 im Licht von Nestle-Aland27 und der sahidischen Ueberlieferung," *NTS* 42.3 (1996) 477

Poewe, Karla, (ed.), *Charismatic Christianity as a Global Cultur,* Columbia, SC: University of South Carolina Press, 1994.

Power, Ward, *The Ministry of Women in the Church: Which Way Forward?* Adelaide, Australia: SPCKA, 1996.

Raming, Ida., *The Exclusion of Women From the Priesthood: Divine Law or Sex Discrimination?* Metuchen: Scarecrow, 1976.

Roberts Alexander and Donaldson James (eds.), *The Ante-Nicene Fathers, Translations of the Writings of the Fathers Down to A.D. 325,* 10 Vols., Grand Rapids: Wm. B. Eerdmans Publishing Company, 1950.

Roger Gryson, *Le ministère des Femmes dans l'Église ancienne,* Gembloux, Duculot 1972; 'L'Ordination des Diaconesses d'après les Constitutions apostoliques', MSR 31 (1974) 41-45.

Roger Gryson, *The Ministry of Women in the Early Church,* trans. J. Laporte and M. L. Hall (Collegeville, MN: Liturgical Press, 1976).

Ruether, Rosemary Radford, "In Christ No More Male and Female? The Question of Gender and Redemption in the New Testament," and "Gender and Redemption in the Patristic Era: Conflicting Perspectives." In *Women and Redemption: A Theological History,* Minneapolis: Fortress, 1998, 12-77.

Ryrie, Charles C., *The Role of Women in the Church,* Chicago: Moody Press, 1978.

Scanzoni, Letha D., and Nancy A. Hardesty, *All We're Meant to Be: Biblical Feminism for Today,* 3d rev. ed. Grand Rapids: Eerdmans, 1992.

Schaff Philip and Wace Henry (eds.), *A Select Library of Nicene and Post-Nicene Fathers of the Christian Church,* second Series 14 Vols, Grand Rapids: Wm. B. Eerdmans Publishing Company, 1952.

Schaff, Philip, *History of the Christian Church,* Grand Rapids: Eerdmans, [1910] 1989.

Schmithals, W., *The office of apostle in the early church,* Nashville, 1969.

Scholer, D. M., "1 Timothy 2,9-15 and the place of women in the church's ministry," In A. Mickelsen, ed. *Women, authority and the Bible* (1986) 193-224.

Schulz, Ray R., "Romans 16,7: Junia or Junias?" *Expository Times* 98 (1987) 108-110.

Schüssler Fiorenza, E., "Rhetorical Situation and historical Reconstruction in 1 Corinthians", *New Testament Studies* 33 (1987) 386-403.

Schüssler Fiorenza, E., "Women in the Pre-Pauline and Pauline Churches," *Union Seminary Quarterly Review* 33 (1978), 153-166.

Schüssler Fiorenza, E.,"Missionaries, Apostles, Co-workers: Romans 16 and the Reconstruction of Women's Early Christian History," *Word and World* 6 (1986) 420-33.

Schüssler Fiorenza, Elisabeth, *In Memory Of Her: A Feminist Theological Reconstruction of Christian Origins*, New York 1983. (The German translation of this same work is titled: *Zu Ihrem Gedächtnis*).

Scroggs, R., "Paul and the eschatological woman, *Journal of the American Academy of Religion* 40 (1972) 283-303.

Sigountos J. and Shank, M., "Public Roles for Women in the Pauline Church: A Reappraisal of the Evidence," *Journal of the Evangelical Theological Society* 26 (1983) 283-295.

Snodgrass, K., "Paul and Women," *Covenant Quarterly* 34 (1976) 3-13.

Spencer, Aida Besancon, *Beyond the Curse: Women Called to Ministry*, Nashville: Thomas Nelson, 1985.

Stark, Rodney, "The Role of Women in Christian Growth." In *The Rise of Christianity: A Sociologist Reconsiders History*, Princeton, New Jersey: Princeton University Press, 1996.

Stegemann, Ekkehard W. and Wolfgang Stegemann, "Part Four: The Social Roles and Social Situation of Women in the Mediterranean World and in Early Christianity." In *The Jesus Movement: A Social History of Its First Century*, trans. O. C. Dean, Jr., Minneapolis: Fortress Press, 1999, (German original, Stuttgart: W. Kohlhammer, 1995) 359-407, 463-74.

Stouffer, A. H., "The Ordination of Women: Yes," *Christianity Today* 20 (February 1981) 256-259.

Swidler, Leonard and Arlene Swidler, (eds.), *Women Priests: A Catholic Commentary on the Vatican Declaration*, New York: Paulist Press, 1977.

Tavard, G., *Woman in Christian Tradition*, University of Notre Dame Press, 1973.

Tetlow, Elizabeth M., *Women and Ministry in the New Testament*, New York: Paulist Press, 1980.

Thomas, W. D., "The Place of Women in the Church at Philippi," *Expository Times* 83 (1972) 119.

Thurston, Bonnie Bowman, *The Widows: A Women's Ministry in the Early Church*, Minneapolis: Fortress Press, 1989.

Torjesen, Karen Jo, *When Women Were Priests: Women's Leadership in the Early Church and the Scandal of their Subordination in the Rise of Christianity*, New York: HarperCollins Publishers, 1993.

Trible, Phyllis, *Texts of Terror: Literary-Feminist Readings of Biblical Narratives*, Philadelphia: Fortress, 1984.

Trompf, G. V., "On Attitudes toward Women in Paul and Paulinistic Literature: 1Corinthians 11, 1-16 and its Context", *Catholic Biblical Quarterly* 42 (1980) 196-215.

Tucker, Ruth A., and Walter Liefeld, L., *Daughters of the Church: Women and Ministry from New Testament Times to the Present*, Grand Rapids: Zondervan - Academie, 1987.

Tucker, Ruth, *Women in the Maze: Questions and Answers on Biblical Equality*, Downers Grove, IL: InterVarsity Press, 1992.

226

Van Leeuwen, Mary Stewart, *Gender and Grace*, Downers Grove, IL: InterVarsity Press, 1990.

Verdesi, Elizabeth H., *In But Still Out: Women in the Church*, Philadelphia: Westminster, 1976.

Waldrond-Skinner, Sue (Ed.), *Crossing the Boundary: What Will Women Priests Mean?* Mowbray, 1994.

Walker, W. O., "The Burden of Proof in Identifying Interpolations in the Pauline Letters", NTS 33 (1987) 610-618.

Walter Bauer, *A Greek-English Lexicon of the New Testament and Other Early Christian Literature*, 2nd ed., trans. William F. Arndt and F. Wilbur Gingrich, rev. F. Wilbur Gingrich and Frederick W. Danker, Chicago: University of Chicago Press, 1979.

Walter, Gross, *Frauen Ordination: Stand der Diskussion in der katholischen Kirche*, München, 1996.

Wayne, Grudem, "Prophecy-Yes, But Teaching-No: Paul's Consistent Advocacy of Women's Participation Without Governing Authority," *Journal of the Evangelical Theological Society* 30 (1987) 11-23.

Wijngaards, John, *The Ordination of Women in the Catholic Church: Unmasking a Cuckoo's egg tradition*, London: Darton, Longman & Todd, 2001.

Williams, Don, *The Apostle Paul and Women in the Church*, Glendale, CA: G/L Publications - Regal Books, 1978.

Winter, Miriam Therese, *"Out Of The Depths" The story of Ludmila Javorova ordained Roman Catholic Priest*, The Crossroad Publishing Company, New York, 2001.

Wire, Antoinette Clark, *The Corinthian Women Prophets: A Reconstruction through Paul's Rhetoric*. Minnepolis: Fortress, 1990.

Witherington III, B., "Rite and Rights for Women - Gal 3,28" (NTS 27) 593-604.

Witherington III, B., *Women in the Ministry of Jesus*, New York, 1984.

Witherington III, Ben, *Women and the Genesis of Christianity*, Cambridge University Press, 1984.

Witherington III, Ben, *Women in the Earliest Churches*, Cambridge, 1988.

Young, Frances M., "On *Episkopos* and *Presbyteros*," *Journal of Theological Studies* n.s. 45 (1994) 142-8.

Zerbst, Fritz, *The Office of Women in the Church*, trans. A.G. Merkens, St. Louis: Concordia Publishing House, 1955.

About the Author

The author, *Chinedu Adolphus Amadi-Azuogu*, is happily married with two boys and one girl. He studied philosophy and theology from 1977-1985 at the *Bigard Memorial Seminary*, Nigeria. He is privileged to have studied biblical exegesis at Biblicum, the prestigious *Pontifical Biblical Institute* in Rome, Italy from 1986-1990 where he holds the *Licenza in Re Biblica*. He is well acquainted with the archeology of the Holy Land, having studied at the *Hebrew University of Jerusalem* for one semester in 1988. From 1990-1995 he specialized in the New Testament at the *University of Bonn*, Germany, with special emphasis on Pauline Studies. He holds a doctorate degree in scripture. Ever since his graduation from the University of Bonn he has been lecturing primarily in different areas of the New Testament. He was the Chair and Professor of New Testament Studies at the *Spiritan International School of Theology*, Attakwu, Enugu, Nigeria from 1995-2000. Currently, he is the director of the Doctor of Ministry Program at the *Southern California School of Ministry*, Los Angeles, California, USA. He published his *Exegetical and Rhetorical Analysis of Gal 2,14-6,2* in 1996 and his *Biblical Exegesis and Inculturation in Africa in the third Millennium* in 2000. In addition, he has written numerous articles.

E

F

Index